Don't Label Me

ALSO BY IRSHAD MANJI

The Trouble with Islam Today
Allah, Liberty and Love

Don't Label Me

How to Do Diversity Without
Inflaming the Culture Wars

Irshad Manji

ST. MARTIN'S GRIFFIN

NEW YORK

NOTE: In this book the author notes that additional materials or related communications may be found at, or sent to, irshadmanji.com and moralcourage.com. Readers should understand that all information on the two websites, whether or not related to this book, is the property of the author. St. Martin's Press has no relation to, or responsibility for, the two websites or any of their content.

Published in the United States by St. Martin's Griffin, an imprint of St. Martin's Publishing Group

DON'T LABEL ME. Copyright © 2019 by Irshad Manji. All rights reserved. Printed in the United States of America. For information, address St. Martin's Publishing Group, 120 Broadway, New York, NY 10271.

www.stmartins.com

Designed by Steven Seighman

The Library of Congress has cataloged the hardcover edition as follows:

Names: Manji, Irshad, author.
Title: Don't label me : an incredible conversation for divided times / Irshad Manji.
Description: New York, NY : St. Martin's Press, [2019] | Includes index.
Identifiers: LCCN 2018049215 | ISBN 9781250157980 (hardcover) | ISBN 9781250223005 (international, sold outside the U.S., subject to rights availability) | ISBN 9781250182869 (ebook)
Subjects: LCSH: Toleration—United States. | Multiculturalism—United States. | Discrimination—United States. | United States—Race relations.
Classification: LCC HN90.M84 M36 2019 | DDC 306.44/60973—dc23
LC record available at https://lccn.loc.gov/2018049215

ISBN 978-1-250-18285-2 (trade paperback)

Our books may be purchased in bulk for promotional, educational, or business use. Please contact your local bookseller or the Macmillan Corporate and Premium Sales Department at 1-800-221-7945, extension 5442, or by email at MacmillanSpecialMarkets@macmillan.com.

First St. Martin's Griffin Edition: March 2020

10 9 8 7 6 5

For my bean.
See you on the flipside, inshallah.

Contents

Introduction

Lily won George over.

George is my editor. I proposed a book to him about healing the divides that are tearing apart these United States. Lily is my dog. Or was. She died unexpectedly during the writing of this book. I miss her fiercely, but I've come to terms with her physical absence because Lil herself recently consoled me with the news that she's fantastic. Nothing less than incredible. We can take heart that the conversation between me and Lil will also illuminate her lessons for the rebirth of America.

I met Lily at an adoption event near Los Angeles. Having suffered a health crisis, and being slow in the self-care department, I didn't realize how much healing I needed—or that Ms. Lil could show me the way. To any lover of animals, the soothing effect of our furry children is self-evident. Not to me. I grew up terrified of dogs and continued to picture them as ferocious beasts. My spouse, Laura, a proud parent of four rescue pups, urged me to evolve.

Given that I teach "moral courage"—doing the right thing in the face of our fears—I had to try. Could I credibly ask others to expand their moral imaginations if I wouldn't go first? Then again, teaching people to be courageous, for as glam as it sounds, had worn me out. On both counts, adopting a dog seemed the right thing to do. Laura and I brought Lily home that day.

But running away from human beings doesn't guarantee that you'll flee your frustrations with them. As Lily and I bonded, I'd confide to her my despair about humanity: that so many of us show so little of it.

I reached this conclusion reluctantly, after three decades of writing (and fighting) about identity. One of my books made the case that my faith of Islam has to be reformed. It offended more than a few of my fellow Muslims, who frequently reacted with personal insults and, on occasion, with physical threats. They jolted me to confront the emotions behind who we think we are.

My follow-up book reinterpreted Islam for liberal-minded Muslims. In it, I showed that the Qur'an, Islam's scripture, encourages questioning. Strident atheists joined the chorus of the offended, some anointing me the latest apologist of a "pedophile" prophet. Evidently, feelings can do the thinking of those who are rational as much as those who are faithful.

The combat zone had long been my comfort zone. No more. Wanting a divorce from my species, I slumped into pessimism and stepped back from the Islam-versus-the-West showdown. Only to behold the next apocalyptic clash: red America versus blue America.

In the lead-up to Donald Trump's election, Lily had one huffy Mama. I grumbled to her that the home of the brave was anything but. What bravery did it take to let "us" and "them" coagulate into us *against* them? Even people who called themselves progressive acted as if progress only meant accosting the other side. Good luck changing the world that way. To achieve justice, devotees of justice must change ourselves, I sighed to Lily, and I suggested how that could happen at a time when almost everybody feels besieged.

While I poured out my thoughts, Lily would tilt her head again and again. It was as if she wondered, *What are you smoking, Mama?* Or, *Can you clarify?* Or, *Have you considered an opposing opinion?* Over time, Lil's questions sent me in search of alternate perspectives—Eastern and Western; scientific and philosophical; radical, liberal, conservative, and populist; each of these a label, and each a reminder that nobody owns the entire truth. More often than not, labels eclipse truth.

This, I learned about Lily's labels. She was old and she was blind.

To love *her*, rather than love my specious assumptions about her, I had to suspend what I "knew" about Lil merely by how she looked. I had to defang the force of ego, the most pervasive and pernicious power there is. Until I tempered my need to be right all the time, I'd never understand her. I'd continue relying on sterile categories. I'd settle for the fake facts that labels hand to us—not only about Lily but about everybody.

Labels keep us all in our assigned places. At root, that's why we're divided. Thus was born the idea to make this book a conversation with Lily.

Enter George, my editor. He'd accepted my plan to write a book on the rupturing of America. I guess I neglected to inform him of the revised plan to feature Lil. Upon receiving my first draft, George flipped. He told me that his "heart sank" and his "head began to ache." Problem number one: He doesn't like dogs. Problem number two: He's sick of books about people and their wise pets. Problem number three: An analysis of the country's sorry state can't be serious if it stars a talking mutt.

Still, George had little choice but to read the damned draft. He downed two aspirins and waded in. The following week, I woke up to an exuberant email. Lily had moved George to see how America's tribal politics can be outwitted by anyone, including the vulnerable.

Lily's method is a form of mental martial arts. At the heart of it lies the practice of respect. Historically, to "respect" meant to "re-spectate"—to turn back and see again. When we see others with fresh eyes, we subvert static labels. If we do it sincerely, we give others the emotional incentive to do likewise for us. Edwin Markham, a poet laureate of Oregon, captured the border-busting, bridge-building power of respecting one's detractors. Imagine Lily reciting these words about George:

> He drew a circle that shut me out—
> Heretic, rebel, a thing to flout.
> But love and I had the wit to win:
> We drew a circle that took him in!

The title of that poem? "Outwitted."

Which is what Lily regularly did to me, revealing her power to communicate tough truths with grace. One afternoon, I slathered peanut butter on my lips to lure a kiss from Lil. She closed in on my face, sniffed out the trickery, and waltzed off, preserving her dignity in the teeth of my pathetic scheme.

Without toiling or spinning, Lily exposed the limits of manipulation as a tactic. She gave me a glimpse into what we humans consistently do to each other, planting the seeds of suspicion and eventual backlash.

Lily's no-nonsense mentoring only started there. Nobody else could have convinced me to stay off social media for two years, during which I discovered the value of time and trust. As she put me through my paces, she got me connecting the dots:

- A rising number of liberal democracies around the world have mega-manipulators at their helm. They wrangle the levers of mass culture, especially social media, to exploit the mistrust that already exists among people.

- Mistrust abounds largely because we the people have been manipulating one another, permitting our leaders to push the bar of integrity even lower.

- Through technology designed to meet our greed for speed, the mistrust is jacked up to emergency levels. Like the teams in a sudden-death playoff, we take refuge in our respective colors.

We resolve to vanquish the other side. We widen the vacuum of public trust, invariably creating the pretext for "strong" dudes to swoop in and restore unity—or uniformity. This is the vintage game of divide-and-conquer, expedited for our time-pressed lives.

The lesson is, people are getting gamed. All of us, regardless of our teams. And our dear leaders won't stop gaming us until we stop gaming each other.

So effortlessly did Lil teach me this lesson that I found myself drawn into deeper conversation with her. That's when I discovered the unabashed cleverness of her "moves." She won over George by intentionally not striving to win. She educated me by letting me educate her. She demonstrated that disagreeing with each other's ideas never has to mean denying each other's dignity. My utter pessimism about the human species was outwitted by an old, blind dog.

"Don't label me," I can hear Lily exhorting a touch tartly. "I'm more than your labels, Mama, and you're more than mine. Can we agree on that much?"

In this book, the issues that Lil and I discuss are provocative. A plea to our readers: Before deciding that you're offended by either of us, kindly pull a Lily. Ask your questions out loud and let us address them in the subsequent pages. For comprehensive footnotes or further context, go to the "Books" tab of my website, irshadmanji.com. There, you'll find information ranging from scholarly studies and research data to recommended readings, podcasts, and videos.

Of course, how I interpret my sources may not be how you do. Feel free to challenge my perspective. If your views—and the respect with which you communicate them—persuade me to rethink, I'll update the corresponding footnote and credit you. Send your grace-laced protests to team@moralcourage.com.

Finally, in the stories I tell, I've altered names upon request and published real names otherwise. In one case, I've used pseudonyms solely to avoid goading U.S. immigration authorities into complicating my life more than they already have. There are enough wrongful deportations to fight.

Amid the ongoing kookiness of our times, Lily remains my guide. She'll be yours, too, if you're willing to see with a new pair of eyes. My respect to all.

Can We Talk?

1

Lily in the Field: Old, Blind, and Badass

Lily, my love, would you please suspend your sniff-fest? Just for a minute. Mama has something to say.

Ever since you trundled into my life with your charcoal fur, your lamb chop legs, and your swashbuckling tail, I've become a more humane human. You've made me less inquisitional. More inquisitive. You're the reason I walk away from my laptop and lose myself in a belly rub. *Your* belly, I mean.

You give me permission to breathe, to interrupt the thrum of anxiety. Around you, I feel no urge to tweet, tap, post, blog, swipe, scroll, or slack. In fact, whenever I'm hunched over my phone, you notice and get bored with me. Message received.

Your gifts to me couldn't have been foretold. How did I luck out? Most people want the entertainment value of a puppy, not a sightless senior like you. Rare is the acknowledgment of puppy privilege. Abundant is the assumption that to be blind, or old, is to be a hassle.

Passersby stare at you in your stroller. Some chuckle at the spectacle of a dog in a baby carriage. A few zero in on your cloudy eyes. Then they get all sad-faced and tell me I'm a saint for adopting you. A saint! They don't know me.

More important, they don't know you. They've never watched you out on the grass, noting the direction of the wind, heading into it nose-first, accepting your power to march right through and blow your own way. You won't be bullied by your vulnerability. You'll hit walls and fences and tree trunks and table legs. Then you'll bounce back, pivot, and carry on. Resilience, thy name is Lilybean.

It's not as if you're immune to hurt. Seems to me you were hurting the first time I scooped you up into my arms. The nipples protruding from your tummy, and your untreated glaucoma, confirmed that you'd been somebody's property—repeatedly raped for a dog breeder who slapped a price tag on your uterus. You had no reason to trust. You could've hung onto past hurt. Yet here you are, giving a second chance to the promise of family.

Maybe it's wrong to compare your behavior to a human's. It might be true that unlike human animals, dogs have no long-term memory and that's why they don't bear grudges or devolve into cynicism. Scientists haven't reached any hard and fast conclusions about this, but I know what I've witnessed: Your memory's perfect when we hop into the car and you doggedly snoop for goodies because the last time we drove, I fed you half a strip of jerky. Now you think I can be convinced that the back-seat treat is our tradition. You've got moxie, Ms. Lil. And magnificent recall.

All to say, "blind" doesn't remotely define you. Neither does "old." Yes, you're both of these. You're also much more than these. Your defiance of simplistic labels has me thinking about the lessons for human beings.

2

Our Division Problem

Math teachers tell us that to solve a division problem, we must find the common denominator. From its birth, this nation's common denominator has been diversity. "I'm not a fan of that word," a neighbor recently snipped. "It divides people." Well, that's one slant on diversity.

The word itself comes from the Latin "to turn aside," or, as some take it, to splinter and separate. But nature would disagree with that interpretation. Every afternoon, Lil, you meander in the park. Here, diversity is the lubricant of a humming engine. Do you breathe in just one aroma?

How about two?

Five?

That's some head-tilt you've got going, Lilybean. You're catching on to my crazy talk, aren't you?

It's bananas to isolate and enumerate the smells enveloping you. None of them, on its own, captures the magic of the intermingling whole. You're gaga about the park exactly for its kaleidoscope of scents that jostle with each other and sometimes get up your nose.

See where I'm going with this? Diversity itself doesn't divide; it's what we do with diversity that splits societies apart or stitches them together. The paradox is, to do diversity honestly, we can't be labeling all of diversity's critics as bigots.

You disagree, Lil? You're entitled to your opinion but you haven't let me explain mine.

Welcome to the real world, you say? Well, this isn't exactly the real world, is it? You're a conversing canine, for God's sake.

Okay, okay, you're right, enough of my defensiveness. Getting my back up won't help you hear me. But if I'm going to work on me, then I need assurance of a fair hearing from you. Deal?

(Note to self: Never expect the mother-daughter relationship to be a picnic in the park.)

As I was about to explain, Lil, there's more than one way to look at a situation. Some people oppose diversity because they *are* bigots. Others, though, are skeptical of diversity because of how we, its champions, practice it. We're fixated on labeling. And labeling drains diversity of its unifying potential.

Since the founding of the U.S. republic, Americans have extolled the ideal of unity in diversity. *E pluribus unum*—out of many, one— became a gallant motto for the union of the original thirteen colonies. No argument, Lil, the colonists were themselves colonizers. Of native people. Of black people. Of women and of poor white men. I acknowledge that such labels didn't drop from the clear blue sky. These groups bore the brunt of keeping the United States united.

So I'll keep it real, too: *E pluribus unum* has always been an uphill battle. Americans fought a gruesome civil war over the obscenity of slavery, whose promoters reduced human beings to labels. A century earlier, drawing unity from diversity proved to be onerous business of a different sort. It demanded that ardent revolutionaries check their egos.

Just before voting on the Constitution, the framers listened to a letter from Benjamin Franklin. He, in turn, had somebody read it out loud. Addressing each signatory as if speaking to him in person, Franklin confessed in the letter:

I do not entirely approve of this Constitution at present, but Sir,
I am not sure I shall never approve it: For having lived long, I

have experienced many Instances of being oblig'd by better Infor-mation or fuller Consideration, to change Opinions even on impor-tant Subjects, which I once thought right, but found to be otherwise.

Take a moment to digest this, Lily. A world-class rebel states pub-licly that he doesn't know it all. That he's missing something obvious to others. That he might be wrong. Was Franklin written off as a wimp? Nope. His fellow framers knew the value of humility in making the impossible happen. For America's revolutionaries, breaking free from a British despot would be the relatively simple part. Much harder would be replacing despotism with something democratic and doable.

The framers' solution? To enshrine and institutionalize *diversity of viewpoint*. Their logic? In a republic of vastly different regions, cultures, peoples, and perspectives, there's nation-building power in airing dis-agreements. Diversity of opinion as a common denominator—sheer ge-nius, Lil. In *Why Societies Need Dissent*, the legal scholar Cass Sunstein describes this funky formula as "the framers' greatest innovation."

Americans, I'm thrilled to tell you, still aspire to that vision. In June 2018, the Harris Poll released findings about what unites and di-vides the country. Among the factors that unite: "being open to alter-native viewpoints." But the deflating reality is, people generally mean that *other* people should be open to *their* viewpoints.

Today, living the revolutionary ideal seems a nonstarter, and for various reasons. Hands down, the most controversial reason is the changing make-up of America. It's a landmine of fraught labels, frail identities, and engulfing emotions.

Can we talk about it?

In this country, brown, black, and multiracial babies outnumber white babies. Beyond our major cities, small towns have started to mix it up. Take Storm Lake, Iowa. An owner of the community newspaper estimates that "88 percent of children in our elementary schools are children of color. We speak about 21 languages." Sarah Smarsh, a jour-nalist from Kansas, says that in the past ten years alone, and thanks to the rise of industrial agribusiness, her farming community has become home to workers from Mexico, Central America, and the Middle East. That's a bundle of change in a flash of time.

Thank God America has a history of muddling through.

Problem is, Americans can't depend on the past to predict that the future will be tickety-boo. Sure, some prejudice has subsided as successive waves of migrants have integrated. On one specific score, though, these are unprecedented days for the nation. That's because a generation from now, white people as a whole will be a minority like everyone else. African American, Asian, Hispanic, and multiracial minorities, taken together, will be the majority.

Think about the implications, Lil. People of color won't need to fit into a white-approved mainstream. If anything, it's white folks who will have to integrate. As stalwarts of diversity, our challenge will be to include them meaningfully—and not just because it's the right thing to do from a moral standpoint. I'm speaking practically as well.

Let me introduce you to the work of Jennifer Richeson, a cutting-edge psychologist. Her experiments shed light on what takes place in many hearts and minds as folks become aware that we're all going to be minorities soon. The more Americans learn about this inevitability, Richeson says, the more attitudes swerve toward conservatism. *But not only among white Americans.* "When you expose Asian Americans, black Americans to similar [information] about the growth in the Hispanic population, they also show a shift to more support for conservative policy positions," Richeson reveals. Which should put a glint in the eye of Republicans from sea to shining sea.

Said starkly, Lil, "old white guys" are dying off but a fresh, diverse crop of Americans could easily perpetuate, even accelerate, the politics associated with old white guys. It's basic group psychology, Richeson emphasizes. Once you're told that your group's losing status compared to another group, you're more likely to feel defensive. Defensiveness triggers division. And division obscures the shared ground on which further progress can be built.

What an incentive to use these next twenty years mindfully—to learn from past mistakes about how, finally, to get diversity right. So far, though, diversity's enthusiasts are committing the same stale mistakes. We're attaching labels to individuals as if those labels capture the sum of who they are. Moreover, we're labeling ourselves to the point of extinguishing our own humanity.

Taking pride in our particulars at the expense of our commonalities has become a hallmark of "progressive" America. Progressive? This was the very mind-set of the colonists! For all of their gentlemanly manners, the most monied colonists sliced and stamped Americans to suit their narrow agendas. These days, that mind-set passes for enlightened diversity. I'm floored, Lil, and worried.

There's the head-tilt. Ready when you are.

Am I equally worried about the current backlash against women and minorities? You bet I am. That's why we have to end our frantic labeling. It fuels the bona fide bigots.

Allow me to elaborate. More and more of us in the diversity crowd label people as ignorant and insidious if they hold opinions that diverge from our script. We rally for diversity of appearance but we flake on diversity of viewpoint. We wield enormous power in American culture, yet we excuse our excesses by claiming to be powerless and therefore incapable of oppressing those who think differently than we do.

No doubt, the expressed enemies of diversity threaten a much worse form of oppression. If we left America to hard-core white nationalists, their women would exist to reproduce and replenish the ranks of the blue-eyed and ruddy-cheeked. The rest of us would be free to take a flying leap into our ancestors' "shit holes" of origin. Some freedom.

But here's the kicker: Hate gets turbo-charged when those of us who bang the drum for inclusion drum out *reasonable* folks—merely because their opinions don't match ours. Labeling our rivals further and further into enemy territory is an unforced error whose repercussions we'll come to regret. How ham-handed can we be?

No, Lil, no. It's just a phrase. There's no ham in my hand. None. You and your nose can heel.

3

Rivals Versus Enemies

Do I have your attention again, Lilybean?

Every rival doesn't need to be an enemy. In 2015, *The Wall Street Journal* and NBC News polled people who identified as Democrats and Republicans. In each party, more Americans wanted an openly gay president than an evangelical Christian one.

And no, Donald Trump hasn't changed everything. Almost a year after his election, Pew Research surveyed Republicans and Democrats on an array of diversity-related issues. Check this out: Most people from both parties endorsed affirmative action in college admissions.

What's more, over half of the Republicans polled said that homosexuality should be accepted. Republicans are also en route to accepting same-sex marriage "at similar rates to Democrats," writes *The Economist*.

For me, Lily, the stunner of stunners had to do with immigration: 92 percent of the Republicans consulted (and 97 percent of Democrats) said that the rising number of people from various ethnicities and nationalities makes America a better country. In 2018, Gallup confirmed that support for legal immigration had reached its highest level ever. Additional polls revealed that most people who'd frowned on immigrants a decade ago embrace them today.

This is a tectonic cultural shift, Lil. Don't let anybody tell you that we in the diversity crowd have been rendered powerless by Trump. The real question is—

Yes, sweet bean, you may interject.

Is it possible that the polls' respondents lied about their support for minorities because they're too ashamed to admit otherwise?

Possible. Researchers have shown that some people will hide their distaste for a diverse America in order to look like they're part of the popular consensus. But this suggests that the popular consensus *favors* diversity. So any liars in these polls would be outliers. Now I have a question for you. If some people are withholding their true convictions, is it because they're actually ashamed? Or is it because they're being shamed?

There's a quantum difference between the two. You can feel ashamed because you realize that you hold immoral beliefs. This kind of shame, generated by your conscience, is healthy. By contrast, you can be shamed into shutting up about your beliefs. In that case, you're probably not going to reconsider them. When the time's right—when you sense that you have backup from people who feel as browbeaten as you—you'll retaliate against your shamers.

Near as I can tell, much of today's polarized politics stems from the shaming that the diversity movement's been doing—not only to authentic racists, but to anyone who's got an honest disagreement with us. I take it as a warning of worse to come. Shaming's a surefire way to alienate the growing legion of Americans who are politically homeless and poised to sway elections. Chief among them: moderate Republicans.

Whoa, Lily.

Slow down, please.

Uh-huh.

You done?

Let me reiterate your questions to be sure I understand you. If Republicans had a scintilla of moderation, then why did most of them back a presidential candidate who ridicules differences?

A candidate who launched his campaign by needlessly labeling the people of Mexico?

Who later parodied a man with cerebral palsy?

Who egged on the Ku Klux Klan?

Who trivialized women?

Let me address, Lil, why I think so many moderates and independents voted for this spoof of a man. It's—

You forgot to add something, little bean? Fine. Finish up.

Alright, to recap: You've just told me it's evasive to say that moderate Republicans voted more against Hillary Clinton than for Donald Trump. Because the question then becomes: Why do large numbers of Republicans still defend Trump? Hillary is a has-been. But supposedly decent Republicans continue to let the president shame, blame, and game swaths of people to puff himself up. How decent is that?

You're a hairy act to follow, Lil. Here goes. In all the ways you've listed, decent Republicans are acting indecently. They have no excuse for averting their eyes to the indignity suffered by others under this president. Let me reiterate: There's no excuse for indifference to the human harm he causes.

There is, however, an explanation. It's called "negative polarization." That's when voters side with a candidate not out of faith in him but out of fury with the other side. Even after their camp wins, they're consumed with ensuring that the rival camp keeps losing; such is the depth of their disdain for the "enemy."

I must tell you about another smart Lily—the political scientist Lilliana Mason. She studies how negative polarization perverts the behavior of voters. According to Mason, whenever we the people form our personal identities as a reaction against the other side, "We act like we disagree more than we actually do.

> Our opinions can be very fluid; so fluid that if we wanted to come to a compromise, we could . . . But we can't come to a compromise because our identities are making us want to take positions as far away from the other side as possible.

Point is, moderate Republicans may very well agree with some of the policies that you and I like—marriage equality, for example, or thoughtful immigration reform—but many of them will choose candidates who stand for the opposite because they want to deny you and me a win, any win. Policy isn't the issue for these voters. The emotions we set off in them are. The more acidly anti-Trump we become, the more egregiously anti-anti-Trump they become.

So, my precious bean, they hate us. Now what?

We could inflate the hate by flipping the bird to these folks. Or— hear me out—we could pose a scandalously compassionate question to ourselves: How have we, diversity's partisans, fed the contempt that many Trump sympathizers have for us? What, if anything, have we done to help incite this level of animosity? I'm not blaming us. I'm not blaming, period. I'm asking, where do we, too, need to mature?

Michelle Goldberg, a columnist for *The New York Times,* dangles one heavyweight hint. When she attended Donald Trump's campaign events, she rarely heard people rail against the economy. In the main, they spat bullets about "political correctness," with its insinuation that certain Americans can't be trusted to discover the truth. *Our* truth. Therefore, we must enforce our speech codes, our approved visuals, our superior values.

Why would anybody give a rip about political correctness, you ask?

I'm on board with you, Lil, that America has more tangible problems. Dead-end work. Generational poverty. Runaway drug abuse. Overpriced health insurance. Gun violence. Mass incarceration. The underfunding of public schools. The overconsumption of junk. On and on it goes.

But as I've learned, political correctness is no mere distraction from these scourges. It's as immediate a scourge as they are. Immediate because without resolving it, we can't advance lasting solutions to anything else. For a solution to be sustainable, it needs buy-in by more than one side. And buy-in requires respect.

From my scores of conversations with Americans who regard themselves as traditional, a common thread emerges. In their eyes, political correctness lays bare the diversity movement's disrespect for others. *Our* others.

4

Who Gets Respect?

I recognize, Lil, that for a lot of diversity lovers, "political correctness" is a bogus term; a label brandished by bigots so they can shunt aside their basic civic duty—to respect all beings as the individuals we are. In demanding respect, though, are we minimizing the individuality of non-bigots?

In 2009, I went on a book tour of the American Midwest. After coming home to New York, I told a fellow educator that people in the heartland seemed to have lost their mojo. Those I spoke with sounded dispirited. Well-informed and obviously part of the book-reading public, a number of them pressed me about "out-of-control political correctness."

They asked, why the knee-jerk vilifying of middle America as "racist"? More African Americans live in the Midwest than in any other area outside the South. Aren't we, the boosters of diversity, being racist in framing the Midwest as white and, by implication, teeming with knuckle-draggers? Above all, they wondered, what happened to giving respect in order to get respect?

Back then, Lil, I couldn't have defined "respect." Did it mean being polite? Going along to get along, whatever the circumstances? Diffusing tension to delay everybody's discomfort? If "yes" on any of those counts, then screw respect. It's just a euphemism for duplicity.

Only after looking into its root did I appreciate its meaning. "Respect" comes from the Latin to see someone in a new light. To be curious about that person's experiences and to spend time finding out about them. In this context, the Midwesterners I talked to deserve no less respect than you and I do. They're as multidimensional as any of us.

You've got a thought, Lil? You can share it in just a moment. Let me wrap up my story.

When I reported my readers' questions to my colleague in New York, the educator, he couldn't have been less interested. Instead, he wanted to know how often I dealt with Islamophobes on my trip. Not whether, but how often. "Truthfully?" I told him. "Never. Not that I noticed." Irritated by my colleague's disrespect for people in the Midwest, I decided to test *his* tolerance. Over several minutes, I held court about my faith in Allah. "By the way," I finally asked him, "if I was a Christian or a Jew, would you indulge all my God-talk?"

He reflected for a couple of seconds and answered, "Probably not." Credit where credit's due, Lil: He could've lapsed into defensiveness. But he chose candor and I thanked him for it. We remain friends precisely because he's open to learning about his blind spots, as I am mine. No blaming and no shaming. End of story. Take it away, my love.

I'm stumbling into a trap? How so?

You think I'm assuming that the more respectable we are to other people, the more respect they'll give to us. And if Martin Luther King Jr. had a dream, then I have a pipe dream.

Ouch, Lil. Your zingers would be devastating in a debate. Good thing this doesn't need to become one.

As for the trap that I'm wriggling in, maybe you've misunderstood me. I don't intend to nit-pick, but I'm advocating that we be respect*ful,* not respect*able.* To be respectable implies that whatever we do, we do so that we can ingratiate ourselves to the people whose minds we want to change. That's a manipulative move. When we see others as the only folks who need to grow, we're imagining them as our objects. We're seduced to game them for gain. Don't be surprised if they resist playing along.

Being respectable is an express ticket to becoming inauthentic.

Being respectful, on the other hand, spreads the authenticity. Martin Buber, a titanic twentieth-century theologian, described the most liberating relationships as "I-Thou" rather than "I-It." In the I-Thou relationship, I presume the other person to be as multifaceted as I am. But in the I-It relationship, I perceive the other person as an inconvenience. "It" is holding up justice. "It" is taking up oxygen. I must get "It" out of the way. Do you smell the rat, Lil?

Do I smell the irony, you ask?

I do. The irony's more than a little pungent. After all, plenty of white people made us their It for generations. But I have to ask you: Does payback equal progress?

To revisit my educator-friend in New York, he turned the archetypal Midwesterner into his It. Suspecting "Midwesterners" of oversimplifying Islam to be violence and oversimplifying me to be Islam, he oversimplified Midwesterners to be Islamophobes. By imagining that they made me their Other, he made them his Other. By imitating his It, he mutated into it. *That's* the trap, Lil. Imitation strangles liberation.

Admittedly, one anecdote about one person in one milieu proves nothing. But I don't share this story to "prove" something to you. I share it to illustrate how I began to understand the ambient feeling of ambush in much of America. Political correctness is the memo that heartland Americans had no input into. It's the command performance that's been sprung on them. It's not the diversity they signed up for.

If you account for the surveys I've cited, most Republicans, like Democrats, have signed up for a consistently diversifying America. Change doesn't necessarily freak out traditional Americans. So what does? For a lot of them, it's the pace of change. Robert Putnam, the famous political scientist, reports that too much diversity too fast can "shock" longtime residents of any community. Putnam likens them to "turtles," scurrying away from the foreign to hide under their shells. But before long, Putnam contends, turtles get past their shock and move forward.

I'm less optimistic, given the shaming that goes with political correctness. As minorities steadily add up to the majority in America, today's turtles should be talking about their anxieties if only to cope with them productively. Yet too many won't talk—not openly, that is—because they fear being humiliated by us.

You heard me right, Lily. We, as much as they, possess the H-Bomb: humiliation. To experience rudeness here or incivility there ain't no biggie. That's life. But serial contempt? Biggie. Arthur Brooks, a behavioral economist, explains it like so: "Anger says, 'I care about you.' Contempt says, 'You're worthless.'" Without worth, you're invisible—the worst of all fates, adds the historian Yuval Noah Harari when he speaks about humanity's looming challenges. Psychologists themselves have found that humiliation's a more intense emotion than happiness. Its claws tear deeper into people than anger does. Its impact outlasts the pangs of occasional shame.

There's an even deeper context to take into account. Sarah Smarsh, the Kansas-based journalist, writes movingly that shame stalks many of the rural poor—often because urbanites can't be bothered to know them as fellow Americans:

> [T]o devalue, in our social investments, the people who tend crops and livestock, or to refer to their place as "flyover country," is to forget not just a country's foundation but its connection to the earth, to cycles of life scarcely witnessed and ill understood in concrete landscapes.

You could say much the same for folks in the U.S. South. They've never really been accepted as "one of us" by the emperors of cultured America, plenty of whom still turn their Northern noses up at "those mother-fucking mutants." That's what one Southerner heard on his Ivy League campus. He reported it to me through tears.

To the incessantly shamed, political correctness dishes out a double-dose of humiliation. It heaps irrelevance on their traditions and indifference on their voices. In the guise of making room for "all," our side, they say, doctors diversity. Under us, diversity becomes selective tolerance: We're selecting who merits membership in this abstract "all"—and, more gallingly, who doesn't. In short, we've fertilized the conditions for feeling scammed.

Donald Trump knows it only too well. When he kicked off his presidential run, Trump claimed that Americans "are tired of being ripped off by everybody in the world." His "everybody" included the proponents of diversity. Later, Lil, you'll eavesdrop on a dialogue I'm having with Jim, one of our neighbors. He maintains that President Trump's only doing to the likes of us what we zealously do to the likes of Jim.

From his perspective, diversity-lovers slap lurid labels on white folks, handing Trump the moral authority to label Muslims.

Our educators label the straight shooters of middle America; Trump labels the unsuspecting citizens of Mexico.

Our press labels Trump voters the enemies of democracy; Trump labels our press the enemies of the people.

Jim overstates. Trump's so-called moral authority? There's nothing moral about it because payback isn't progress. But try telling his emotions. He's done with being labeled because, as he puts it, "labels distort." I don't disagree. Labels distort you, Lil, and I can assure you that they distort me.

5

How Labels Distort

I've duly noted your tilting head, Lilybean. Have at it.

You're curious as to how you and I, both of us women of color, can bring such different lenses to reality? Hey, just because we share an identity doesn't make us identical.

Let me clear up another confusion that I sense in your question. The lenses I'm wearing right now aren't my own. They're the lenses of people unlike me, and I'm putting them on because to have an informed viewpoint about what others are doing, it helps to understand where they're coming from.

You want to know where *I'm* coming from? Why, that is, I'd care to view life through lenses that make me uncomfortable? Thank you for asking, Lil. I'd be glad to confide my back story. Besides humanizing your slightly demented mama, my experiences will fill in the blanks about what makes me passionate enough to raise these thorny issues at all.

Over the years, I've called for freedom and human rights within Islam. My books kindled controversy, violence, and courageous resistance to that violence. In Indonesia, young Muslim women threw their bodies onto mine to protect me from face-smashing militants who showed up on roaring motorbikes and swung iron rods, lasso-like. In the Netherlands, my supporters organized themselves into my shields as jihadists from Belgium crashed our gathering at Amsterdam's main community center.

I've been privileged to encounter a groundswell of bravery on the part of ordinary human beings. But may I confess another privilege, Lil? I've always been squeamish about this: My labels have played an outsize role in bringing attention to my ideas.

Journalists take advantage of my user-friendly identities—none of which I've earned, each of which I've been born into, and all of which convey that there's something bizarre about this Muslim: She's also a lesbian!

Cringe-inducing. To my ears, "lesbian" has the ring of "alien." Maybe I'm overly sensitive, having been deemed an "alien" by U.S. immigration officials.

That's a joke, Lil. I'm a person off-color.

That's another joke.

Moving along.

In taking issue with the "Muslim lesbian" label, I'm not disputing the facts. Your mama's both queer-ish and Qur'an-ish. It's just that facts alone don't add up to truth. As the media critic Brooke Gladstone writes, people interpret facts through their biases. So even when labels are factual, they don't innocently describe someone. They come with heavy baggage that can distort, or outright hijack, who someone really is.

I'll be specific. There are some conservatives whose bias is to bomb Muslims into oblivion. They interpret my "Muslim" label to mean that I'm a stealth jihadist. Then there are particular atheists who take it on faith that as a Muslim, I'm a dupe of superstitious cave dwellers. Either way, I'm not an individual in my own right. I'm an involuntary avatar of other people's projections.

Do you see how labels can manufacture realities? And do you pick up on how the labeled get used so that those who do the labeling can score points for their rendition of the truth?

Two more examples come to mind. Many traditional Muslims regard me as a stooge of the corrupt West because of my "gay" label. Apparently, I'm rubbing my decadence further in their faces by having a wife. (Just one, mind you.) Meanwhile, certain progressives envision all Muslims as victims-in-waiting. To people with that bias, I'm an enabler of discrimination because, they assume, in being gay I give cover to Islam-haters who can claim, "We're tolerant of minorities. We love that Muslim lesbian!"

I must clarify that I'm not speaking about all progressives or all conservatives or all atheists or all Muslims. I speak of certain ones, particular ones, many, or some. But I do detect a pattern among this motley crew, and it's twofold. First, they've fallen for the illusion that labels allow them to know a person when they only know *of* that person. Second, by only knowing *of* that person, they can treat him or her as a plaything of their broodings, the better to fuel their warring versions of reality.

When we let labels stand in for people, we end up manipulating people. Our shared humanity, along with our distinctive individuality, loses out. Do I sound naïve?

No, Mama. You sound like Bruce Lee.

Lily, you're speaking!

Yes, because it's my turn. Mama, do you know the name Bruce Lee?

You mean the martial arts master and movie star?

He was also a philosopher, Mama.

Hold on, Lil. How do *you* know about Bruce Lee?

You're asking about my own back story now, Mama. I'll throw you a scrap. The lady who owned me listened obsessively to Bruce Lee's interviews. Maybe she hoped to learn how to resolve the conflicts in her life. I overheard some hostile calls with her son; every time she slammed the phone down, she'd then log onto YouTube and play a video clip of Bruce Lee. I couldn't help but absorb his philosophy.

Which is what, Lil?

Bruce Lee believed in "harmonious individuality." By this he meant that you can be a unique individual, with dreams all your own, and be in harmony with your surroundings even when those surroundings contain forces that oppose your dreams. The opposition could be a person, or a government, or a culture. Whatever it is, if you attack the opposition head-on, you harden its resolve to defeat you. But by developing harmonious individuality, both you and your opposition win. Think of it as self-defense without defensiveness.

Practical, Lil. How would I start?

Be like water, Mama.

Gotcha. Not really. Float that by me again?

Here's the long and the short of it, Mama. Bruce Lee said, "Be like water, my friend." Water respects the obstacles in its midst by treating them as a natural part of the surroundings. Consider all the rocks that speckle the ocean. Water could choose to view them as the It, the Other, since they get in the way of its flow. But to focus energy on pushing the rocks aside, or to demand that they disappear, would be to wage war against the life-breathing universe that gave rise to both the water and the rocks. Water's going to lose that war. Besides, in its petulance, water never learns to be agile. It thereby defeats itself.

Thankfully, Mama, water knows better. To keep flowing, it approaches the rocks with grace, washing over them, gliding around them, seeping into them, loosening them, reshaping them, and, with time, eroding them. Water wins without the rocks having to lose.

Dang, Lil. I've thought of Bruce Lee as a tough guy, but he points the way to taking the tough guy out of our politics.

Let's assume that supporters of diversity are water and skeptics of diversity are the rocks. Water's been rippling through American culture for a while, gathering such momentum that it swirled past driftwood, tree branches, shrubs, and other potential obstructions. What I mean is, in America's culture wars, conservative Christians recently came close to whipping out the white flag. Some actually did.

All of a sudden, smack-dab in water's path, a wall of rocks appeared. Individually, they've long been there but now they're collectively asserting themselves. The rocks have formed a wall to teach water that they exist. Undoubtedly, a cluster of them aims to stop water from circulating. But most of the rocks just want water to recognize that they, too, have a dignified place in the landscape.

Water acts from defensiveness and labels the rocks "racists." Feeling more harangued than ever, the rocks reject the lesson that water thinks it's teaching. Out of their own defensiveness, the rocks label water a cesspool of elitism.

Although they've been gifted life by the same universe, each element—water and rock—clots into lifeless conformity. Water needs to move, yet it's hit a dead-end that it helped bring into being.

What then, Mama?

The rocks have no incentive to change, Lil. By staying put, they demonstrate both their presence and their power. It's water that must change in order to flow again. And water can't flow—or irrigate the land—as long as it interprets justice as a win-lose game. Even if the rocks "lose" because water has crashed through them, water's current has weakened. Water's integrity has dissipated. A win-lose outlook produces a lose-lose outcome.

But if water espouses the win-win, then it'll use its power differently. Water will make room for the majority of those rocks. Not the ones that seek to keep water out, but the ones that water itself has prematurely kept out. When we, diversity's supporters, clear space for diversity's skeptics, then diversity will be consistent. It'll have integrity. It'll cease to be a shtick.

Some of the rocks will fall away from the wall and enrich the water with their nutrients. Now we've got a wobbling wall and a swelling current. Watch out for the waterfall! Dr. King taught that when we avoid humiliating our adversaries, the tide picks up momentum on its own. As he wrote with biblical panache, "Let justice roll down like waters"—justice is like water, Lil!—"and righteousness like a mighty stream."

I'm with you, girlfriend! I, too, am panting with excitement!

Oh, you're thirsty. I knew that.

Here's your drinking bowl, sweet bean. Hydrate to your heart's content. Be like water.

6

A Dog-Loving Muslim Pundamentalist

Lily, I've been researching Bruce Lee. What a fascinating figure. No wonder he advised us to be like water. He personally experienced how labels clog perception. The ethnic box that Hollywood executives stuffed him into restricted their imaginations as well as his opportunities.

You've unveiled my bias, too. The label that I attached to Lee, "martial artist," overshadowed a related part of him: student of the *Tao*. In ancient Chinese philosophy, the word "Tao," pronounced "Dow," means "the way"—the way our universe works. But according to that philosophy, the word itself counts for nothing because the universe outwits any attempt to label it. So, the philosophy goes, don't try to prove that your perception of reality is right. Hell, don't try to be right. Don't even try to not try. Just be.

Like water.

When Bruce Lee applied this insight to martial arts, he transformed the discipline. Pre-Lee, classical martial arts stressed tradition and rules. Post-Lee, martial arts became much more creative, freewheeling, nondefensive. Funny thing is, Lee's often credited as the father of Mixed Martial Arts, but that's a label he'd probably spurn. Precisely because he didn't want his fluid approach to decay into dogma, he hesitated to brand it. Lee told *Black Belt Magazine* that "truth exists outside all molds." Whatever he'd name his anti-method, it's "just a name used, a boat to get one across, and once across it is to be discarded and not to be carried on one's back." Labels, in short, can be burdens.

Yes, Lil?

Ah, terrific point. If I'm going to be like water, then shouldn't I open my mind to the alluring upside of labels—namely, that they comfort us with an identity?

Granted, humans are social animals who yearn for belonging. Labels provide that sense of security. And if we choose them for ourselves, labels feel ennobling. I voluntarily identify as a Muslim because I believe in Islam's original principles. A monumental principle is *tawheed*: the oneness of God and, by extension, the unity of God's vast creation. It's an honor to be created alongside you, Lil, despite inheriting a nose that's far less sophisticated than yours. Thanks for never making an issue of my disability.

Another core proposition in Islam is that God's gender-neutral. This tickles me pink (and blue). It's a rational idea since an infinite Creator, being infinite, has to exist beyond man-made categories—"outside all molds," as Bruce Lee said of truth. Yes, Lily, color me Muslim.

But my identity as a Muslim shouldn't have the power to freeze me in time or fix me in place. Because then I'm the opposite of water. "Beware of confining yourself to a particular belief and denying all else," the thirteenth-century philosopher Ibn Arabi cautioned, "for much good would elude you . . ." That speaks to me, Lil. If I cocooned myself in my Muslim identity, you and I probably wouldn't have met.

Here's why. It's common for Muslim parents to warn their children that dogs are *najis*, the Arabic word for "unclean." Apparently, doggiekind's so contagiously unclean that I'd risk poisoning my soul if I touched you. Nothing personal, of course.

How, you ask, can Muslims degrade dogs when our own religion teaches *tawheed*, the community of all God's creatures?

Think culture. Culture is the collective habits of a group. The group could be members of a religion, a nation, a company, or a movement. You've heard people sigh, "That's the way things are." Most people take the rules of their culture as a given. It's inconceivable to question whatever you take as a given, which is why even book-smart people tend to go brain-dead under the sway of their cultures.

I'll plead guilty, Lil. Oh, I adore you now but for most of life, I stayed away from the likes of you. Inculcated with a fiendish fear of dogs, I bought into that aspect of my culture until very recently. With the help of trusted friends, I overcame my fear, kept my faith, and ta-da, baby—it's you, me, and our shared weakness for peanut butter.

Again with the head-tilt? Okay, one more for now.

How can I call myself a Muslim when I violate Muslim culture? I'll answer with a story. Growing up, I attended a public school from Monday to Friday, followed by an Islamic school on Saturday. Like you, Lil, I exuded curiosity. I meant no harm by it; whenever I asked why or why not, I genuinely wanted to understand. At the age of fourteen, I posed a simple question that triggered a seismic test of my faith.

The teacher at my Islamic school announced that Muslims can't take Jews and Christians as friends. Full stop. "Why?" I asked him. That question burbled in me because at my public school, I had two teachers— one Christian, one Jewish—who stepped up as my mentors. Let me tell you, Lily, those men cared more about me than my own father did. Both made the time if I needed their guidance.

It's with them in mind that, when I heard Muslims must never be-friend Jews and Christians, "why?" went from gurgling in my gut to surging up my throat to spilling out of my mouth. For years, my Islam teacher had confronted my questions. But confronting isn't the same as addressing, so I'd never walk away feeling content with our ex-changes. I persisted in the hope of having an actual conversation. The existence of Jews and Christians made my teacher defensive, I sup-pose: He booted me out of the Islamic school. "For good!" he decreed.

There *is* a God.

Going forward, I spent every Saturday in the public library, explor-ing different religions, excavating the cultural sludge that concealed gems of wisdom. Eventually, I discovered that Islam has its own tra-dition of independent thinking.

Eureka!

Mashallah! (Praise God!)

And, being an American history buff, huzzah!

The civil war inside of me began to simmer down. Realizing that questions are *halal*, or permissible, I could finally reconcile being a faithful Muslim with being a searching one. What I learned that day prepared me for you, Lil. The lesson is universal: Most of us have our sacred cows, but when a remarkable mutt ambles in, we're not bound to renounce the cow for the mutt or to disregard the mutt for the cow. Any god worthy of worship makes room for both. Canines and bovines. Water and rocks. Us and Them.

Chinese and non-Chinese. When Bruce Lee became an instructor of Gung Fu (what we used to know as "Kung Fu"), he embraced non-Chinese students. You can't do that, classical teachers warned him, because Gung Fu belongs exclusively to the Chinese. Lee, born in America, raised in Hong Kong, educated in both, and living in San Francisco, embodied inclusion. To resolve the conflict with his critics, he challenged one of them to a Gung Fu fight.

It's like Bruce Lee brought a butter knife to the epic shoot-out at sunset: non-defensive self-defense versus time-tested and culturally authoritative Gung Fu. No contest, right? And, in fact, it wasn't much of one. Lee's more harmonious, less plotted maneuvers frustrated his opponent's moves. Bruce Lee won, effectively striking an obsolete, fear-based method from the manual of Chinese martial arts.

Which returns me to whether I can call myself a Muslim. Am I breaking sacrosanct rules by loving on a dog? Far from it. Typically, the rules of a group are little more than customs, those strands of culture that group members have woven, without question, into their "normal." Well, I've got questions. I question why you're labeled too dirty to go near, let alone to bring home. I could stifle my questions, as many do, but then I'm allowing culture to oxidize *tawheed*, one of my religion's most luminous ideals. I won't do it, Lil. Only when identity has integrity does it represent me. That's how I can be smitten with you and be an honest-to-God Muslim.

By the way, yesterday a university colleague informed me that I'm, in fact, a humanist. Broadly speaking, a humanist turns to humans as the ultimate source of reason and wisdom. Count me out of that club. To my mind, Lily, you qualify as a more sage, more sane being than most humans I know. Does that make me a dogmatist?

Roll those eyes if you must but I have to come clean: I'm a dog-loving Muslim pundamentalist.

What, too ruff a pun for your high-brow tastes?

Alright, alright, I'll paws.

Rescue me, Lil.

All in all, I accept that labels have their purposes. When I can afford to, I buy food that's labeled, "Locally Grown." It's helpful information—provided I can trust it. Anyway, labels save time. A shoe's a freaking shoe regardless of any other function it may serve. We need to name things to get on with life.

Trouble is, people aren't things. No sentient being's a thing. That's where diversity's gone wrong.

7

People Aren't Things

People are "huge waves of happenings," in the language of the physicist Carlo Rovelli. We're unfolding mixtures of genes, emotion, ego, memory, aspiration, and more. This means you don't fall off an assembly line as an interchangeable replica of all the others who share your labels. "You meet one Jesuit, you meet one Jesuit," jokes Father James Martin, one of America's spunkiest priests. Chew on this, too, Lil: Unlike things, humans aren't here to satisfy each other's desire for convenience. Not if relationships matter.

Emphasize *if.* Salma Hayek, the actress and movie producer, reports that she had to fight off Harvey Weinstein's repeated demands for sex. She'd later write that, to him, "I was a thing: not a nobody but a body." As #MeToo has made transparent, she's not alone.

On the opposite end of the celebrity meter was a black-bodied "nobody" named Eric Garner. A handful of New York police officers considered him a thing—good for padding their performance statistics but otherwise expendable. They pounced on Garner's petty crime of selling loose cigarettes and choked the life out of him.

Why? Is the answer as overt as his race and their racism? I'd assume so, since nonwhite neighborhoods too often crackle with police brutality. But according to the *Rolling Stone* journalist Matt Taibbi, Garner's story reveals something more layered than off-the-shelf racism. Garner suited the officers' need for a body, any body, to satisfy their quota.

In almost every major American city, Taibbi reports, police are "given a quota."

> *We want you to stop 20 people a month, we want you to seize one gun a month. So cops have to make stats. . . . [This] creates a factory-style approach to policing where you're not waiting for real probable cause, and you're just sort of pulling over people willy-nilly. . . .*

You know, Lil, I can't shake the parallel between factory-style policing and the supposed antidote to it: diversity training. In America's transactional culture, diversity amounts to slapping labels on individuals. People wind up packaged like products—crammed into prefabricated molds, presumed indistinguishable from others in the same category, handy for a momentary purpose and destined to be disposed of afterward.

The factory churns out units. "How many wings have we sold this week?" the fast-food manager asks. She must deliver for her bread-and-butter customer, the franchisee who has the power to fire underperformers. "How many minorities have we recruited this year?" the university president asks. She must deliver for her prestige customer, the color-conscious student who has the power to brand that university as woke, extra-crispy woke, or original recipe hostile.

The fast-food chain makes commodities out of nonhuman animals. The university does it to human animals. The fast-food chain strives to meet quotas. The university strives to please a quota-conditioned mentality, as if the value of an individual depends not on who each is but on whether each can help fill an order.

Factory-style diversity uses people for their labels. On the conveyor belt, we become instruments to advance a commercial agenda. Such diversity inadvertently does the grubby work of "the system"—to dehumanize.

A diversity that objectifies has spread so far and wide that it implicates avowed system-smashers, too. Later, Lil, I'll tell you about a couple of African American guys who came to my office for advice. An organizer with Black Lives Matter eagerly recruited their bodies for rallies, but in between protests she waved off their rather astute minds. The guys struggled with a question: Did the organizer want them only to the degree that she could capitalize on the color of their skin?

Martin Luther King Jr. would, I believe, have welcomed this question. He visualized a "beloved community" in which more of us are seen for our innate worth, not for our potential to add to a body count. You'd thrive in the beloved community, Lil, because you'd never again be someone's property. This isn't a place of rainbows and unicorns, though. We can't build the beloved community through child's play. As toddlers, we learn to master our toys. As we age, many of us treat people and animals as yet more toys—to be traded or tossed for shinier trinkets. "But when one matures," Dr. King preached in 1957, "when one rises above the early childhood years, he begins to love people for their own sake."

Put bluntly, quota-driven diversity fails to love people for their own sake, and this signal failure has earned diversity a reputation for hypocrisy.

Lil, you and I agree about the hypocrisy of many a Christian conservative. I've joined others in challenging Christians who evangelize the love of Jesus but then damn anyone who doesn't sing from their hymnbook. That's how chunks of America view the temple of diversity. From their vantage point, diversity's devotees belt out sweet songs of dignity but pick out whose dignity should prevail and whose should be assailed.

Witness what diversity's people so often do with the word "love." We craft hashtags from it. We hoist placards that blare it. We vow to reimagine the planet with it. Then we lose it. We come across people who disagree with us and, more frequently than we care to admit, our fear trumps love.

Some time ago, Lil, you met Brie Loskota. The three of us had lunch at the University of Southern California, where she directs the Center for Religion and Civic Culture. Loskota says, "Love that's reserved only for people who agree with you isn't love. It's narcissism." She's all for diversity, but she's put her finger on the way we're going about it: as a win-lose game.

Instead, let's go for the win-win. Just as water accepts the presence of rocks, people can accept that different elements inhabit the same surroundings and that a common denominator brings them together in one place at this particular time. Call that common denominator the Tao. Call it evolution. Call it God. Our universe has no need for people's labels. But people have a need for the integral message of our universe: Unity isn't uniformity.

Give that message a good, long whiff, Lil. Somewhere in there is the solution for America's division problem. As a starting point, let's label it *honest diversity*.

Why are you laughing at me, Lil?

You're just emulating the universe, are you?

Everyone's a comedian.

8

Honest Diversity

Dishonest diversity labels people as a substitute for understanding them. *Honest* diversity moves people beyond prefabricated labels—whether "white male" or "queer Muslim." Honest diversity begins with labels, sure, but it surges past them because it induces us to ask others why they believe what they believe. Practicing honest diversity, we listen without having to agree; we cultivate common ground even as we stand our ground; we act from a place of grace.

Cue the sarcasm. "I'm sorry that you feel bad," the journalist Jelani Cobb imagines bleeding hearts like me gushing to Trump voters. "What is it that caused you to destroy democracy? Perhaps we can hug you and move on from there."

Hug-a-thug is not where I'm at. Hugs, however, can come in handy when approaching non-thugs. To attract people to your vision, Lil, you first have to develop trust with them. This "happens more in the first hug and hello than with a big argument from smarty-pants me," Sarah Silverman discovered. She's the stand-up comic who hosts *I Love You, America with Sarah Silverman*. For all her progressive politics, she puts honest diversity to the test by engaging with Trump sympathizers in different parts of the country. One week, she told some of them about the time that she pooped her pants. They then revealed their own pooping accidents. I think they did so because Silverman showed them grace.

Absurd, you say?

Embarrassing, too?

Suck it up and stick with me, Lil.

Victor Tan Chen, a sociologist, writes that grace "is about refusing to divide the world into camps of the deserving and undeserving." By divulging her secret to people whose politics conflict with hers, Sarah Silverman telegraphed that they belong to her world. That they're vulnerable, just like she is. That everybody has shit to contend with. That we all, each one of us, deserve to laugh about it. No exceptions. Grace.

Oh, and by disclosing her story first, she earned that much more trust. In effect, Silverman communicated that whatever she wants from her new friends, if anything, she's prepared to give before she'll expect to get.

Barack Obama perspires grace. He celebrated Nelson Mandela's one hundredth birthday in Johannesburg the week that President Trump literally winked at Russia's Vladimir Putin in Helsinki. Obama could've gone low. He could've sniveled about the monopoly on political power still held in some domains by white men. But he did the opposite.

In a stadium bursting with people of color, Obama announced that the "reality of people who are different than us" must be a central concern in any democracy. "You can't do [democracy] if you insist that those who aren't like you because they're white, or because they're male . . . that somehow they lack standing on certain matters." That's a strategy as worthy of Bruce Lee as of Nelson Mandela. Obama acknowledged the dignity of any white man while paying homage to the valor of a black man. He replaced the suffocation of either/or with the imagination of both/and.

Let's brainstorm, Lil, how grace can work in other arenas. For instance, who "deserves" to speak at colleges? Grace would permit varied viewpoints, including ones that will probably offend you. But remember, whoever offends you may well be offended by you. Wouldn't you want them receiving your perspective with grace?

I know: What, then, are we to do about truly disgraceful values such as racial supremacy?

Oppose all forms of degradation. "There are different ways to go about it, though," adds Victor Tan Chen. The win-win way—honest diversity—will tax your patience but in the end it's efficient because, like water, it avoids humiliating others. Therefore, honest diversity has a higher chance of preventing blowback than reactive labels do.

I swear to you, Lil, I haven't been smoking a thing. Honest diversity isn't some pie-eyed hallucination concocted in a psychedelic state, at least not on my part. I can't vouch for the justices of the U.S. Supreme Court. In 1978, they mandated a form of honest diversity in higher education. At the time, the affirmative action debate was raging and the justices tackled this question, among others: Is race-based affirmative action constitutional?

The court thundered "no" to quotas. But in a 5–4 decision, it also said that race could be one of many factors in admitting students—as long as universities invest the time and energy to ensure that diversity of appearance results in diversity of viewpoint. That way, all students, whatever their complexion, would gain from fresh thinking in an educational environment. Win-win. In theory.

Not yet in practice. It may be that student leaders need the course, Be Like Water 101. On YouTube, I can watch screaming matches at campuses throughout America. Social justice activists face off against free speech warriors, each tribe preferring to be controversial over being constructive.

I must stress, Lil, that the militants don't represent most students. Calm exists in spades at every university. Yet, even in those mellow corners, I've observed how diversity of viewpoint gets casually dissed. At one workshop that I attended, a white woman was told to check her "ample privilege." Being large, the woman pinched her bulges. "I just checked it," she said with a smile. "Still there. Still ample. We're good."

Her crack infuriated the self-identified Latina two seats down, who accused our amply privileged friend of being a "white supremacist." To which Ample Privilege replied, "We haven't said two words to each other until now. What could you possibly know about me?" The Latina walked out without another word.

In front of everyone, I asked Ample Privilege a bit about herself. Whitney was her name—not to be confused, she quipped, with "Whitey." As the child of alcoholic parents, Whitney survived tension in the house by lightening the mood. It's a habit that also helped when kids fat-shamed her at school. These days, the same reflex kicks in whenever she's "white-shamed." Hearing that phrase, a number of the students in the workshop hissed. Not one of them asked for details about what she'd experienced.

Whitney shrugged at the disapproval. "It's too easy to be offended," she declared to the room. "Get to know me."

Clearly, Lil, diversity of views can't be attained by laws or secured by policies. Only relationships can guarantee real inclusion. Only people can stop gaming, blaming, and shaming each other with labels. Only then will diversity be honest.

I'm advocating a simple switch: *View labels as starting points, not as finish lines.* Starting points, that is, to ask each other questions. In doing so, we learn how individuals construe themselves and their world, not what's been decided about them without them.

I've got a searing story for you about what can happen when people take labels as finish lines. Rohith Vemula was a young PhD student in India. He identified himself as a Dalit, a member of the caste that used to be labeled "untouchable."

Vemula had academic potential like nobody's business. The first-class scholar made it to a prestigious university without relying on affirmative action, which speaks volumes: India, a multiethnic, multilingual, multi-everything country, has the most gargantuan affirmative action program anywhere.

So here's a child of society's bottom rung. Couple this with the fact that his mother endured regular beatings from a higher-caste man. For both of those reasons, Vemula was expected to follow his culture's script about the poor and seemingly dim-witted. Per the script, he should've been a mediocre student at best. He should've needed, desperately, one of those university seats reserved for marginalized groups. He should've been brought to his knees with gratitude for affirmative action, ignoring that in India it's primarily a vote-getting scheme.

But Rohith Vemula wouldn't conform to his society's mold for him. On campus, he became an activist for the most downtrodden—those too far in the fields to hear about any affirmative action program. The further off-script he veered, the more enemies Vemula made.

At one point, he and his fellow activists denounced the death penalty for a convicted terrorist who was also Muslim. Given India's Hindu-Muslim animosities, Vemula might as well have painted a target on his backpack. University authorities took aim. Over a single semester, they stripped him of his housing, his fellowship money, and his right to walk into campus facilities.

Within days, Rohith Vemula hanged himself. In the note that he left behind, he accepted full responsibility for his suicide. Still, listen to the very first words of that note: "The value of a man was reduced to his immediate identity and nearest possibility. To a vote. To a number. To a thing. Never was a man treated as a mind."

That, Lil, is why diversity of viewpoint has to be an inherent part of diversity itself. People aren't numbers or votes. We're capable of thinking, dreaming, and doing. We have relevance beyond our labels.

Head-tilt registered, sweet bean. Be my guest.

Why do I believe that human beings are capable of honest diversity? Because I've watched sincere questions tease out different perspectives, especially among young people. Would you like me to share a story about how we might give diverse viewpoints a real go?

Is that yawn a yes?

You're so good to me, Lil.

Years back, the media went ballistic over the radio shock jock Don Imus. He'd smeared a university women's basketball team as "nappy-headed hos." Racist and sexist, without a doubt. African American organizers joined with feminists to bombard cable TV in outrage. A rotating roster of them proclaimed that Imus had made all young women of color feel like victims. One of the pundits referred to "our" girls. I wish I could've asked him whether the girls had consented to being owned.

That week, I visited a school for young women of color in New York. Do you, I asked, agree with those speaking on your behalf that you've been victimized? Some responded no, fewer said yes, and one raised a piercing question: Why would she let anybody, white or not, male or not, define who she is? A classmate replied that white people will define her regardless of how she acts. The first girl then pointed out that some of their teachers are white and if they intended to stymie students of color, why let this conversation take place at all?

After a vibrant back-and-forth, another student, silent until now, lifted her hand. "Why is it," she wondered, "that when rappers say the same stuff about us as [Don Imus], they keep getting rich and famous?" More students chimed in, asking if the difference between "white" and "black" meant a difference in who's responsible for justice. The word "power" came up. Does a millionaire rapper have power even if he barely survived a rough childhood? I asked the students what they thought. An awkward pause. A muffled laugh. Darting eyes. Furrowed brows. Then a polyphony of views.

On it went—"our" girls proving to be neither the property of a tribe nor the output of a factory. These young women needed a chance to speak for themselves because, it turns out, they're textured.

I'll bet the Latina who called Whitney a white supremacist is textured. I'll wager that she has a story or six. Too bad she didn't come back.

9

The Way Forward

Zadie Smith, the novelist, says that we're all "internally plural." I like that, Lil. Each of us, including the white guy, is so much more than meets the eye. If we're willing to be honest about ourselves, we're plurals—an identity that fits even misfits like you and me. You can't know plurals by looking. You come to know them only by engaging. Which entails listening.

Easier said than done, isn't it? For twenty years, I've stood in front of audiences and debated attacks on my motives, not just on my ideas. Buttons pushed, blood pumped, ego bruised, defenses up, temper flaring, I was fast with the comebacks but slow to ask my critics why they believe what they do.

Trying to win every "game" sucked me dry. One Friday, preparing for a debate at the University of Oxford, I struck a pact with my exhausted spirit: If you hear a good point from the other side, say so. If you're antsy to jump in, slow down. If you need time to think, take it. What do you have to lose except yet another showdown that opens no minds, least of all yours?

That night, the pressure to be right yielded to the freedom of being real. My critics had expected me to stay in character. But when I pulled out of performing, it was game over. The debate became a conversation; one that led to more conversations, culminating months later in an invitation to speak about religious reform before a gathering of imams.

Strangely, listening didn't translate into losing. It generated trust. Lily, just wait until I tell you how trust changed the relationship between me and my mother. And no, honey, that's not code for why you should listen more to your mama. We're golden. Trust me, my treat-seeking missile, I'll keep the snacks coming.

Trust is such a retro concept. I've taught in New York, Los Angeles, and Toronto—three of the most diverse cities on earth. But few of my students would dare to be curious about people with backgrounds other than theirs. In our unforgiving call-out culture, asking the "wrong" question can get you slammed.

How self-defeating for a society. If diversity's going to drill deeper than labels, if innovative insights are to be heard, if derelict systems will ever evolve, people have to risk giving offense. Equally, we'll need to take offense as an opportunity to ask: What would water do? Then we'll be smarter about next steps.

You, Lily, are teaching me that this isn't a fantasy. When we met, I hadn't fully transcended my fear of dogs and you couldn't know whether I'd be an owner or a mother. We came to one another wary. And in my case, weary. I felt like an old dog who has adjusted to people's tricks: our antisocial antics on social media and our pretenses in person. How could human beings flourish in the pandemonium of our colliding values, priorities, and obsessions? Intellectually, I've been studying, speaking, and reflecting on these puzzles forever. Now you're schooling me in a force at least as potent as ideas: relationships.

May I make a proposal inspired by you, Lil? Let's equip a new generation to grow trust in relationships. Specifically in one relationship, just one, with someone whose opinions feel unsettling—even shocking.

As mass migration speeds up around us, as technology shoves confusion at us, and as "us" narrows from fragment to faction, it'll take courage to expose ourselves to uncomfortable points of view. It'll take more courage to display grace as we question those views. Above all, it'll take moral courage to cop to the limits of our own views.

I see at least three advantages to cultivating honest diversity. One: We'll wake up from the false certainty of labels. Two: We'll sober up from the addictive high of tribal loyalties. Three: We'll grow up from the juvenile need for validation at every turn.

Sums up a certain U.S. president, no?

There's the rub, Lil. *Dishonest* diversity helped elect him. Through the eyes of people as human as we are, dishonest diversity labels and frames white men as props in a drama that's intended to shame them. Dishonest diversity erects walls in reaction to existing walls. At rock bottom, dishonest diversity cements the border between Us and Them.

The cycle now feeds on itself. Donald Trump, the impresario of finger-pointing, shames much of humanity. He spares no one his mockery, not even a sexual assault survivor whom he earlier lauded as "a very fine woman." At the same time, he's empowered by our chronic shaming of his supporters. What do we ritually intone to them? "Shame! Shame! Shame!"

My question for those of us looking ahead: Do we want more of the shame? If not, then we'll have to risk unusual conversations. Lead the way, Ms. Lil.

"Straight White Male"

10

Lily in the Field: "I'm Not Your Bitch"

Ever since you came home with me, Lil, you've insisted on a leash-free life. The stroller is how you roll. The collar? Not so much.

Whenever I've tried to hitch one around your neck, you've refused to budge. It's like you're waging a campaign of noncooperation. I can imagine you growling, "This thing holds me back. Yeah, Mama, it makes you feel more secure when I can be controlled but the truth is, I don't exist for your convenience. With all due respect, I'm not your bitch."

Boom. Thank you for the thunderbolt. *You're not my bitch*. If more of us understood this unvarnished insight, we'd be on our way to honest diversity. Beauty is, your statement holds water from very different points of view. Let's start with the perspective of the Trump voter next door.

Scratch that. Let's start with a morsel of jerky. Then we'll call on the neighbor.

11

A Good Neighbor

Ms. Lil, do you remember Jim? You'd know him to smell him because he's always been gentle with you, extending his hand to your nose, and sweetly calling your name before slowly stroking your back. Jim's proud to have voted for Donald Trump, the most unscrupulous politician in my lifetime. I won't pussyfoot around: I detest the content of Trump's character.

But Jim? I love him. He's a father figure for me. Gregarious, kind, reliable, and reliably annoying. Jim and I met at a conference in Los Angeles. I spoke about the need for reform in Islam, after which he stood up and asked, "How can I help? I'm a Reform Jew but I wouldn't want you being labeled a puppet of the Jews."

"Too late," I told him. "'Puppet of the Jews' is one of my sturdiest labels. You might as well make it worth my while." Since then, we've been tight.

In my pre-Lily life, drab as it was, I taught at New York University. Jim would call me from Southern California simply to check in. Whenever I came to Los Angeles, I'd stay with him and his wife, Liz. One summer, I confided to them that I was depressed and had, a few days before, been hospitalized for a seizure. Jim instantly offered to hop a plane and whisk me home to his family. He promised that I could "eat like it's going out of style, shuffle around in pajamas, and defend Barack Obama."

At the time, Obama fired up in me a feeble "meh." His administration had lied, spied, and spun like the rest of them. I defended him only around Jim. But before I had a chance to say so, Liz snatched the phone to remind me that no Muslim (or Jew) ever escapes a doting mother. This would be her role until I could break it to my own mother that I was in bad shape.

For years, Jim watched me disintegrate from a firebrand to a zombie. In my never-ending travels to profess Islamic reform, I confronted every disagreement, epithet, and threat, fancying myself a slayer of all dragons. Guess who got slayed in the end? Your mama.

Needing to recover in solitude, I took a rain check on staying with Jim and Liz. But I had no idea how much they continued to worry for my well-being. Jim knew that lecturing me about the primacy of health wouldn't slow me down, so he adopted a subversive means of being fatherly. He also scheduled his subversion with a strategist's acumen.

I'm about to give you the details, Lilybean. Pay close attention now.

After recuperating, I resumed my travels for work. Five time zones and three weeks later, Jim picked me up from Los Angeles airport. As we caught up in the car, he said that he'd like me to meet a new neighbor of his. She's a "really neat lady," he cooed.

I'm crabby when I'm jetlagged, Lil. And L.A. traffic drives me bonkers. Without thinking, I snapped at Jim, "I don't have the time or the bandwidth for the emotional complexity of a romantic relationship."

He shot back, "I'm not asking you to marry her!"

The next day, we walked across the street to a common green space. Laura strode up in funky jeans and blue suede loafers. Her puppy, Rocky, pounced on Jim's dog, Romeo. Yelps of bromantic joy broke out.

For the next fifteen minutes, Laura and I flitted from her passion—animal welfare—to my fear of dogs to her profession as a medical tattoo artist to mine as an educator of moral courage to our mutual rejection of law school to the meaning that we both draw from having pursued our callings.

Laura then aroused the butterflies in my stomach. "Who we are," she mused, "is God's gift to us. Who we become is our gift to God. Does that make sense?"

Uh, yes. Seriously, yes. When can I see you again?

I glanced at Jim as he sat beaming on a nearby bench. As we sauntered home, I took his arm and whispered, "Well done, sir."

He chuckled. "Not bad for a homophobe, huh?"

12

Is He a Homophobe?

On more than one occasion, Jim told me that some family friends labeled him a homophobe because he votes Republican. The fact that now and again he'd mention being slandered as a homophobe made me realize that it gut-punched him, and he couldn't let it go. Having been Jim's "daughter" for a decade, I already knew that he didn't judge people by their sexuality.

Months after the Supreme Court confirmed marriage equality as a constitutional right, Jim took me to lunch. I watched how respectfully he interacted with the woman who waited on us at her family's restaurant. Jim asked her whether she planned to run the place when her mother retires. No, she said. She and her wife had other dreams. As a retired sales executive, Jim volunteered that if those dreams involved business, he'd be honored to advise.

His conversation with her shines head and shoulders above the one I had with a gay activist just before I came out to my mother. "Prepare to be disowned," the activist told me. "They all disown their gay kids." I should've asked, *Who are "they all"*? He didn't know my mother—at all.

Same goes for Jim's accusers. They don't know him. They presume that knowing his party label is to know him as an individual. They've done to him, one of those Republicans, what too many white people do to African American people, what too many African American people do to queer people, what too many queer people do to Muslim people, what too many Muslim people do to Jewish people, what too many Jewish people do to goys. The philosopher George Yancy spells out the "what" well: "As black, I am possessed by an essence that always precedes me. I am always 'known' in advance."

Like when all black men in America are "known" to be gangbangers. Or absentee dads. Or ice hockey incomps. Or dumb lugs who can play football, but not those positions that demand thinking. Several coaches in the National Football League admitted to assuming this, Lil. That's why African Americans have been wildly overrepresented in defensive roles and dramatically underrepresented as quarterbacks. Like Yancy says, when you're black in a white-defined setting, you can't take for granted that you'll be seen as an individual. You're often prejudged to be a mascot of some amorphous, ominous blackness.

"Black" is itself a made-up category. Exactly one hundred years before the American Revolution, African slaves and European laborers, all exploited by landowners, rebelled together in the English settlement of Jamestown, Virginia. Over the next many decades, plantation bosses resorted to dividing and conquering.

An Act Concerning Servants and Slaves, passed in 1705, legalized a hierarchy based on skin color. Under this law, "Christian white servant" would sweat for his master from ages nineteen to twenty-four but no longer than that. By comparison, the "negro slave" would be lashed for life, and "baptism of slaves doth not exempt them from bondage." In other words, being a Christian wouldn't save the Negro and being a Negro would most definitely sink him. Race—a pure fiction—ruled.

Ever since then, being perceived as black has been the catastrophe to avoid for every immigrant in America. People whom we'd now consider white sometimes met a grizzly end if Southerners deemed them no better than black. A slice of family history for you, Lil: Your Mama Laura had a great-grandfather, Angelo, from Sicily. In 1910, he was lynched. Laura showed me the tattered newspaper photo of his body hanging from a Florida tree next to the corpse of a fellow Italian. Their "in-between" skin tone—not quite black but manifestly not white—made them prime targets.

In fact, Italians had to watch their backs throughout the U.S. South. They came to these shores unstained by hostility toward African Americans, but after arriving they learned to keep their distance in order to pass as white. A lot of poor Italians even quit working alongside African Americans.

Hispanics also knew to market themselves as white in order to get ahead in this country. The writer Richard Rodriguez, who immigrated from Mexico, remembers hearing, "*No somos negros*—we are not black. We are a different people."

What all this says is that in America, there's no aspiring to white status without consciously or unconsciously putting down blackness. "White" establishes its credibility by *using* "black"—and using black people.

Really, Lil? I sound radical? Then call me radically real. Because I'm drawing directly from Jefferson Davis, president of the slave-holding Confederate states during the Civil War. "White men," he noted, "have an equality resulting from [the] presence of a lower caste . . ." But, he went on, such equality will collapse wherever poor whites "fill the position here occupied by the servile race." I'll translate these words plainly: If blacks ever disappeared, the white fraternity would be at war with itself. By Davis's own admission, white doesn't hold together without black. White has stature only because it isn't black. The moment white approximates black, the stature's as good as gone.

So, you ask, why not dump the vile black-and-white vocabulary associated with "race"? I'd love to, Lil. I'm told, though, it's exactly because racism persists that these labels remain relevant. My question is, how can racism recede if we continue relying on the categories invented by racists?

Beats me. I'm as guilty as anyone for recycling their rancid language. I hope to redeem myself a little later by suggesting an identity that respects you, me, and whomever else wants to bust out of the racial cubicles that we're herded into.

All I know for now, going back to Jim, is that being "white" or "straight" or "male" or "conservative" shouldn't blot out the fact that he's an individual. The categories assigned to him don't automatically make Jim a homophobe, just as the category "black" doesn't destine someone to be a hockeyphobe. Puck all labels.

13

Who You Calling Fragile?

Getting to know Jim as an individual means discussing with him how he decided on his politics. It doesn't mean debating him—not yet anyway—but asking sincere questions so you can figure out for yourself the caliber of his character. If anyone asked, Lil, they'd know that Jim's been complaining for twenty years about the perks and privileges amassed by the people's representatives in Washington—including Republicans, he used to be the first to fess up. They'd also know that his passion for American democracy is why he kvetches about political correctness. He's convinced that when you repeatedly tell people what they can and can't say, they stop seeing themselves as capable of self-government.

But Jim's accusers didn't ask him a solitary question. Instead, they seized on what they assumed a conservative to be. Then they mistook their subjective perception for objective proof that Jim's a bigot. Social scientists call this move "motivated reasoning." Motivated by an agenda, people cook up tripe that "proves" they're right about how the world works.

Yikes, Lil. Apologies for mentioning tripe.

Hang on. You're salivating because you're going to challenge me? Go on with your bad self, girl.

It sounds like I'm giving Jim a pass for playing the "fragility card." Hmmm. Okay. Could you add meat to those bones?

Ulp. Sorry, my little carniwhore. Could you clarify this "fragility card"?

Yes, I know about the theory of "white fragility." It states that white people are brittle. They haven't had to grow thick skins because they haven't had to deal with being stereotyped. So it's no shocker that if a white guy's labeled a homophobe, he lapses into sulkiness or bitterness. According to the theory, what Jim's really steamed about is the sudden questioning of his power—the power he's always had, as a white man, to set the terms that the rest of us will live by. His white fragility is a woe-is-me excuse to block the power-sharing that goes with true diversity. Did I explain the theory to your satisfaction, Lil?

Grand. May I respond?

There's some truth to it. In popular culture, white men tend to get away with being individuals wherever black men will be typecast. When black people gun down other black people, the squawking about "black-on-black violence" can be deafening. By the same token, almost 100 percent of America's mass shooters are white men, and yet each enjoys the benefit of being uniquely berserk. "White-on-student violence" isn't a coinage that I'd welcome, but it's only fair to juxtapose "white-on-student" with the "black-on-black" business that keeps getting recycled. Of course, both are crocks. All blacks, all whites, all of us, are individuals with back stories. Which is why I can't buy the theory of white fragility as a full-on truth.

Let's face it. More and more people *are* stereotyped simply for being white and male and heterosexual.

Say again, Lil? Don't forget "cisgender"?

Set me straight if I'm wrong about this, but to be "cisgender" is to be privileged because you retain the gender that you came into the world with. Those of us who aren't trans are, by default, cis. Do I have that more or less right?

Phew! I mean, phat! Far out. Super duper. And no, I'm not jittery. Don't label me.

Back to my point. More and more people *are* stereotyped for being white, male, heterosexual, and cis. But for diversity defenders to shame cis white males for being cis, white, and male, then accuse them of fragility when they fight back, and ultimately resent them for not being fragile enough to wilt is beyond passive-aggressive. It's Trump-grade gaslighting.

Jordan Peterson has surfed this wave to global superstardom. A psychology professor at the University of Toronto, he confronted students who tried to push him into accepting certain pronouns for transgender people. Peterson spoke with them on-camera but remained unconvinced. His critics then sheathed him in the label "transphobe." Peterson fulminated about their tactics, escalated the dispute, and detonated into an internet sensation.

His advice to would-be revolutionaries—clean your damn room before presuming to change the world—lends Peterson an aura of homespun authority. When combined with his pox on political correctness, his wisdom serves as both a balm and a bomb. He's God to the many (not only white men) who fervently believe that it's time for the shamed to rise up against the politically correct set. And he's Lucifer for the many (not only women) who suspect him of dragging the father-knows-best attitude back into fashion.

The fallibly human Jordan Peterson has become a whiteboard for whatever stereotype people now associate with the white man as Daddy. No need to read between the lines or parse semantics. Just listen to the sociology professor and preacher Michael Eric Dyson. During their May 2018 debate on a stage in Toronto, Dyson denounced Peterson as a "mean mad white man."

Once more, Lil?

I should remember that earlier on, I lamented our unforgiving call-out culture and now I'm contributing to it by calling out Dyson?

I'd stop myself if Dyson's words to Peterson—"You're a mean mad white man"—had been an honest mistake. But this wasn't a mistake. When given the opportunity to retract or rephrase, Dyson repeated his racial profiling. He then luxuriated in applause from a hefty portion of the audience, which tells me that he speaks—and stereotypes—for many more people than himself. As for Peterson, he retorted that he's not a caricature but an individual whom Dyson doesn't know.

That's how Jim, our neighbor, would've responded. For him, being stereotyped as a homophobe wounds; adding to the wound is a willful ignorance about him on the part of those who slur him. If white fragility applies to Jim, he's no more fragile than students of every color who petition for safe language, safe ideas, safe spaces. Designating fragility as a "white" condition, rather than a human condition, smacks to me of a double standard—and a graceless one at that.

Jerky?

14

Humiliation Nation

Please don't get peeved, Lil, but as I see it, you're relaying to white guys that they don't deserve the very understanding you expect them to show for us. It's yet another double standard. More, it has the makings of humiliation—an emotion that anti-diversity crusaders feast on. Humiliation can radicalize.

Ask young Muslim men across Europe. Many feel humiliated because mainstream society demonizes their religious and cultural heritage, all the while flaunting its apathy about their potential as contributing citizens. (In some cases, their own parents, nostalgic for their homelands, also discourage integration and further derail their dreams.) A fraction of these young men land on the digital doorstep of ISIS, the "brothers" who shrewdly empathize with their search for meaning. God knows I'm not condoning this choice, Lil. But without the intervention of skilled mentors, the tormented can become tormentors.

American kids aren't immune to humiliation, either. Many conduct their online lives lax about the fact that they're just a post away from a public shaming. Inevitably, some of these kids share a photo or comment that's pounced on as despicably prejudiced. They're battered by blame. Then come the Hitler references. You're a Nazi, they're told. Kill yourself. Drop dead. The line between virtual self and actual self blurs in the haze of emotion. How could it not? Most people, never mind the young, are stupendously devoid of self-awareness. Reeling from judgment, a subset of these kids gets gamed directly into the arms of the "alt-right," a label for the pro-Trump cavalry that, like their hero, makes sport of offending. Especially online. We'll take that label as a starting point to explore more deeply.

Before I continue, Lil, a nuance: Every backer of Trump isn't a backer of the alt-right. Plenty of smart young people with right-of-center thoughts have made the internet their sanctuary from schools with vehemently liberal cultures. They've followed in the footsteps of bright progressive minds who, for years, have used web spaces to push back on the traditional values rammed down their throats. Simply said, if you're put off by a Trump fan online, don't assume she's a shill for the alt-right. Roger that?

On to the alt-right. Their cockiest offenders have our number, Lil. They love to incense us diversity types with their vulgar "jokes" about women, queers, people of color, and assorted others. The louder our conniptions, the louder they laugh—at us and with each other. Now let me tell you about the craftiest of the cockiest. These cats are constantly trolling for recruits to their army of offenders. They count on kids feeling hunted by the liberal language police.

Excuse me, Lil? You say there's no such thing as the liberal language police?

Believe it or not, I agree—technically. The very existence of an alt-right testifies that in America, anyone *can* say anything. But *do* they? As I've learned from heartland Americans, no. Which is how some in our diversity circles want it. After all, their logic goes, listen to the dreck that dribbles out when people think they can spew whatever they like.

You know what I spew, Lil? Two words: "confirmation bias." This is the human tendency to zoom in on information that confirms our pre-existing assumptions. Here's a scenario. You're tweaked by three or four provocateurs who recently made scurrilous remarks just to rebel against political correctness. If you've already decided that our society's overrun by jackasses, then it's reasonable to conclude that jackass comments are the totality of what can be expected when Americans freely express themselves. But in your haste to confirm that bias, you neglect to zoom out and consider the panorama: that ordinary people say perfectly benign, even beautiful, things when they're not scared to pay a compliment, or be of assistance, or simply open their mouths.

Groups will energetically expose confirmation bias in other groups while denying it in their own. But the cold reality is that every group selects its facts. That's why, Lil, it does no good to insist that the "liberal language police" is a lie. Anti-PC brigades exaggerate, it's true. Yet everyone knows that imperious individuals, pretending to speak for all liberals, intimidate decent people into clamming up. So what that there's no authorized and organized squad of censors? Freelance censors do the job and that's a fact of the diversity scene we've got to deal with.

The sooner, the safer. Just as jihadists poach young Muslims who feel bilked and barren inside, alt-right crusaders target secular kids who feel the same. The crusaders invite their recruits into an exclusive club with private rituals, a members-only speech code, and consolation for being persecuted by liberal society. Lazy recruits get to weasel out of responsibility for their personal failures, which they now pin on conspiracies.

Best of all, Lil, willing recruits get to be warriors. They commit character assassinations and, from time to time, flesh-and-blood homicides. Involuntary celibates or "incels"—men whom no woman will sleep with—can prove their virility this way. That *they* might be the reason for women's rejection is unthinkable. It must be the fault of those "feminist cancers" and the "cucks" who stoop to them.

Whatever their specific grievances, alt-right soldiers are sold a spiritually transcendent test: Will you be man enough to avenge your liberal crucifiers? Will you subdue them once and for all or will you submit to a life of licking their boots?

Such tasty gruel for the snake pits of the internet. And for pleasant places within mainstream society. The alt-right's chatter about being subjugated bolsters the humiliation that many Americans already feel offline.

Stay alert to this feedback loop, Lil. It dangerously compounds "competitive victimhood," a phenomenon in which your group tries to one-up every other group in the sweepstakes of suffering. You recall those sweepstakes, don't you? They used to be parodied as the Olympics of Oppression. The gold medal went to whatever group announced itself the worst off. Invariably, the competitors would be women, minorities, or—jackpot!—both. Countless Americans in the heartland (and not a few on the coasts) would scoff at the whining, as they saw it. Today, those scoffers consider themselves among the victims, only more victimized for having been discounted by the courts, maligned by the media, and shunned by "the diversity regime."

Perceived humiliation has radicalized many voters to stand behind the world's most manipulative politicians. We, diversity's defenders, counter-scoff at our own peril.

15

"I Love You Just the Way You Are"

Riddle me this, Lil: From what you've been able to ferret out, are human beings born to cooperate as much as to compete? Or does your mama belong to a staunchly dog-eat-dog species?

Oh, come on. "Dog-eat-dog" offends you? They're only words, honey. No, not like "mean mad white man." That's different.

Can we talk about this later? Mark my words—er, I promise—that we'll go there.

Where did we leave off? Ah, yes. Human nature. I'm asking about it because "populist" politicians, ascendant around the globe, appreciate that humans are lone wolves and pack wolves all at once. And these politicians adroitly channel both instincts.

The label "populist" describes politicians, right, left, or otherwise, who appeal directly to the people. Like every label, this one's crass and sloppy. After all, "the people" are diverse. I'm as much "the people" as Jim is, but I can't stomach populism whereas he laps it up.

So let's treat the label only as a starting point to dissect what populist politicians do. They pitch themselves as servants of the forgotten folks, vowing to restore their long-lost pride. But it's smoke and mirrors, Lil. In blowing rhetorical smoke and priming us to mirror our tribe members, the Trumps of our time lure people to pridefulness, not pride. Their exploitation of human fragility undercuts much that there is to be proud of—character, for openers.

Such politicians prosper by playing to our kill-or-be-killed instincts. As Jim puts it, "Do unto others before they do unto you." It's not that populists kiss off cooperation as a fairy tale. In their telling, cooperation *among Us* will seal our survival. But cooperation *with Them* will be our demise. Outsiders, they warn, are out to defraud Us.

To pound this fear in, populist politicians manipulate frustrated human beings in two ways. First, they present clear-cut enemies— whether they're foreign investors, destitute refugees, corporations, minorities, "the one percent," or the media. We the people are never responsible for our mess. Other people are. Don't just name Them, the politicians hint. Blame Them. Second, to leave Us feeling that much better about ourselves, they promulgate a squishy message of self-esteem: *I love you just the way you are.*

That insight comes from Ivan Krastev. He's a scholar of democracy who, being based in Eastern Europe, is extraordinarily familiar with strongman tactics. Have you read him, Lil?

What, you can't pick up a book? I have two hands. You have four paws. Methinks you're well-equipped to crack the odd cover. Sheesh. Regardless, I love you just the way you are. Let's take Krastev's insight out of Eastern Europe and travel to different parts of the world with it.

In America, "I love you just the way you are" means, *I love the poorly educated. The Ivy League snobs want to confiscate your buckets of chicken. Tell 'em: Fry, fry again! Your traditions are terrific. Hold on to them. Your hometowns are the backbone, not the backwater, of this country. Stay in them. You don't need to learn about computers. Geeks are losers. Trucking and steel-making and coalmining are great skills. We're great people. But we're tired of being the patsy for, like, everyone!*

In France, "I love you just the way you are" means, *Guard with your life your pork, your wine, your cathedrals, your liberty. Our honorable civilization will neither crumble nor so much as crumple amid the swords of our Muslim aggressors. We will swarm their useful idiots, the multiculturalists who scream that we are racist but who cheer the woman-hating prophet of the Muslims. We, the nation of France, shall take our cues from Joan of Arc. We shall die at the stake before we live on our knees!*

In Turkey, "I love you just the way you are" means, *You no longer have to hide your religion. The secular cabal connived against us. But almighty Allah knows best. Islam is back in splendor! Young women: You will not have to leave Turkey to graduate from university. Our Turkey gives you the right—and responsibility—to wear your hijab as you pursue medicine and motherhood. Young men: You will not have to adjust to the heathen bandits who steal your human rights. Our Turkey gives you the right—and responsibility—to uphold your identity. We were a glorious empire. We will be again.*

In India, "I love you just the way you are" means, *We Hindus will finally stand up for ourselves. We will protect our cows from the Muslim butchers. We will protect our women from the Muslim rapists. We will protect our symbols, our speech, our status from the intellectuals who defile our values. We Hindus lead the world's maximal democracy! We will not be pushed into acting puny.*

Our final stop, Lil: Canada. Your floppy ears heard me right. In the outer reaches of Toronto, the ditched man and woman propelled Rob Ford to the mayoralty of Canada's biggest city. "Ford Nation" swept to power in 2010, six years before Trump Nation. Unlike Trump's base, Ford's brimmed with recent immigrants—black, brown, white, the spectrum. They seethed about shelling out their hard-earned tax dollars to Toronto's downtown, populated (in their view) by ingrates who gleefully disparaged the suburbs. Rob Ford, on the other hand, always returned the little guy's calls. He also smoked crack, talked smack, and consorted with sketchy characters. Finally, exulted his base, authenticity!

By electing His Worship Rob Ford as the chief executive of Toronto, Ford Nation symbolically seceded from cosmopolitan Canada. And not for the last time. In June 2018, Canada's largest province elected Ford's slightly milder brother as its premier. The capital of that province is Toronto. Downtowners may as well be sputtering, "I can't even . . ."

Say again, Lil?

I'm lapsing into labeling the voters who like populism? What gives you that idea?

Because I'm judging their leaders, eh? Let's hash this out. We'll take Donald Trump as our example.

I won't pretend to be neutral about this president. I repeat: In my judgment, he's the sultan of blaming, shaming, and gaming. My call to distrust labels shouldn't prevent us from judging; it should prevent us from judging *prematurely,* as in stoking *prejudice.* But when someone has a long, demonstrable history of comments and positions, the truth about his character can be deciphered. Donald Trump, an amateur commentator for decades, eminently qualifies on that front.

Now to my supposed labeling of Trump supporters. Equating them with Trump makes no sense unless I know each of his backers as the individual he or she is. Since that's impossible, I'm careful not to label them—not consciously, at any rate. Well, I did once. In a snarky mood, I condensed my philosophy as, "Love the Trumpian, hate the Trump."

You had to be there.

Look, Lil, if Trump fans take my castigation of him as a criticism of them, then I wonder: Might they be stereotyping themselves? I'd gently ask his voters to accept their diversity. Still, if I'm the one who's overlooking their diversity, then I ask that they educate me, and do so with grace. That's the only way I'll hear them.

I hope it's transparent by now that I'm against prejudgment on more than moral grounds. Strategically speaking, prejudging Trump defenders backfires on Trump opponents. Populists milk their support from people who are fed up with you and me lecturing, hectoring, almost scoring them on their values—or what we *speculate* are their values.

Let's return to those who label Jim a homophobe. He feels that they've demeaned him three times over: by assuming the worst about him before conversing with him; by using their assumptions about him to justify their biases about how "the system" operates; and by trying to guilt him into atoning for something that they've fabricated about him in the first place.

In essence, Jim has told them, "I'm not your bitch." Now, multiply by millions his fury at people who pay lip service to love but who leap to judgment—*pre*judgment. It's one way of understanding why Donald Trump won the White House and why he has such a good shot at being returned to it.

16

The Disadvantage of Being White

Shall we peer further through a white man's prism, Lil?

Yes, of course I'll share what I see. For context, let's first discuss election night 2016. In the frenzy of analysis that followed, a consensus quickly formed about what happened. Apparently, white working-class men in middle America revolted over their looted jobs. And their long-term economic insecurity. And their embattled identity. Jim, who lives in comfort, relates to the last of these—identity.

I believe it held the key to Trump's triumph. In May 2017, a survey was released invoking a sizable sample of Americans. The research showed that economically anxious folks favored Hillary Clinton for president. White working-class people who worried about their bills chose her nearly twice as much as they chose Donald Trump. He compensated by pandering to the culturally anxious. Feeling like "a stranger in my own country," to use the lingo of the survey, overwhelmingly motivated his supporters across class divides.

Mind you, Lil, Clinton didn't help by plunking half of Trump Nation into her "basket of deplorables," prejudging them that much more as "irredeemable." She meant the alt-right and white nationalists, not the family farmer. I'm sure of it because in practically her next breath, Clinton described "the other basket": those "who feel that the government has let them down, the economy has let them down, nobody cares about them, nobody worries about what happens to their lives and their futures." At the glittering fund-raiser for queer equality, where Clinton was speaking, she made clear that in this other basket are "people we have to understand and empathize with as well."

Too late. She'd been recorded and edited. When the "deplorables" video aired—without any mention of her call to understand struggling Americans—a colossal proportion of on-the-fence voters swung to Trump. According to the Clinton aide who monitored undecided Americans, that moment marked "the single biggest spike" of the campaign.

One offended voter compared Clinton to a big-league bully. Whereas Trump bullied Clinton, he said, Clinton bullied the masses. How could he identify with someone who repudiated old-school Americans just for being different?

Yes, Lilybean?

Definitely. I agree that Hillary Clinton was misunderstood, not malevolent. Indeed, she was malevolently misunderstood by the Trump campaign and its media cheerleaders. But the very word "deplorable" activated in a sweeping segment of America what it had already been feeling. You guessed it: deplored. Clinton's language vindicated a question that's been gnawing at Jim for a few years now: *As a straight white male, do I belong anymore?*

Lil, you wandered the streets after being released. You know it's natural to feel fear when you're unsure about where, or whether, you fit. If that's true for dogs, it's no less true for people. White Americans increasingly find themselves doing what you and I have done: negotiate for a purposeful place in the culture. Jim feels that much more dislocated because, as someone with conservative values, he prioritizes social order. The society he thought he understood is unremittingly opening up. From his perspective, it's disorderly. No wonder he's disoriented.

But even white Americans who want *openness* can feel fear—and, this I can't stress enough, those fears aren't always telltale signs of hatred toward others.

In 2014, I delivered a speech at the Wise campus of the University of Virginia. Afterward, several students hung around to talk. Among them was Sam. "Why," he asked me, "are the best things about the culture down here never, ever considered part of multiculturalism?"

"Best things?" I responded, intrigued by his boldness. "Like what?"

Sam told me that in Appalachia, "How are you today?" is a sincere question. "We really do care," he assured me. "Same when you're in trouble. If you've got a flat tire, lots of us will stop to help you out. Does that happen much where you are?" In New York, I'd grown accustomed to watching people from all over the world interact and transact. On the streets, though, I hadn't yet come across a common routine of generosity.

Sam continued. "Scholars and activists praise multiculturalism because of what immigrants bring to the country. Awesome. My girlfriend's family comes from South America and I love learning from them. But nobody's asking about the American South and what folks born here can bring to the multicultural scene. Except maybe a famous chef who does that whole farm-to-table act for a Food Network show." I smiled at the jab about tokenism and invited Sam to tell me more.

"The hicks in Virginia are supposed to be leery of outsiders, right? Isn't that how we're portrayed?" Sam cursed the hillbilly stereotype, larded as it is with assumptions about whose culture deserves respect. Precisely because he and his white male friends buy into an inclusive future, they won't sit there and take it while filthy memes about people like them ricochet around the internet. Not even if they're just jokes. Progressive dog whistles are still dog whistles.

Pardon the dog reference, Lil. It's a common expression in politics.

It's a microaggression against dogs? Nah. Nahahahahaha!

For real?

Hold that thought. You have my word that we'll discuss microaggressions.

For the moment, let's stay focused on Sam. He woke me up to a generation that's going to feel more disaffected as diversity's pledge becomes more corrupted. The pledge, quite simply, is that everybody belongs by dint of the dignity we're born with. If you're going to stand out for good or ill, let it be because of the character you've built and not the traits you've inherited—gender, color, sexuality, class, or otherwise.

Wasn't that the deal tabled by the civil rights movement? To judge and be judged by the content of one's character, not the color of one's skin? This covenant can't be credible when it's executed as though white people must view people of color for their individuality but not the other way around. If there's a double standard, then there's no deal.

Sound off, Lily.

The same can be said by African Americans about the double standards they face? True enough. We're still ensconced in a system designed to erase the individuality of nonwhite people. It brings up the paramount issue of power: who has it and who doesn't. I'll think on this, Lil, and I'll speak with you about power a bit later. In the meantime, I'm grateful for your red flag.

But—and this is my red flag—progress won't ramp up by giving white America a taste of the putrid medicine dispensed to black America. That civil rights covenant of judging by character rather than by color still holds the secret to keeping each of us accountable for our part in the pursuit of happiness. If we abandon the covenant now, we're bending the arc of history alright. Backward.

Moreover, Sam wants to help seal the deal's promise. He's down for equality as long as he knows that it's neither a swindle nor a setup; that it's being sought in good faith. Which is why he questions any multiculturalism that excludes some people under the banner of including all people.

I asked myself: *Is Sam alone in his questions? Or does he reflect an impending crisis of identity among young white people, with repercussions for everyone?*

I've read and heard a litany of opinions about what it's like to be white in the new America. Richard Rodriguez, an author of several books about identity, offers the least voiced yet most interesting angle. "I give a lot of lectures about being brown, by which I mean mixed," he says.

And kids will come up to me afterwards. A girl said—this is a preface to her question—"I'm white. I'm nothing." Or another will say, "I'm white. I have no culture." The price of being white in America is that you obliterate memory. . . . That you have no history. That all the things that might colorize your life—grief, joy, a tradition of hard labor—is obliterated in this bleach of whiteness.

Blatantly put, Lil, young white people risk becoming invisible in the American tapestry. They're denied the ethnic roots that kids of color can call on for recognition. In truth, Rodriguez says, young whites are as "varied and complicated" as he, the child of Mexican immigrants, is. "[T]o give a Mormon kid *that,* to give the son of divorced parents *that,* that you have had a life, that there's something in you, that you're not simply white, is important."

As I listened to Rodriguez, I reflected on Sam, a thoughtful son of the South. Thoughtful enough that he took the time to ask why the best of his culture escapes notice when students and academics stick up for multiculturalism. In my view, Richard Rodriguez nails it: These days, to be labeled "white" is to learn that you're a cultural nonentity.

I've got another example of being whitewashed, as it were, from empathy's embrace. A former student of mine emailed me for advice. He'd made the move from an investment bank on Wall Street to the environmental unit of the Clinton Global Initiative. There, at the gold standard of good works, he faced the same office politics and ego trips that infected the bastions of finance. He then proceeded to discredit his heartbreak as "a white people's problem." I reminded him that the search for meaning is both timeless and borderless. Absolutely, his circumstances are first world, but his dilemma—how to persevere when you're thoroughly dejected—is nothing if not universal.

It occurs to me that if Sam had inherited infinitesimally different genes, his quest for belonging, for integration, would probably be encouraged. "Let's do something about it," I can hear an urban teacher telling a brown boy who's hurt that the school doesn't make space for his family's cherished customs. Sam has no such privilege. He grew up in suburban Boston with a divorced mother and no visible disadvantage. Therein lay his disadvantage. When students ridiculed his old-fashioned chivalry and occasional accent, he couldn't call it racism; only kids of color could claim that affliction against them. Unsure of what category he fell into, Sam just fell silent.

Grappling with his identity crisis, Sam waited until everyone else had exited the university auditorium before bringing his question to me. His first words as he shook my hand: "I come in peace." I left our conversation realizing that Sam doesn't belittle diversity as it's meant to be. Diversity as it's practiced belittles Sam.

Wait, my inner New Yorker then piped up. *Are you being conned? How do you know that what this guy says about the South is true?*

Choosing to trust but verify, I contacted my friend Genesis, who at the time toggled between New York and her hometown of Biloxi, Mississippi. Biracial and raised a Muslim, Genesis isn't prone to romanticizing the South. Lately, in fact, she's been drawing on her talents as a hip-hop artist to advocate replacing Mississippi's state flag, which honors the civil war soldiers who fought to retain slavery. Whenever that flag snaps, it signals to Genesis that she should salute the enslavement of her forebears. Salute this, groupies of the Confederacy: She's not your bitch.

Sam, however, has it right as far as Genesis is concerned. She affirmed what he pinpointed as the best of their shared culture—sincerity, hospitality, active intervention for someone in trouble. In a phone call from Manhattan, Gen said softly, "That's why I love coming home."

17

This Is Progress?

We started with Jim, Trump's fan boy and my father figure. His story about being smeared as a homophobe seems petty on its own. But add all the context we've been discussing, Lil, and you see why it strengthens Jim's suspicion that in multicultural America, his dignity doesn't rate. That he can be toyed with. Singled out for a moral takedown. Robotically accused of crimes against diversity.

For some of us, to engage with Jim is to simper, "Boohoo, bruh. You think you're under siege? Get over yourself—and welcome to payback time." Yes, he admits, white men in earlier generations did mistreat entire classes of people as property, and yes, more than a few continue to. As we talked about this, the Fox News star Bill O'Reilly was being accused of sexually harassing several women. Jim didn't defend him. "O'Reilly has issues," he mumbled to me.

I hear you, Lil. It's nowhere near an acknowledgment that sexism saturates our culture. From Jim, though, it's a refreshing bit of honesty since his home marinates in the talking points of Fox News.

For all that, Jim remains as baffled as I am about the unspoken question: When white male gasbags become rhetorical punching bags, how's America truly better off? No dispute that their language can be atrocious, so yanking them off the air feels gratifying. I won't hide the side of me that savors O'Reilly's comeuppance and gets positively giddy at the thought of Trump in an orange jumpsuit. He'd be tremendously coordinated from head to toe.

But what does my malice for their malice accomplish beyond a spiteful snicker? Does it address the demoralizing of those who feel they're being unwoven from the American tapestry? If I accept that kids like Sam are collateral damage in the war for a just world, if it's fine to throw them under the revved-up diversity bus, isn't the hackneyed pattern of Us against Them repeating itself? If so, then payback can't be progress. Jim has a valid point.

Jim also has a lot of nerve. Not once has he tipped his hat to Barack Obama's attempts at reconciling Us and Them on the racial front. Again and again, Obama urged African Americans to empathize with white Americans. When he delivered his famous "race speech" from Philadelphia in 2008, then-candidate Obama explained that "to wish away the resentments of white Americans, to label them as misguided or even racist, without recognizing they are grounded in legitimate concerns" will boomerang badly. Instant judgment "widens the racial divide" because it "blocks the path to understanding." He set the same standard for white Americans. To no avail in Jim's heart.

As president, Obama persevered. In a 2016 commencement address at Howard University, the nation's premier black college, he encouraged graduates to connect their drive for equality with the hardships of other Americans, especially "the middle-aged white guy who, from the outside, may seem like he's got all the advantages, but has seen his world upended by economic, and cultural, and technological change."

When I informed Jim of President Obama's sentiments, he was unmoved. I then told him that Obama reiterated those sentiments in his farewell speech to a mostly young throng in Chicago. On that night, the president added, "We have to pay attention and listen." Frankly, Jim does neither when it comes to anything Obama-blessed.

Every once in a while, my pre-Lily impatience makes a sudden appearance. Late one evening, during a Fox News broadcast about Black Lives Matter, Jim griped that Obama will be leaving the United States more racially fractured than ever. "Ever?" I asked. "Does American history begin after the genocide of Native Americans?" Jim shot me the stink-eye and smoldered.

Minutes later: "Obama's the reason for all this. What would he have to say about black-on-black violence?" I'd been dozing off in Jim's living room, but sprung back to vertical life.

"Are you kidding me?" I spat. "Obama's been so outspoken on the need for African Americans to own their shit that some black leaders complain he lectures them." Statistics don't speak to Jim, but values do. Framing the issue as one of personal responsibility, I figured I'd have a chance of being heard.

"You've got your iPad right in front of you," I motioned to Jim. "Google 'My Brother's Keeper.'" It's an organization that mentors African American boys to develop the content of their character and choose honorable lives for themselves. President Obama founded the program. Jim hadn't heard of this effort; he must have missed Bill O'Reilly's coverage of it.

"Okay, well, good," Jim said after he read what My Brother's Keeper had already achieved. Then he tacked on, "Do you enjoy making me look stupid?" For the record, I don't think Jim's stupid. I respectfully submit that he has "alternative intelligence."

The next day, as he digested our conversation, Jim sounded energized. "I really got a kick out of that," he raved, "and I learned a few things." You understand, Lil, that I can't badger Jim day in and day out. To get in his face would turn every issue into a matter of saving face—a diversion from the issues themselves. Besides which, I don't want our relationship being defined by cage-matches. Where's the joy in that? And what's a relationship without joy?

"Marriage"? Is that what you just snarled, Lil? Troublemaker.

Where was I? Oh, yes, having more joy than oy in my relationship with Jim. It explains the final reason that I won't suit up and try proving him wrong at every opportunity: To do so is to game him, and Jim's not some plastic figurine to be roughed up for my ideological amusement. He's not my bitch. To love Jim for his own sake is to sustain the conversation—while testing our trust by venturing into uncharted territory. Come with me, Lilybean. I'll take you there.

18

Beware of Your Brain

Three weeks after Donald Trump took office, Jim and I went out for ice cream. We sat in the car, talking about the Muslim travel ban and polishing off our trashy soft serves. I'd been wanting to discuss how annoyed I felt with him. His blanket condemnations of Barack Obama bugged the bejeezus out of me. Was he a racist, pure and simple?

If my question comes off as dense, Lil, I ask it because Jim's complicated.

On the one hand, he radiates civic virtue. Among other volunteer gigs, he works with a local group that houses low-income families, immigrant and not. In fact, he's counseling the group to respect those families; to stop seeing them as charity cases and start viewing them as agents of change in their own right. That's the reason My Brother's Keeper touched Jim. Barack Obama respects young black men to be more than victims.

On the other hand, Jim sprays bile at Obama—actually, at all Democrats. I don't know what he'd do without them. If I bring up Trump's latest lie, Jim mechanically fires back, "What about Hillary?" Partisans of every cause share the "what-about" reflex. But no practitioner of what-aboutism has perfected it quite like the Soviet Union.

For decades, it's what Moscow mouthed whenever reporters investigated human rights abuses in the U.S.S.R. "What about racial segregation in America?" the Kremlin's flunkies regurgitated as a way to deflect accountability. What-aboutism solves exactly nothing. It only sharpens the claws of negative polarization. In its grip, we're obsessed with crushing Them instead of improving Us.

I was busting to hold the mirror up to Jim. Knowing that he labels Barack Obama a socialist and therefore a treasonist, I put it to Jim point-blank: "Do you realize that your addiction to what-aboutism is more socialist than anything Obama ever did?"

Crickets, Lil.

Ice cream in my right hand, I curled my left hand into a fist, lightly punched Jim in the arm, and risked a rather brusque question. "Who's undermining American democracy more: Russian trolls or patriots like you?"

"What about liberals?" Jim replied without irony.

"You're right," I attested. "Liberals push the 'what-about' button all the time. And I say so all the time. But you don't say it about your side. Why not?"

Jim bit into his cone and stared out the windshield. "Bad habit."

That's it? I thought to myself. *Bad habit? Bullshit.* But you've taught me, Lil, that to love someone is to learn from them. So I took inspiration from Jim's claptrap. I began researching why so many good people tumble into the quicksand of Us versus Them. It turns out that there's a ton of truth to Jim's "bad habit" jive.

The human brain plays a habit-forming trick that dates back to our time as hunter-gatherers. When people slaughtered their prey, circuits in their brains lit up to give them the momentary feeling of being rewarded. Get this, Lil: Those same brain circuits are activated whenever we're *agreed with*. Recent research shows that if we're validated in our beliefs, we experience the fleeting exhilaration of victory. Exhilaration can be addictive. The more we feel it, the more we crave it. The more we crave it, the more we go after it again. And again.

Apply this scientific insight to Jim. Hearing his opinions repeated and applauded has a chemical impact. It makes him feel good. What an impetus to wall himself off, take refuge in his chest-thumping tribe, and defeat those who threaten the tribe's preconceptions.

Now apply this to all human beings. Our biology guides us toward the easy pleasures, so even highly educated people scamper into pods of purity, where they can bask in emotional warmth. That's how those of us who advocate the opposite of conformity—namely, diversity—too often end up creating conformist platoons.

That's how we succumb to the seduction of labels.

That's how we unintentionally practice exclusion camouflaged as inclusion.

Above all, that's how we mirror Donald Trump. On the campaign trail, Trump announced, "The only important thing is the unification of the people because the other people don't mean anything." Wait, what? Asinine. But if we leave diversity to our most base instincts, we become *that*. Labeling Trump supporters instead of understanding some of them lures us to a Trumpian result: We unify ourselves and brush off "the other people" because they "don't mean anything."

Don't tell me, Lil. It's a false equivalence to compare Us to Them. We have brains.

Consider this a mixed blessing. Typically, human beings submit to the ancient part of our brains rather than exercising the more evolved regions of our brains. In doing so, we kowtow to our Us against Them impulses. At that point—and with apologies to the lovely state of Louisiana—diversity congeals like spoiled gumbo. The layer called "us" separates from the goop it leaves behind. Although "our" layer may be foodier, chewier, more substantial than "their" layer, both layers have turned gnarly.

Please give me a minute to retch.

Better now.

I don't want to insult your intelligence, Lil. There's no single cause for any single act. Nothing that humans do can be demystified by study-ing the brain on its own. Alongside it churns an intricate mix of genes, hormones, environment, and culture. But the brain is the last tunnel traveled by these different influences. It's the "final common pathway," according to the neuroscientist Robert Sapolsky.

Hilariously, he observes that researchers of the brain unconsciously cave to the brain's knack for grouping: They classify themselves into ever-more specialized fields and reach ever-narrower conclusions. These cerebral professionals somewhat ape the loyalists of any political party. How's that for hope, Lil?

The next time you're having a lousy day, I recommend that you read Sapolsky's masterpiece, *Behave: The Biology of Humans at Our Best and Worst.* It'll make you feel like you bypassed a bullet in being created a dog.

Shoot, I forgot. You don't do books. That's a pity because I'd love to coauthor our mother-daughter memoir down the road. But your choices are yours and I accept them. The choices of humans, however, I struggle with because the stakes involved couldn't be higher.

Not steaks, honey. Stakes. S-t-a-k-e-s. Here's a tissue if you want to mop up around your beard.

Beauty.

Throughout the world, including here, more and more people are choosing to use their brains mindlessly. As in tribally. To be accurate here, Robert Sapolsky doesn't believe we choose anything. He says that human beings have zero free will because in the final analysis, our biology dictates our behavior. But then how do we explain "consciousness"— which another neuroscientist, Timothy Wilson, defines as "that wonderful ability to reflect, ponder and choose"? What do we make of Bruce Lee, who challenged tribalism in both the Chinese and American cultures? And Sarah Silverman? And Barack Obama? And Benjamin Franklin? Don't they demonstrate that we can choose to override the brain's either-or instinct?

Aren't populists demonstrating that we can also choose not to? If America literally were a gumbo casserole, Lil, then at this moment I wouldn't feed you a spoonful of your country no matter how much you begged.

You've got the floor.

I certainly do care about your appetite, honey. It's entirely understandable that you don't want gumbo going to waste. Polarization jeopardizes your pleasure. I feel you.

What am *I* going to do about it? No, my love, I alone can't fix it. Any solution will be an array of tiny solutions, which means a lot of hands on deck. But I can testify that we won't solve Us against Them strictly by sloganeering at Them. In a polarized society, truth dies in part because of Us. While we collectively resist the other side's truth, our own official truth emerges. Although we differ among ourselves at the edges, our core assumptions about Them hold our orthodoxy intact. Ditto for theirs. As the orthodoxies square off, we self-congratulate and self-segregate behind our "gated realities," in the astute words of Brooke Gladstone. How can the consequence be any different than polarization once again?

Rest assured, I appreciate that human beings, social animals that we are, gravitate to wherever our friends go. Mass events tingle our brains and titillate our spirits, if only for that hour. To all our peeps, Lil, I say: Congregate away. Snag the feel-good moments that quench our parched souls. Careful not to kid ourselves, though. If we care about solidarity—those social ties that ensure the *durability* of progress—we'll also have to chip away at polarization.

Best as I can tell, the big-picture antidote to polarization is raising young people to invite, actively and regularly, a diversity of views into their lives. We can role-model this M.O. with personal conversations that bring out what we don't yet know about our Other. And if we want the visceral rush of thrusting our fists in the air, hey, nothing prevents us from doing both. Nothing, except our willingness to be played by our brains.

I confess, Lily, that Jim might never be changed by my conversations with him. Or that, if he is changed, he might drift in a direction that disappoints me. It's possible that Jim will become more savage about political correctness, whose manipulation he despises down to his fingernails. Possible, too, that he'll become even more oblivious to the manipulation that he construes as information—courtesy of the far-right's multimedia rage machine.

But I can tell you this. If Jim pulls himself out of the Us-against-Them quagmire, it won't be because I tore into him with verifiable facts. It'll be because I loved him enough to wonder where he's coming from, and because he trusted that my questions spring from a desire to challenge myself.

I must make a second confession. Jim has changed me. Around him, I can't settle for the vacant thrill of name-calling. In democracy as in matrimony, you amend the Other, if at all, by reforming yourself.

May I let you in on a recent development? Jim sent me his rabbi's sermon about breaking the habits that inflame polarization. He actually took the time to request a written copy. He's thinking about the privilege we humans give to emotion. He's thinking about democracy's need for a better balance between feeling and contemplating.

Well-functioning humans never stop feeling, but more of us could try, like Jim, to think about how much we're emoting when we argue with our Other. Because we're emoting out of a desire not to do what's right, but to show we're right. And yet, all we're showing is that we resist the very introspection we demand of our opponents.

Sure, we're human. So's our Other. Empathy for Them is compassion for ourselves.

By the by, Lil, without Jim you probably wouldn't be in my life. I told you that he introduced me to your Mama Laura. Together, they introduced me to the dignity of doggiekind. See? Jim's "alternative intelligence" paid off at least twice. First, I fell in love with you. Second, a few weeks after you adopted us, Laura and I got married. That day, Jim joined my devoutly Muslim uncle in walking me down the aisle.

"Muslim Refugee"

19

An Upper, a Downer, and a Mother

Lilpill, what do you think of when I say, "Muslim woman"? Do you think of someone who's her husband's bitch? You can be honest with me. There's no shame in having biases; we all do. What I'd fault you for is leaving it at that because then *you* become the bitch of your biases.

Sometimes, I tell you stories about my mama. Her name's Mumtaz. To describe her, you can start with the labels, "Muslim woman." But to end there would be to deprive yourself of a kindred soul. Mumtaz is so much scrappier—and funnier—than any container can hold. One day, when my sisters and I were kids, Mumtaz pestered us to pick our socks up off the floor. My sisters advised her to take a downer. "No," she vented. "You take an upper!"

Like you, Lil, Mumtaz won't be corralled.

It's from her perspective that I'd like to explore one of your key teachings: that people don't exist to be pawns of our personal agendas or bit players in our private dramas. We humans keep our pantomimes going through sheer manipulation. We stuff others into roles of our choosing and we forego the surprises that can't be scripted.

At your mamas' wedding, Lil, Mumtaz read from the Qur'an to bless my union with Laura. An unforgettable overture that made history. Even more special for us, however, was her bumble. Mumtaz meant to call us "creations" but accidentally referred to Laura and me as "creatures." Catching herself a little too late, she burst into laughter and couldn't stop. As we watched Mumtaz bust a gut during a sacred moment, Laura and I doubled over. So did our guests, especially the judge who married us in his solemn black robe. How fitting that the gathering erupted, emulating the once-active volcanoes that watched over us. Unity without uniformity.

If Mumtaz were a movie character animated only by her labels, you'd have to cut that scene. An observant Muslim woman sanctifying the same-sex marriage of her daughter? What the hellfire? Looking back on it now, Lil, I realize that Mumtaz was revealing her leash-less identity. And I'm sorry to say that I'd misunderstood my mama for most of my life.

20

The Unexpected Rebel

For too long, Lil, Mumtaz was in fact her husband's bitch. Born into drastic poverty in Dar es Salaam, Tanzania, she entered an arranged marriage with a man whom her family deemed respectable only because of his middle-class status.

We'll call him Bash (the nickname that he went by with his colleagues at work). Bash compulsively beat Mumtaz. When she needed grocery money for their three daughters, Bash flung bills on the ground and glared as she reached for them. There would've been a fourth daughter, or a first son, but he forced Mumtaz to get an abortion, lest she produce another female. To this day, Mumtaz begs her unborn child to forgive her for not wanting to leave me and my two sisters mama-less. She intuits that the baby was a girl. She's named the girl Zahra. Bash would've killed Mumtaz, she believes, had Zahra seen the light of day.

For what it's worth, Bash took no interest in Islam. He identified as a Muslim but attended the mosque only for show. Mumtaz, on the other hand, cried and confided to Allah. She'd never spoken with God as a child. "Religion for me really came later," she says, after her spunk as a nonconformist was stolen by cultural tradition and she had no place to turn except the prayer mat.

You see, Lil, as a teenager Mumtaz honored her rebellious nature. Despite already being engaged—against her will, I must repeat—she fell in love with a different man who loved her right back. He was best friends with Mumtaz's brother and, for a while, her bro served as their intermediary. Every other day, the man she loved would drop by the corner store where she worked, just to flash a smile at her. They began to exchange secret letters.

Meanwhile, Bash also mailed letters to her. He filled them with mundane details about how life would be after the nuptials—the duties she'd have toward her in-laws, what he'd do with the money she'd collect as a seamstress, that sort of thing. Mumtaz determined that she had to escape, but in a way that brought the least amount of shame on each family. Her strategy: Convince Bash to be the one who calls off their wedding. Her problem: Speaking with Bash about breaking up would make him go haywire and quite possibly exact revenge, if not against her then against her brother. Her sole hope would be to create the conditions under which he'd no longer want to marry her. "I was ready to spoil my reputation," Mumtaz admits.

Hence this plan: Mumtaz allowed the man she loved to intercept a letter from Bash and reply to it. When Bash received the reply, he immediately protested to a relative that there's another man in the background. The news spread, compelling Mumtaz's mother to inform both families that her daughter was miserable about the engagement.

Finally, Lil, someone had spoken the unspeakable. The door to liberty and love had been unlocked. The worst of the deed was done, at least in Mumtaz's head. But culture dies hard. Her father's ancestors came from Gujarat, a state in India and the birthplace of Gandhi. Yet they had none of Gandhi's countercultural courage. Family honor dictated what took place next. Her mortified grandmother approached Mumtaz in tears.

I remember that she used a Gujarati proverb, "You are throwing sand in my gray hair." I think she meant I was making it grayer. She was very upset with me. She said, "Mumtaz, I have loved you so much"—and she did!—"I have loved you so much. What are you

doing to my reputation . . . ? In an upstanding family like ours, we
don't do this . . . People will talk."

They already were. Like a Twitter pile-on, the village gossips in-
flated the truth all out of proportion. "So," Mumtaz sighs, "I told my
grandmother that I would not break the engagement. I said I would
just take their prayers and go with it." She adds, "In the first week of
our marriage he beat me up. In the very first week."

The thrashings didn't abate. I remember nights, Lil, that Mumtaz,
my sisters, and I spent in the family room, each of us busy with her
own task. The tranquility would be punctured by the *clunk-clunk-whrrr*
of our garage door opening. We'd exchange glances as if to ask, *Is this*
the last time we'll all be together—alive?

Yet the child in Mumtaz wouldn't die. One evening, I heard her
belly-laugh at the neighbors' house. They'd invited us for dinner and I
begged off early to finish my homework. All the way across both lawns,
a voice of full-throated fun reverberated. I needed more of that, Lil.
More shots of happy. I had to believe that Mumtaz wouldn't remain a
victim. I desperately wanted liberation for her.

For us.

21

Real Liberation

You have a question, Lil? Probe on.

OMG. This is spooky. You ask, "When you're under the thumb of a tyrant, how are you supposed to be like water?"

You're giving me chills right now. I've been contemplating the Very. Same. Question. Sometimes, Lily, I think you've invaded my head because you've got this zany flair for finishing my sentences. Let's see how simpatico we really are. What's your answer to the question?

I know you asked me first, and I'm not trying to pull a fast one on you. I'm just queasy. Listen, the reason I have the same question as you is that I also have a dilemma. For you to make sense of it, I have to say more about the saga of Mumtaz and Bash. You game to hear the story?

Yes, Lil, I agree to stipulate that you're not my therapist. May we proceed?

Five years after my parents got married, a civil war rocked Uganda, the East African country where they settled. It was the early 1970s, a time of idealism and liberation—as well as the betrayal of both. Africans demanded independence from their European colonizers, but a justified movement for black freedom spiraled into an all-out assault on nonblacks. Uganda's military dictator, General Idi Amin, announced that Africa belonged only to blacks. He handed brown-skinned Ugandans an ultimatum: Exit or be exterminated.

It counted for nothing that many of us had lived in Uganda for several generations. Britain had transported families from India to East Africa so they could build the colonial railroad—the foundation of an economy that exploited brown, black, and white bodies. South Asian workers in Uganda later became businesspeople who wrung their own profits from cheap black labor. For Uganda's freedom fighters, liberation from the British went hand in glove with avenging the bitches of the Brits: Indians.

Prowling for riches, Idi Amin's soldiers went after entrepreneurs, Bash among them. They jailed him on rumors that he hoarded foreign currency. Untrue, Mumtaz says. But whatever earnings he did stash would clearly be looted any day. From behind bars, Bash managed to bribe the jail wardens, smuggle in his checkbook, and funnel money to Mumtaz for the entire family's plane tickets to Canada—the only country willing to admit us as refugees.

Mumtaz describes it as "the hardest time of my life," partly because of all the changes she endured as a new Canadian and partly because of what didn't change. Her husband's continued torment, coupled with her isolation, nearly broke Mumtaz. She recounts that he "did not speak to me for six months, because, number one, I had given birth to another baby girl"—that was before the fourth, aborted, pregnancy—"and number two, we had lost everything in moving to Canada.

> I hated him so much for punishing me for nothing that I did! I went through a depression at the time, with three young children, not knowing the language or anything about a Western country, not knowing where to go or what to do.

The inconspicuous humiliations by Bash hurt Mumtaz the most.

> When we went to bed at night, if my feet accidentally touched his feet, he would kick me so hard [that] it would wake me up. Now, someone might ask why I did not sleep in another bed . . . [I]f I tried that, he would beat me, thinking that I was thinking too much of myself, so it was really darned if you do and darned if you don't.

Thus, Lil, my dilemma about Bash. He tortured his family with physical, mental, and emotional assaults every day for years. But he saved our lives with those plane tickets to Canada. In fact, Bash risked his own life to access the funds for our safe passage. I respect those deeds. Gutsy as all get out. Do I owe it to him to say so? Is it possible to be grateful for someone's caring side without legitimizing their cruel side?

I don't know either, my sweet bean. Maybe that's why God made Judy, my therapist.

After two decades, Mumtaz separated from Bash. She says she left for her children—the same reason that she'd stayed, guilted by culture into the illusion that two parents are always better for the kids even if one parent mercilessly degrades the other.

But as soon as they separated, Lil, Mumtaz ruminated on disaster scenarios. "If I died," she told herself, "the law would give my children to a father who didn't want girls in the first place. Who would take care of my daughters? How would they eat or get a good education?" As a manual laborer, she worked every holiday to earn time and a half, yet she hardly made ends meet. Suppose she was laid off? What then?

Mumtaz seriously considered getting back together with Bash. Well aware of her vulnerabilities, he offered to deposit $20,000 into her bank account on condition that she, and we, return to him. From her perspective, reconciling with Bash would give their daughters enough means to complete university. From my perspective, any "reconciliation" instigated by fear would be extortion. We didn't need his frickin' money. We could earn scholarships. To trade our emancipation for the pledge of coin would be to sell us out.

I lashed out at Mumtaz. The next day, I passed out in class. The day after that, my professor called home to check in on me. Mumtaz picked up the phone and learned in no uncertain terms what a basket case I'd become. That's when she broke it to Bash she'd be filing for divorce.

If she was liberated, Lil, I wasn't. In my stringent refusal to be a victim, I became a bully—toward my own mother. I persistently prejudged Mumtaz, which is another way of saying I misjudged her.

22

Mistaken Identity

Six years after Mumtaz and Bash divorced, she and I sat down for the conversation. I told her that I'd fallen in love—"and not with a man." Through her tears, Mumtaz assured me that nothing would change between us. Her love for me, she repeated, is unshakeable. She wanted to understand, though, whether Bash's violence drove me to become gay. Probably not, I said, because people don't "become" gay or straight. We choose our partners but not our biology. Besides, girls all over the world watch guys pummel their mothers, and most of those girls remain straight.

I swore to Mumtaz that I don't hate men. Truth is, Lil, I hadn't gotten past my hatred for *that* man. All I'd done is made up my mind not to be his victim. I'd assumed this would be enough. Convinced that I'd conquered my fantasy of having him whacked, I pulled off a molten performance of resilience in front of Mumtaz. But it was a mirage. Despite feeling at peace with the multiple strands of my identity, I lacked wholeness, and the fraying within me had implications beyond me.

Let me put this in context. Over the years, my mother has suffered from an illness that swells her feet and saps some of her mobility. No specialist could figure out how she contracted it or how to cure it. For Mumtaz, the disease felt like a sadistic tease, showing up right after she tasted independence as a divorced woman. I watched her wither into bitterness and, at times, selfishness. Chronic pain will do that.

But I couldn't, or wouldn't, empathize. I ignored her phone calls. If I responded at all, it was briefly and curtly. I decided that Mumtaz had resigned herself to being a victim for life. To guard myself against the prospect of turning into her, I kept my mother at arm's length.

Notice, Lil, that I foisted my fear-heavy baggage on Mumtaz, tagging her with the label "victim" as if she'd taken that identity for herself. She didn't. Nonetheless, I framed her as my bitch, a prop to be handled rather than a person to be heard. Had I given Mumtaz the room to speak for herself, precisely as she'd done for me when I came out, I would've known just what a victim she's *not*.

At her mosque, the imam's wife had tried to shame Mumtaz, accusing her of encouraging me to go gay. Instead of fumbling through a frantic defense of her piety, my mother spotted the game of gotcha and did an end run. "My daughter," she responded, "actually, all of my children, are their own person. And it is okay."

"If I were you," the imam's wife prodded, "I would disown her."

Over to Mumtaz:

I said, "Never. I will never do that. She will always be my daughter and I will always love her just the way she is. That part of her, it doesn't make any difference in my life. It does but it doesn't. In my heart, it doesn't. When I'm seeing the world, yes, it does. But that's the way life works. . . ."

I said, "Since you are so religious, you tell me: One morning, do you wake up and tell your daughter [to] go ahead and be gay . . . ? God has created her and that is the way she is. God does not make any mistakes. And it is okay. I am okay with that. If you guys are not okay [with it], that is not my problem."

Steely, huh, Lil? Not quite the victim's pose. Man, did I ever miscast Mumtaz so I could dodge my long overdue date with the mirror. I'd learn about her confrontation at the mosque much later. For the time being, I remained holed up in the ranch of self-deception, fully confident that she, not me, is the reason for our ruptured relationship.

Back at the ranch, I couldn't keep avoiding my mother's calls. So I took them but treated her as a damaged good. Every time Mumtaz brooded about her health—or, from her point of view, shared updates—I urged her to try one or another remedy. Ponder these words from Narcotics Anonymous! Or that observation from Gandhi! Or this saying from the prophet Muhammad! Nothing stuck. She still didn't listen because I still didn't listen.

Clean out of solutions for Mumtaz, I surrendered. Not in the sense of packing it in and walking away. Rather, I let down my defenses and opened up to the lesson at hand. Like water in the midst of rocks.

Only then did it dawn on me that all the proverbs I'd pushed onto Mumtaz could, and should, be *my* marching orders. Had I taken Gandhi's advice to be the change I wish to see? Did I stop doing the same thing over and over and expecting a different result—the definition of insanity coined by Narcotics Anonymous? Was I faithful to the prophet Muhammad's assessment that the best of us address our anger issues?

Zero for three. Yet I had the temerity to sermonize to Mumtaz. Mea culpa.

I let go of fixing my mother and focused on quieting the self-righteous clatter in my head. On cultivating my curiosity about her many dimensions. On loving her for her own sake.

No relationship worth its name is linear, Lil, but something intriguing unfolded. Each of us won. We've healed enough, me and Mumtaz, that we're now laughing without worry of offending. Fear has left the building.

There's the time that Mama Laura privately asked my mother for my hand in marriage. Mumtaz agreed and then, in Laura's presence, blurted to me, "Are you sure you want to marry this piece of shit?" Today, Mama Laura calls Mumtaz her "personal Muslim terrorist." For her part, Mumtaz confirms that she *will* kill Laura at some point. "I love you to death," she sincerely and sinisterly tells your Mama Laura.

Whatever else Mumtaz is—Muslim, woman, working-class, person of color, Canadian citizen, African refugee, domestic abuse survivor, pro-choice feminist—the most meaningful identity for her is "mother."

How unexpectedly unexotic. But there you have it, Lil. When her children are happy, she's deliriously so.

Which is why Mumtaz couldn't stop laughing in the wake of her "creature" gaffe at the wedding. She kept cracking up because she felt the permission to be real, comfortably accepting the discomfort at hand. Out of her realness that afternoon, our wedding guests relaxed and relationships grew stronger. The unity of God's creation seemed closer.

At brunch the next day, one of our guests approached Mumtaz with a question. How difficult was it for an observant Muslim to participate in yesterday's ceremony? Mumtaz told him that "under the open sky, I thanked God so many times. God, this is such a bonus to me. I never, ever dreamed about this wedding. And seeing my daughter so happy—I could not be happier. I could not be happier."

False. The liliko'i cream wedding cake sent her happiness over the cliff. In Hawai'i, even the sugar highs hang glide. Now, Lil, allow me to ruin the romance of this moment.

23

Can Words Be Violence?

Being real will lead to disagreeing about issues, some of them life-and-death. For example, Lil, Mumtaz rejects my faith in free speech. We got into it over *Charlie Hebdo*, the French satire magazine whose editors were murdered by Islamist extremists. "Why do these people jab, jab, jab?" Mumtaz grumbled, referring to *Charlie*'s editors.

"They're not just 'jabbing,'" I said. "They're standing up for a bigger principle. Freedom of expression for Muslims in France depends on everyone having freedom of expression, including atheists."

"But you do not see Muslims offending atheists," she tossed off.

My disbelief almost cut the conversation short. "The very fact that mosques in France—no, mosques everywhere—segregate women and men is offensive to a whole lot of atheists. But you don't see them, week after week, shooting and killing Muslims for being offensive."

Mumtaz grinned. "That is such a lame argument. You do not see Muslims going out to offend. That is not their intention. Their intention is to be true to what they believe is their religion. But *Charlie Hebdo*? Their intention was to offend—and that is the difference."

I knew Mumtaz wasn't excusing atrocity. Not for a second. She simply thought that my blanket defense of free speech smothered a point worth considering: If you intend to offend, then at least concede that your words will hit some people like violence, especially those who already feel beleaguered, one or more of whom might retaliate with violence of their own. *Charlie's* editors accepted that risk. Therefore, Mumtaz seemed to be saying, they should accept the result.

However logical, her point just didn't sit right. To preempt another person's violence, I should bottle up words that may very well set off that person? Isn't this a prescription for self-censorship, eliminating the "honest" from honest diversity? Personally, I'm not interested in offending for the sake of offending but would you agree, Lil, that sometimes the intention to cause offense serves a greater good? Like blowing open an urgently needed conversation that nobody would bother to have unless they felt provoked to talk?

You disagree. How come?

My perspective makes objects out of people? Are you serious? Tell me what I'm missing.

You say there's a difference between violating the status quo, which can be good, and violating human beings, which can't be good. I hadn't thought about it in those terms. According to neuroscience, you're onto something. Words and images *can* do violence.

It takes a boatload of slurs repeated for a long time to wreak the trauma that, say, one physical attack can inflict. That's a high bar for bad speech to meet, and yet the bar gets met every day, everywhere— at home, at school, at work. For years after her divorce, Mumtaz rode out the racist bullying of a coworker. Nobody laid a finger on Mumtaz, but the toll of verbal violence could literally be measured: The near-daily taunts worsened her chronic stress. Which, in turn, weakened her body's ability to heal, both from her illness and from Bash's abuse.

Is that, Lil, why you take the phrase "dog whistle" as a microaggression against you? That it doesn't constitute violence in and of itself, but that a lifetime of being disparaged as mere property makes the negative connotation of "dog whistle" feel like you're being disparaged all over again? That instead of belittling those with your point of view, I should listen to their stories? And that they should listen to the stories of the people they belittle with their labels?

I'm feeling you, Lil. Free speech isn't cost-free for someone on the receiving end if she's struggling with the anguish of past violence. I'd missed that nuance. For me, freedom of expression has always been a hallowed principle of liberal democracy. But if I'm willing to violate a fellow human being in order to defend liberal democracy, then how liberal or democratic am I? Then again, none of this means that disagreement on its own causes harm. If my viewpoint injures another person's convictions and not much else, have I really been violent? Honest diversity deserves a reckoning with these questions.

But how do we reckon, reason, deliberate, or discuss when we get bent out of shape in nanoseconds? Honest diversity doesn't stand a chance if we ramp up everything in our heads to a fight-or-flight crisis. With our permission, the primitive foundation of the brain will keep us in reactive mode—scoping out immediate threats, seeking out instant rewards, blurring crucial boundaries between fear and fact.

I'm saddened that in making claims about violence, many of us don't draw distinctions anymore. A clumsy phrase rubs a bunch of us the wrong way and we'll think nothing of labeling the person who spoke it. He must be a hater of this or that group. If the offender has any public influence, we fear that his comment will enable wiping out the group. Our pulse quickens. We tell ourselves, "History proves that words kill." We omit, "sometimes." In our mind's eye, the sketch of a slaughter takes shape. Gaunt bodies. Roads strewn with corpses. To our emotions, annihilation is more than a fear. It's a "fact."

"Not so fast," Brie Loskota warns. She's the researcher we met with, Lil, at the University of Southern California. "There are lots of stages between words chosen in haste or ignorance and the genocide of a people." Precisely. And precisely why it's so important to give speakers the chance to clarify themselves. To contextualize, to reword, or, as long as it's their call entirely, to rescind. Not everybody who loves free speech has the motive to spread hate.

Brie Loskota adds one last consideration. "When we erase distinctions between free speech and genocide, when we leap straight from one to the other, we lose people." Because we lose credibility.

We'll gain perspective, and regain cred, by taking to heart Loskota's three small words: Not. So. Fast. To tap the evolved regions of our brains, the parts through which we can balance reflexive feeling and conscious thinking, we've got to slow down. It takes time to burrow beneath the labels with which we quarantine people. But, especially in case of someone you love, time spent is time invested, not time lost.

I'm kind of bowled over, Lil. I never anticipated that my mother's got an opinion about free speech, let alone an opinion that pokes holes in mine. Poverty denied her an education beyond third grade and she's worked with her hands all her life. So she doesn't play up her ability to analyze issues. But ask Mumtaz a question and watch her mind motor. She might get carried away; that'll happen in a juicy joust. The joust itself tells us something more: She's open to being taken on. My mother's the kind of surprise that the crude labels "Muslim" and "refugee" tend to conceal.

Over tea with me and Mumtaz, a friend said that she'd read about a group of Christians who blame climate change on gay marriage. "Global warming was happening thirty years ago," Mumtaz hooted, "and there was no gay marriage then! How stupid some people are!" She did say *some*.

24

Freedom, Finally

Ah, there's the head-tilt. Make it a doozie, Lil.

If my mother can surprise us, isn't it possible that my father can? Doesn't he deserve a hearing? Wouldn't that be an act of grace?

First, congratulations, you wily rascal. You made me say, "my father."

Second, you're spot-on. My mother's more than the sum of her labels; we all are. There's no reason for my father to be less. Who knows why he slung chairs at Mumtaz and intimidated the rest of us with his erratic belligerence? Bash has his story, I'm sure. But I'm not sure he cares to be heard. He's never apologized to Mumtaz; not an ounce of contrition offered. Whatever his state of mind during my childhood, he's chosen to be unaccountable after all these years. Shouldn't conscious choices have consequences?

Fine. I'll tell it to the therapist.

I've been thinking, Lil. The woman who forced you to breed—your tyrant—let go of you. Do you owe her?

Mama, my owner didn't let go of me. I let go of the tyrant inside of me and my owner realized that she could do the same for herself.

The tyrant inside of you, Lil?

For longer than I'd like to admit, Mama, anger warped me. Now you know why I'm a little gruff.

And here I thought you might be a dog-identified cat.

Watch the labels, Mama.

I'm only saying you have a maverick streak, Lilybean. You call it "gruff"; I call it "pluck."

That's because you're my mama and your love for me is boundless, just as your mama's is for you. But I know the brute truth about myself and you're helping me to heal. Thank you, Mama Dearest.

Oh, Lil.

I was angry, Mama, because I was property. My owner's livelihood partially came from selling my pups, so I had to accept that I couldn't stop the rapes. But because I can't see in the way most beings see, I perked my ears and listened closely.

To what, Lil?

To the messages that my owner conveyed about her life, Mama. Those phone calls with her son? Turbulent, to say the least. All that time glued to Bruce Lee interviews? It signified her yearning to live differently. I started a conversation with her about it.

Say what? Did the specter of a talking dog discombobulate your owner?

She wigged out, Mama. Unabashedly. But then she dipped her toe into the current because who else cared to ask about her dreams? One conversation led to another. Eventually, I "saw" the tyrant inside of her: She had this voracious need to win the war with her son, someone she also treated as her property. She'd slam the phone on him and sob that she couldn't understand why he didn't understand her.

But, Lil, didn't she learn anything from Bruce Lee?

She had to hear his teachings from someone she trusted, Mama. Our conversations gave rise to trust.

What did you do with it?

I asked my owner if she owned her son. She said, "He owes his existence to me."

"Therefore, you own him," I echoed. Then I asked, "Are you owned?"

I waited. It might've been dusk by the time my owner spoke again. When she did, she said, "The more I own, the more I'm owned." Her son and I owned *her*.

Not sure I follow, Lil.

I'll guide you, Mama. And I'll speak slowly. The more things and beings you own, the more you're owned by them. As the owner, you expend energy controlling, maintaining, and protecting merely for the sake of possessing. Your walls go up, your spontaneity goes down, and the sweetness of discovery goes away because you're consumed with hanging on.

I've got the shivers, Lil. Your owner pieced all of this together for herself?

No airhead, that woman.

No kidding. What happened next?

I thanked her for a down-to-earth distillation of Bruce Lee. Then I suggested that Mr. Lee would take it further: You win when you don't seek to win. When, in other words, you quit legitimizing the win-lose game in your relationships. And you quit legitimizing the game when you no longer participate in it.

By not trying to own someone else, you opt out of the game. Is that right, Lil?

You're making strides, Mama!

But I'm only human, Lil. Humans are afraid to lose what we assume we own.

Like you said earlier, Mama, choices have consequences. When you *choose* to possess a being, then as night follows day, fear will possess you. The owner becomes the owned. Win-lose turns into lose-lose. But refuse to participate in the game and you'll emancipate yourself to be . . . ? Work with me, Mama! To be . . . ?

Like water, Lil!

Booyah, Mama! You'll emancipate yourself to be whomever you would be were you not deformed by fear. Exactly like water, which takes innumerable forms but is never deformed.

It's all starting to sink in, sweet bean.

At heart, Mama, this is how my owner released the image that she chose for her son. She first released *her fear* of relinquishing that image. In the process, she released me, too.

Aha! Which is why I must ask again, Lil: Do you owe her—forgiveness, I mean?

Here's the thing, Mama. There's no need to forgive unless you assign blame. I don't blame. In my less angry moments, I understand that my wounds can be gifts. They remind me to stay grateful for my strengths by making prudent use of them. I still have my nose and I sniffed *you* out, didn't I, Mama?

Smooth, Lil. I see politics in your future.

Dream on, Mama Dearest. I see a nap in my future.

25

Lily in the Field: Wake-Up Call

I don't want to weird you out, Lil, but some mornings I wake up early, kneel on the floor, and lay next to the chaos of fur that you've exploded into overnight. One ear droops over your bed, your head's tucked into your chest and—bam!—you're a festival of fluff from the neck down. That's what you look like right now, a snoozing sprawl on the grass. Sorry for rousing you, Your Royal Hot Mess.

Dr. Daffner phoned. She says you have a tumor in your belly. It could be cancerous. Your surgery's next week but before then, let's get a little more meat on you.

Aw, Lil. How callous of me to mention meat. Just for that, I've got a nugget of jerky with your name on it. Hoover it in good health.

Atta girl. Now that you're up, where were we?

Yes, yes. Whenever I need a good giggle, I think about the fact that Mumtaz, my mother, and Jim, my father figure, agree about Barack Obama. They both believe he's a Muslim. Difference is, Mumtaz takes pride in that prospect whereas Jim gets agitated over it. Of course he's afraid. But, frankly, some of the people who'd accuse him of racism have no shortage of fear themselves. We're on the brink of an epiphany, Lil. I can feel it. I need you to dog me with more questions. Let's keep it honest. Hold me accountable for my own baloney, okay?

Not the edible kind of baloney, love. Sorry for triggering you again.

What are you looking at me like that for? I see right through your deprived doggie act.

Right through.

Here's a cluster of jerky strips. Knock yourself out.

What Change Means

26

Do All Black Lives Matter for BLM?

Lilyboss, two young African American men swung by my office. They announced themselves as Edward and "D." A former student of mine recommended that they look me up because of the predicament they're in. I'll get to it in a moment, but first a bit of background.

The guys participate in Black Lives Matter, the global antiracism coalition. BLM took off on social media after a teenager named Trayvon Martin died from gunshots in February 2012. His confessed killer pleaded self-defense, but defense against what remains anyone's guess: Trayvon was unarmed and snacking on Skittles. He was also black. In July 2013, Lil, a jury acquitted his nonblack killer on all counts. BLM was born. Other deaths of black men followed—symptoms of police brutality. Edward, D, and many more people demonstrated in the streets.

One day, D told a local BLM organizer that he'd like to sit down with a few cops and listen to their experiences. "Not to excuse them," D assured her, "but to understand what's going through their heads when they lunge at a brother or pull the trigger."

Edward backed the idea. "We wouldn't be going in there with the delusion of solving anything. But rallies only get you so far. If the police are feeling smacked down all the time, why would their hearts change?" He said that in any dialogue with police, he'd ask them if they see why smacking down black youth doesn't motivate change in them, either. Their approach, Lil, seemed to me a smart mix of empathy, education, and justice-oriented jiujitsu.

So how did the BLM organizer respond? D shook his head numbly and spoke with a WTF tone. "Shot. Me. Down. She preached to us about the tragedy, travesty, whatever, of betraying our people." He transported himself into that moment:

> *Sister, you're cool with having my black ass at your protests but I've got to turn off my brain? Are you telling me that my body's my only asset? Like the [slave] master told us for centuries?*

D drew a deep breath and grudgingly apologized. He knew that one organizer does not represent all of BLM and, moreover, that BLM has comforted people of color worldwide. Still, D resented feeling like a bauble to advance the movement's marketing. He and Edward wanted guidance on how to avoid becoming bitches of the BLM brand.

I counseled them to keep the organizer's remark in proportion. Are they sure that they understood her intent? They assumed so. Did they venture beyond that assumption and actually speak with her about it? No. Then that's step number one, I suggested.

Step two: Engage the police. BLM considers itself leaderless, or, in the movement's argot, "leader-full"—decentralized, democratic, and therefore full of leaders. Since BLM claims to have no hierarchy, why seek an organizer's approval for a conversation with the cops?

But before pulling up a chair with them, I asked, how could D and Edward show that they're genuinely interested in the perspective of these officers? By "genuine," I meant interested first out of sincerity and only second out of strategy. They mused about going on a ride-along. A superb thought, isn't it, Lil? Such an investment of time would tell the police that D and Edward care about how the world appears from the interior of a patrol car. They'll be credible at the discussion table.

Finally, step three: Start a conversation within BLM about how to avoid doctrinaire identity. Movements, to keep moving, need creative energy. D and Edward came up with an innovative idea, only to see it treated as a stab in the backs of "our people." When liberators cleave to a rigid identity, they contort themselves into bigots. Both the unrepentant racist and the antiracist operate from a fear of losing control.

For diversity to be honest, diversity's enthusiasts have to face the purity problem within.

27

When Purity Pollutes

Purity contaminates diversity. To be pure is to wall ourselves off from influences so novel that they could transform us. But many of us don't want to be transformed; we want the other side to be. Behold a flagrant contradiction, Lil: In rhetoric, our side touts diversity yet, in action, we prioritize purity.

"Some of us engaged in struggles for social justice have been incredibly naïve about what has been happening in our own psyches," noted the progressive Christian philosopher Walter Wink a generation ago. "Our very identities are often defined by our resistance to evil. It's our way of feeling good about ourselves: If we are against evil, we must be good."

We're fooling ourselves, Wink emphasized. "The very shrillness of our opposition may indicate that a part of us secretly desires to emulate what we oppose.

> How often have I heard people say that the greatest violence they have ever personally encountered was from colleagues in the peace movement! Sometimes people are attracted to peace issues because they are fighting inner violent tendencies that they have projected on the 'enemy.' Whatever the source, this unattended shadow can erupt in vicious language and acts that endanger others and undermine the effort.

Andrea Dworkin, a famous feminist of the 1960s and '70s, under-stood this truth viscerally. Her sexuality might have been flexible, but in public she adopted the identity of a lesbian. A segment of the American women's movement doubted Dworkin's queer credentials and let her know it. Instead of emboldening a woman to define herself—the entire point of feminism—the custodians of lesbian purity bullied her.

"Women shouting at me: slut, bisexual, she fucks men," Dworkin recollected. Upon being showered with vitriol, she girded herself for the greater indignity:

> *In that room, to answer the question, "Do you still fuck men?" with a No, as I did, was to betray my deepest convictions. All of my life, I have hated the proscribers, those who enforce sexual conformity. In answering, I had given in to the inquisitors, and I felt ashamed. It humiliated me to see myself then: one who resists the enforcers out there with militancy, but gives in without resistance to the enforcers among us.*

Vault ahead twenty years, Lil. In the late 1990s, a bisexual person still got villified by gay and lesbian prudes. I had words with several LGBT activists who charged bisexual "fence-sitters" with collecting a bonanza: They benefit from the ooh-la-la of being queer while they savor the privilege of passing as straight. "The bisexual is a bi-schemer," a gay man complained to me back then. Incredible, I thought, how he imitates the judginess of homophobes. Even more incredible that he hadn't clued in.

Today, trashing someone's sexual identity in the name of diversity would be patently obnoxious, yet movements for justice remain scar-ring. Frances Lee is a self-identified Queer Trans Person of Color. "They" (the pronoun Lee chooses) personifies the inclusion that my di-versity tribe seems to embrace—

Uh, no sweat, Lil. Ask your question.

Why am I using the pronoun "they" even though I oppose political correctness?

My choice to say "they" isn't one bit about political correctness. What makes any speech politically correct is compulsion. The speaker's compelled by fear—the fear of being shamed for breaking legal or cultural codes by not using certain words. But I'm saying "they" out of respect. Frances Lee has the right to identify any way they wish.

Even as a shoe, you ask?

People aren't things, Lil. If Frances Lee wanted to identify as a shoe, I'd ask them why. If I'm criticized as disrespectful simply for seeking clarity, I'd again ask why. If I'm then criticized as childish, I'd recommend distinguishing between "childish" and "childlike." And, after attempting to have the conversation, if I'm not persuaded to call them a shoe, I'd thank them for their time. Then I'd shoo.

Glad you liked that pun. May we resume, *mon petit chou*?

No, Lil, I did not call you a shoe. I called you "my little cream puff" in French. May we resume, Puff Lily?

Merci beaucoup. I was saying that in light of all their labels, Frances Lee represents the wide tent that we juggernauts for diversity have pitched. Or have we? Let's mosey into the tent and poke around, shall we?

In a summer 2017 blog post, Lee declared a willingness to be "excommunicated" from the "church of social justice." Forced in a previous life to follow evangelical Christianity, Frances Lee couldn't abide the equally "disturbing" dogma that has polluted justice movements. Lee reported having "countless hushed conversations with friends about this anxiety," this "fear of appearing impure."

They then revealed how the purity problem twisted their behavior to the point where they were "performing" justice, not actually practicing it:

> *I self-police what I say in activist spaces. I stopped commenting on social media with questions or pushback on leftist opinions for fear of being called out. I am always ready to apologize for anything I do that a community member deems wrong, oppressive, or inappropriate—no questions asked.*

That, Lil, is the price of being "respectable." It's the death of authenticity. Activists rightly carp about the pressure to be respectable in the eyes of mainstream society. But we seldom take exception when the same pressure pulsates through our movements.

Why, you wonder?

For starters, there's the fear of punishment. Frances Lee itemizes the penance for going rogue within social justice movements: "shaming," "scolding," "isolating," and "eviscerating someone's social standing." The question that Lee *does* ask, however, is arresting: "Punishment has been used for all of history to control and destroy people. Why is it being used in movements meant to liberate all of us?"

Bang. Bloody. On.

If diversity of opinions, ideas, and perspectives won't be tolerated in movements that prize emancipation, then what kind of a utopia are we being emancipated into? I have a second question for diversity's proponents. If you won't make peace with different points of view, what's inclusive about your diversity?

Allow me to bring back D, the activist whose proposal to engage with police got "shot down" by an organizer with Black Lives Matter. D speaks truth to power when he wonders, *If my ass is my only asset to the cause, then aren't I only an object? How does objectifying my black body square with proclaiming that my black life matters?*

To be fair, Lil, BLM's founders aren't like this. Frances Lee heard one of them—Alicia Garza—deliver an "explosive" address in a hall packed with activists. The line that stuck with Lee? "Our movements must include people not like us, people with whom we will never fully agree, and people with whom we have conflict."

I heard another founder of BLM, Patrisse Cullors, speak of activism as "healing." She lifted the lid on questions that leaders everywhere would be wise to pose. In her words, "How do we show up in this work as our whole selves? How do we be in it as our best selves?"

Oh, chill, Lil. I'm not going all self-helpy on you. Trying to be our best selves transcends Oprah and spills over to the teachings of Timothy Snyder. He's the historian who wrote *On Tyranny: Twenty Lessons from the Twentieth Century.* The nineteenth lesson is, "Be a patriot," and Snyder unpacks it with aspirational zest. A nationalist, he explains, "encourages us to be our worst, and then tells us we are the best." In contrast, a patriot "wants the nation to live up to its ideals, which means asking us to be our best selves." What a yummy distinction.

As you can surmise, we're not talking about self-absorption. We're talking about self-awareness—the sort of awareness that holds a mirror up to each of us and whispers, *Can you honestly fix your society without first fixing yourselves?*

28

Meet the Egobrain

A moment ago, Lil, you asked me why Frances Lee held back the questions they had for the powers-that-be in their justice movement. My answer doesn't leave it at Lee's fear of being punished. Rather, we have to examine why human beings have a proclivity to punish at all. In a word: ego.

"Ego" derives from the Latin for "I." It's who, or what, I believe I am. Ego makes identity a possession; a thing to be polished, presented, controlled.

The BLM organizer warned D not to sell out "our people." Did she treat him as someone who belongs or as a belonging? To my mind, the latter. Her ego jealously screened what a member of the tribe may or may not do if he's to stay loyal and his identity to remain pure in her books.

But was D really the problem? I don't think so. The organizer's ego took it out on D for a fear that *she* felt but wouldn't face. The possibility that one of Us from BLM could be consorting with some of Them, the cops, naturally made her anxious. It jeopardized the certainty of her identity. Much like an object that cracks open under stress, her identity—static and brittle—needed assuaging.

Say hello to the ego. This isn't some mystical force best addressed by a meditation retreat in Bali. (Although if you go, Lil, I'll happily schlep your bags.) Ego's a function of the brain and therefore essential to living. To douse the woo-woo mythology and hammer home the neuroscience, let's rename it the "egobrain."

You dig that, do you, Lil? Careful not to flatter my egobrain.

The egobrain does its work cleverly and naughtily. A discrete region of the brain detects any thought or feeling that causes me tension. When my life's in immediate threat, my brain will protect me by sounding the alarm that I have to repel this threat or run like there's no tomorrow. In that deadly scenario, the egobrain's my best friend.

Not so under other circumstances. In a situation where I'm merely on edge, my egobrain wants to skirt the slog of figuring out why I feel that way. It's more efficient (read: easier) to suppress whatever's behind my distress. So my egobrain devises fishy ways to defend me. They're known in psychology as defense mechanisms.

Denying my fear, rationalizing it, projecting it onto someone else—these and many more, Lil, are defense mechanisms. They literally make me defensive. They turn others into scapegoats for my problem. And they let me off the hook for fixing myself.

I'm not proud to admit that I used to be a raging ego-brainiac and that I relapse all too readily. Remember how I behaved toward Mumtaz, my mother? I feared the image of her as a victim. Then I projected my fear onto her and concluded that she's the epitome of what I needed to avoid becoming, at any cost. By visualizing Mumtaz as the thing I revile, I rationalized treating her as my bitch.

At the same time, Lil, I lobbied for immigrant women's rights, wrote speeches for Canada's most feminist members of Parliament, and gave my own public talks about equality. During these performances, defending me from acknowledging my fear may have been efficient for my egobrain. Through the years, though, burying my fear of being a victim proved highly inefficient. I diluted more physical and mental energy by ducking change than by making change. It's a story that far too many activists can relate to.

What change means is taking responsibility for managing our defensive egobrains. Change means understanding, and never underestimating, the egobrain's power. Then and then alone can we work intelligently with it. Short of this, we'll keep manipulating each other as our property. Along the way, even our points of view will become possessions. We'll calcify our opinions so we can feel control over them. At which point, they'll control us.

This has deep implications for democracy. If someone makes an argument that questions mine, about anything that gets my blood racing, I'll double down on my view because I've equated my view to my identity. So any threat to my view becomes a threat to me.

That's how authoritarians behave, Lil. That's why the politics of identity—whether Trump's or ours—devastate democracy.

29

Choosing Integrity

Your turn, Lily.

You ask if I'm being impractical. Expand on your question, please.

Let me repeat what I hear you saying: Any movement for justice will collapse if activists second-guess who they are. They've got exorbitant inequalities to combat and taking their eye off their identity, the one certainty that they all share, will spell chaos.

When you put it like that, I agree. But I wouldn't put it like that. I'm calling for integrity, and having integrity differs from second-guessing yourself. Integrity's about being consistent in what you advocate and how you act. If you advocate justice, then act just.

Frances Lee catalogs some steps that any of us can take to be consistent. Integrity might mean:

- "checking in with myself about how I have let my heart grow hard";

- "cultivating long-term relationships with those outside my (not that) safe and exclusive community, understanding that I will learn so much from them";

- "seeing them as individuals, not ideologies or systems."

In other words, putting the brakes on objectifying human beings, even when they're adversaries. In this regard, Frances Lee has given us three excellent tips to evaluate how we're doing.

What if we developed a *habit* of self-evaluation? Couldn't it be a hedge against leading bifurcated lives and, ultimately, disintegrating? I'm thinking about the disintegration not only of ourselves, but also of our movements. As you've reminded me, Lil, the most electrifying movements also have gigantic goals. To move the needle, they need to cultivate rules about how to do what they'll do. But from the perspective of D and Frances Lee, the rules in practice stomped on the ultimate goal of their movements: human dignity.

Which means they had an excruciating choice to make. Often, as members of a pack, we're pushed to choose which matters more—identity or integrity. It's a lose-lose game but the egobrain, out of defensiveness, falls for it. The question is, *Will I let my egobrain dictate my conscience?*

If so, then I'll choose the path of least resistance—identity. I'll clam up and conform to the group. I'm scared stiff of renouncing the security that comes from belonging to something. I'd sooner justify my community's rules by fearing the worst that could happen if they cut me loose. Among my cataclysmic thoughts:

Who will I be once I'm excommunicated from the movement?
When I'm no longer one of Us, will I be accused of joining Them?
How will I prove to Us that I'm not part of Them?
Where will I go now for approval?
What will I endure to get there?
And if "there" doesn't exist, why roll out of bed?

To fend off the agony of asking myself such questions, my egobrain arms me to stick with the familiar. It hates the stress of anticipating the unknown, so it throws everything at preserving the status quo. For a time, I'm hoodwinked into feeling more safe by going along with the dishonesty around me than by reckoning with it.

Can you fathom a bit better, Lil, why people who decry society at large may be petrified of speaking up against abuses within their intimate tribe? Our tribe's massively more personal than society in the abstract. To my egobrain, my tribe's my home.

And can you appreciate how the stakes feel that much higher when society's already polarized, so that the accusation of having ditched Us and defected to Them can seem too much to bear?

To this dog's breakfast of a psyche—sorry, Lil, to this hodgepodge of a psyche—add a biological reality that you and I talked about earlier: The brain rewards humans with a chemical high every time we mimic the opinions that drew us to our tribe in the first place. We don't perceive those highs as they happen but we sure feel it when they don't. To say we feel untethered, out of sorts, or out-and-out lonely would be achingly accurate.

Given the barrage of incentives for human beings to keep our heads down, it's a marvel that Frances Lee displayed the moral courage to stand up. Those who choose moral courage show that you don't have to be a bitch of your identity.

You have another option: integrity. This word stems from the Latin for wholeness. Choosing integrity may well heal social cleavages by first reconciling the cleavages within ourselves.

To develop integrity, Lil, we'll need to be aware of the egobrain's stampede to safety. In effect, the egobrain assumes that any discomfort indicates a lethal threat. We'll hear the ensuing racket in our heads. But for the sake of integrity, we'll listen for the softer voice of conscience—which is another function of the brain, yet one that doesn't traffic in fear. That's how we'll become mindful, not reckless, rule-breakers.

By reflecting a little each day on the mischievous power of the egobrain, we need never be defensive, or divisive, like the BLM organizer. Her ego tried to game D and Edward for supposedly driving a dagger into "our people." As if all black lives are the same by virtue of their label. It's a bias that the organizer would want the police to drop. Maybe she could go first. Defensive self-defense leads many of us to spend our waking hours unwoke to the gap between our ideals and our impulses.

I once delivered this message to BLM activists in Toronto. We can best defend our cause, I said, by being nondefensive in our dealings with the police, the public, and each other. Whereupon I was sternly told that making nice doesn't end racist policies. Except I didn't recommend making nice, since that would be pretending. Instead, I clarified to a particularly offended activist, I'm for parking the pretense and role-modeling the justice of which we speak—in the name of integrity and thus credibility.

I'm for exhibiting that our justice is positive rather than punitive.

I'm for demonstrating that it's doable on the ground, not pickled in the brine of theory.

And I'm for recognizing that policies can't end systems of domination, such as racism, until more of us have the humility to question our own domineering ways.

Of course, Lil, I could be wrong. But that's my point. Any of us could be wrong. Why have we seen umpteen examples of principled policies with dismal outcomes? It's not because our principles suck, but because the people who ideate, legislate, and execute policies wear blinkers. All humans do. Yet very few ask themselves: *Who disagrees with me and how can I secure their help in coming up with a Plan B if Plan A gets bungled?*

Consider the landmark policy of desegregating public schools. It resulted in half of America's black teachers getting fired! Meanwhile, most white teachers kept their jobs. That's because government officials closed black schools and rerouted black students to white areas where white faculty stayed on. Almost never did schools with black faculty absorb white students. Most of those schools were shuttered by the policymakers. To this day, the United States suffers an immense shortage of black teachers.

Chalk it up to unintended consequences, Lil?

Well, yeah. You just proved my point for me. The unforeseen happens regardless of how much you believe you control. Who provided the "authoritative" analysis of segregated schooling and who supplied the "expert" reasoning for its solution? I'll tell you who: all nine justices of the Supreme Court. All exceedingly educated. All human err-heads.

Who wrote the desegregation policy? Err-heads.

Who implemented it? Err-heads.

Might it be that we, paid-up members of the Great Resistance Against Trump's Ego, must also resist *our* egos?

30

The Show Must Go On

Permit me, Lil, to dismount my high horse and step into some hooey of my personal making. Humans have a terrible track record of learning despite being taught. I'm a textbook case. After misunderstanding myself and my mother all this time, you'd think that I grew to value my integrity over my identity. Think again.

After 9/11, I became a media darling on the knotty issues of Islam. A repeat guest on the most popular TV shows, I delivered every sound bite just so. But the dread of going toe-to-toe with detractors, week upon week and year after year, ate away at both my endurance and my tolerance.

I let the cacophony of my egobrain drown out the cues from my frazzled body—frazzled by the 24/7 clamor as well as my precarious future. Why precarious? Because I didn't know who I'd be without the nonstop noise and not knowing terrified the integrity out of me. I pushed myself to keep playing my "role": the go-to Muslim reformer.

During the Arab Spring of 2011, I practically slept in cable news studios. When President Hosni Mubarak fled Egypt, U.S. broadcasters went LIVE well into the night. My final appearance of that day was on *Hardball with Chris Matthews*. He hailed the uprisings as democracy blossoming before our eyes. I said that the military remained in charge. His brusque reaction felt personal when, in fact, it was performance. By now, I'd come to loathe performance. As I left the

Hardball set, I also loathed myself—not for being a buzzkill but for being a brand.

Look at you, my conscience sniped. *You're an educator who doesn't educate anymore. You're just another talking head in the rat race for media exposure. Are you happy with your persona? Are you fulfilled being one?* Obviously I wasn't, Lil. But I had an identity with no apparent exit. None that I could imagine amid the clash and churn of my egobrain scrambling to bury the voice of conscience.

Then another blockbuster development in the news: U.S. Navy Seals snuffed out Osama bin Laden. The media calls poured in. Twice in two weeks, I flew cross-country to appear on LIVE programs. During one of the flights, a fellow media whore goaded me into a debate. It lasted four hours, much more time than I'd spend contemplating why I refused to give him the last word.

For three months, I had panic attacks over nothing that I could point to. The message from my conscience—*Have the guts to get out*—was gaining ground on my fear that I'd be a nobody if I gave up this gig for a while. Straining to breathe, I prayed to Allah for serenity. The Qur'an teaches that "God does not change the condition of a people until they change what is inside themselves." I, not God, had to go first.

One afternoon, I pulled a knife from the dishwasher and wondered how it would feel if I plunged the gleaming blade into my neck. It would've been a gratuitously painful way to die. That's how I knew I wasn't thinking right. A few hours later, I did CNN to discuss—what else?—breaking news from the Middle East. I could barely hold myself together. "I think I'm depressed," I whispered to a producer. Her already frenetic tone turned frantic.

"Oh, no, not right now," she begged. "You're needed on-set in forty-five seconds!" My eyes welled up. "Don't ruin your make-up!" she implored. The show went on, as it must.

After my segment, the producer consoled me in the greenroom. "Depression wrenches the life out of you," she affirmed. "Is that why you're not eating?" I hadn't thought about my abnormally thin frame. Weeks before, a producer at MSNBC raised a similar question: "Are you on a hunger strike?" Back then, her comment sailed over my head. Now it landed with a thud.

Better late than never, wouldn't you say, Lil?

Yeah, I'm not sure, either. Let me explain why. The morning after my quasi-meltdown at CNN, I'd been scheduled for the interview that would launch my next book. That evening, the signature event of my tour would be held for several hundred ticket holders. I'd been busting my hump for this day. It finally came—and I couldn't have been sadder. When I got out of bed, I fainted. As soon as I came to, I phoned my book publicist and confessed, "I don't know why this is happening."

"It had to happen sometime," she claimed matter-of-factly. "You're a Muslim lesbian." Um, what? On reflection, I trust she meant that years of soaking up venom from the haters had shredded my immune system. And to a blistering degree, she'd read the situation right. But the clock kept ticking and the show had to go on.

I trooped into the shower, stayed upright, and made my way to NBC. Once I slid into the make-up chair, my egobrain—that soothing source of uncompromised identity—worked its wizardry. I envisioned powering through the interview. From the TV monitors mounted above, the painted and perky hosts yapped away. I'd be joining them shortly, I resolved again.

Their babble rang in my head. Then it clattered and clanged. My body broke out in a sweat. Inside me, the voice of conscience added to the bedlam. *Is this what you've worked so hard to do? To be the filler between commercials? Why do you keep feeding a beast that's insatiable? Does it give you meaning? Are you proud of what you've become?*

Down I went, slumped and unconscious, but with perfect eyeliner.

As I opened my eyes, the make-up artist, Barbara, had her face in mine. (She's a hard-core New Yorker.) "Do you know where you are?" Barbara demanded. "Do you know *who* you are?" There it was, Lil. My identity crisis. Up close and personal.

I later emailed Barbara a thank-you note. She responded with un-solicited details. "Your eyes rolled into the back of your head and were white. To me you didn't just pass out but had a seizure because of the shaking you did in my chair. You almost fell out . . ." When the convulsions ended, "I seriously felt no pulse on you." With a finishing flourish, she wrote, "You drove me to drink!" Glad I could be of service.

After my release from the hospital, Lil, I cancelled my book tour on physician's orders. I would've protested but Dr. Davis read me the riot act: Either I quit for the summer or she quits as my doctor. In the following days, I eased into an antidepressant, renewed my gym membership, chugged protein shakes, and logged off social media.

For two months, the silence in which I recuperated kicked my butt to a new awareness: As a brand, I'm entirely dispensable. Most "friends" and "followers" didn't notice one iota my evaporation from their feeds. For them, the show went on. But for those who knew me, not merely knew of me, I went missing a while ago.

I'd closed my mind to the possibility of stepping on the brakes and breathing. A decade of dropping hints about health got Mumtaz and Jim nowhere. Didn't they see that somebody needed to fight for freedom of conscience in Islam? What *I* failed to see is that in the process of fighting, I'd spurned my own conscience and become a prisoner of freedom. My egobrain rationalized away the truth that I'd become a hostage to identity and a stranger to integrity.

In mind, body, and soul, I had some serious reconciling to do. Not unlike American society now.

31

America's Seizure

Indulge me in a thought experiment, Lil. Partisans of diversity usually talk as if identity is a compass with which you "find" yourself. What if it's more like a scrambler? In that case, obsessing with identity gets us lost. It leads us down a rabbit hole of caricatures, absurdities, and lies not only about others but also about ourselves. Tribe-building egomaniacs clench the microphones. They play us into picking sides. Reconciliation is for pansies, one trumpets. In reaction, another bellows that reconciliation is for traitors.

They never let on that puritanical identity will destroy whatever it's meant to defend. Because a society attacking itself, like a body inundated with the fear of losing control, seizes up and finally conks out. Before then, it would be healthy to ask: Can a seized-up society always rebound from seizure or, sometimes, is it too late?

Yes, Lil, I heed your head-tilt.

Yes, I'll be more specific. Let's reflect on the chasm between white nationalists and those of us who'll go to the wall for diversity.

White nationalists scorn diversity—not just of appearance but also of thought. For a good long time, they marginalized themselves by resisting the cultural current in America, a current that embraces multiculturalism. Over these past few years, though, white nationalists have traveled with the current. Today, they parrot the worst of multiculturalism by insisting that, as a budding minority, they've got the right to self-segregate.

Strategically, white nationalists became "like water." They got the culture's drift and waded in. Then they dove in. Spiritually, of course, nationalists are nothing like water. They're sopping with fear, the current that now courses through America.

As champions of diversity, Lil, we have to outwit the fear-carrying current. We can do that by refusing to be part of the lose-lose game that I call "segregate-and-imitate." America practiced racial segregation by law. It continues to practice racial segregation by habit. And, with each passing culture war, supporters of diversity fortify racial segregation by label.

Hold the heckling, Lil. Let me explain how we're contributing to this contagion.

We talk a blue streak about the mass incarceration of black and brown men in the United States. We want more Americans to understand that it's a perversion of justice. We work for the day when most Americans will vote out the opportunists who prop up this perversion. But do we identify our own opportunism? When we shame white people for their privilege, we become *their* jailers.

What are you jumping around for, Lil?

You're hopping mad?

No, no, by no stretch am I diminishing the impact of real imprisonment. God, no! Let me clarify. A criminal justice system that incarcerates too many people of color has something in common with a social justice movement that locks up the hearts of too many white people. Both types of "justice" come from an impulse to dominate. It's an impulse that throbs in every human, thanks to our egobrains.

Until we bust out of the bars that our brains are behind, we'll keep setting off this habitual spiral of suspicion: White folks step back and stew. White nationalists step in and spin. Diversity's battalions fiercely condemn them but deploy rhetoric that feels to loads of white folks like they're being indicted for every one of the nation's ills.

Which legitimizes their sense of siege.

Which incites in some of them an indignation that fertilizes the soil for white supremacy.

Which repulses many of us and downright terrorizes some of us. We shout louder about white supremacy and take to jeering about white fragility.

Which leads to fresh outbreaks of mutual incrimination.

Which strengthens what many more Americans feel about the unity, the integrity, of the country: abject defeatism.

Which translates into a final sneaking suspicion that the experiment of *e pluribus unum* is doomed.

Overwhelmingly, it's white people who've sheepishly told me that the time has arrived to throw in the towel; that the body known as these United States is beyond repair, seized up by spasms in its self-image. No melodrama intended, Lil. One of America's foremost historians, David Blight, describes the state of the union this way: "It's not only racial polarization but a seizure about identity."

This, I've come to see, is how the most despondent Americans justify their meager expectations of Donald Trump. Why bother demanding better of the president, or of themselves, when America can't be salvaged anyway? Far more amusing—and less naïve—to watch the moral panic that Trump induces.

Right you are, Lil. It's unpatriotic. Yet the same Americans who've given up on the ever-perfecting union will think nothing of demanding that we all stand for the national anthem. And, hand on heart, many will call for heads to roll when a few Americans exercise their lawful right to kneel. Nationalism is its own kind of political correctness. Nationalists would do well to take the advice of the psychologist Jordan Peterson: Launder your sulfurous sheets before instructing others to clean house.

From their choir, I've heard only one note of uplift: Christ is coming. But even he admonished people to remove the log from their eyes as they pray for redemption. Because on the off-chance that Jesus doesn't show, what then? Should we pray for intergalactic aliens to storm Planet Earth so we can all band together in fear of the new Them? What if they've got higher priorities than raiding Us?

Then we the people have only ourselves to rescue us from ourselves.

Which doesn't exactly inject me with optimism. We're biologically coded to form tribes and culturally conditioned to be deformed by them. How do we work with identity as a fact of life?

What's more, social media magnifies our tribal tendencies. Realistically, can anything be tried online, where all too many of us live, so that human beings become vaguely humane?

Talk to me, Lil.

I'm spent, Mama.

Me too, *petit chou*. Go on back to your jubilee of odors and aromas. We'll pick this up later if you still think I'm capable of making scents.

A New Identity

32

Lily in the Field: Many-Sided, Many-Sighted

Have I told you lately how much I love your questions, Lil?

Your individuality teaches me that the way we do diversity needs a rethink. Diversity is dishonest when it squeezes you and me into predetermined labels. How short-sighted. Labels can inform us about *things* but they cloak the truth about *beings*. A label is static. A being is "a net of interactions," as the physicist Carlo Rovelli eloquently puts it. From the antiracism campaigner to the Trump admirer to the Muslim refugee to the misfit mongrel, we're all many-sided.

Honest diversity is about becoming many-sighted: willing to see the sides that I don't yet know; ready to be surprised and not raring to be offended; committed to ending a supremacist system by looking hard at my own supremacy complex toward those who disagree with me. Mine might very well be the better—morally upright—position on a given issue, but my supremacy complex seduces me to believe that I've got nothing to learn from the so-called Neanderthals.

My bad, Lil. Neanderthals are people, too. I take it back and repeat that there's a win-win way out of all our pinched moralities: honest diversity—treating each other as more than a jumble of labels. Respecting the individual, even as she, he, and they append themselves to groups. Wondering, *What do they think?* without assuming the answer. Asking them.

You've got a question, sweet bean? Bring it.

Do I realize that I sound like a chump? That I'm asking to be steam-rolled by the haters who are hell-bent on demolishing lives and not just disagreeing with us?

Sure, Lil, I'll give you that perception. But are you prepared to be surprised?

33

We the Plurals

Liliko'i, my Hawai'ian passion fruit, most days, I could you eat you up in all your scrumptious irresistibility. Some days, though, your sourness stops me cold. You cautioned that I come off as a "chump." Attitude aside, I'd like to set the record straight. Human beings will always tribe out. It's nested in our biology. The barely evolved brain guarantees that we'll succumb to some relic of Us and Them. And this means labels won't disappear.

But I don't believe it's frivolous to ask, can we tribe out differently? For many of us, to be categorized is to be minimized. We don't fit into manufactured molds and, frankly, we don't want to. Who are "we"? We are the plurals. And we are real.

- *I was an action movie hero who first appeared on-screen at the age of three months. I played a girl. As an adult, I epitomized manhood for my fans worldwide. People say I'm Chinese American but what does that mean when I'm also part Dutch and a fraction Jewish? Let's discuss it over a drink, my friend.*

- *I'm an Iranian student who lives a few miles from the White House and I'm plotting. My plan is to land a premier seat for my favorite Cole Porter musical,* Anything Goes. *If you and I get together for coffee, I won't be able to say much about the mullahs in my country because I'm not all that religious. If you're interested, though, I'd love to tell you about the shows I've caught this season at the National Arts Center.*

- *I'm a teenager who invented the app ReThink. It gives users a chance to think twice (or once) before they get involved in cyberbullying. I passionately believe that technology can help people to stop harming themselves and each other. Oh, and in case you think I'm obsessed with computer science and math, ReThink. ☺ My favorite subjects are history and English. Tell me something about you that assumptions get wrong.*

- *We're white guys in Appalachia. We're also out-of-the-closet atheists. Our whiteness and maleness are plain as day but because of our godlessness, life around here is no breeze for us. Rather than assume that all white men have it easy, how about getting to know us? Ask anything. There are no forbidden questions.*

- *I'm an improv artist born in Pakistan, raised in Britain, and living in Brooklyn. As a child, I aspired to be an astronaut. But my* abbu *(that's Urdu for "father") explained that girls don't fly into space because they're needed at home. Now my dad's my most vocal supporter. Why did abbu change? He's going to be at my show tonight. Feel free to ask him directly. He won't be offended.*

Get the picture, Lil? To be a plural isn't exactly to label yourself. It's to leapfrog over labels because everyone's a puzzle whose pieces shift with time and experience. Plurals recognize this about themselves and, out of self-respect, they commit to recognizing it in others.

Committed plurals are therefore conscious renegades. They're wise to the influence of the egobrain, which prods humans to fear the Other. If plurals assume anything, it's that the Other has a back story and they ought to hear it. Which is why they'd ask how you came to believe what you believe. They'd also invite you to ask them whatever you wish.

For plurals, a conversation with the Other is like water. Try to control the conversation and, like water, it'll squirt right through your fist. Let the conversation undulate and, like water, it'll reveal abundant room to flow in a new direction. By stepping up to be the first listeners, plurals set the conversation's culture—its tone, vibe, sincerity, and reciprocity. Plurals thereby steer expectations without ever having to manipulate. They claim their power through grace.

At the same time, plurals accept their limitations. They're busy, dammit. They can't pay this amount of attention to everyone. So in any given chapter of their burgeoning lives, plurals build one relationship where disagreement can be elevated to conversation, and conversation can lead to shared action.

Make no mistake, plurals have personal views that differ from each other's. But among their values is the humility to understand that their views will modify if they hear better arguments. For plurals, free speech is more a gift to pay forward than an inheritance to squander.

Go ahead, Lil. Speak your mind.

Since plurals honor individuality, Mama, how do they forge community?

So—

And how do plurals escape feeling alone if they belong to neither an Us nor a Them?

Yep—

And how do plurals make their way through emotional situations where there's a blazingly clear right and wrong, where compromise just won't do, where injustice blows the mind?

Breathe, Lily. Let me address all of your questions through a story so dope, it'll maul you with hope.

34

Friends on Opposite Sides, Part 1

Earlier in our conversation, Lil, I mentioned my friend Genesis from Biloxi, Mississippi. She's the "source" I called when I needed straight talk about the culture of the American South. I trusted Genesis to give me the skinny because she's both an ambassador and a critic of her home. "The people are all beautiful down here," Gen says of Mississippi. "You go by any local place and you'll hear more thank-you's and pardon me's and yes, sir's—just genuine hospitality—than anywhere I've ever been."

As a rapper, Genesis represents Mississippi wherever she performs, and she reps with humble honesty. To paraphrase the psychologist Karl Weick, she speaks as if she's right but she listens as if she's wrong.

You'd never know it from her theatrics, Lil. At a concert she headlined in April 2016, Genesis railed against Confederate Heritage Month. That month, the state of Mississippi paid tribute to its slave-holding past, and for Gen (among many others), it was an expression of contempt. Genesis takes history personally. It's understandable: Southern segregationists repeatedly trailed and tailed her grandfather, a Christian minister who kept African American voters safe on their way to the ballot boxes. He died under circumstances that can be linked to the known tactics of the Ku Klux Klan.

Now that you've got a bit of Gen's back story, Lil, let's return to her onstage protest. She placed a noose around her neck. She then whipped out Mississippi's flag, whose symbolism hollers Confederate pride. Gen held a lighter to it. Her fans roared their approval. She didn't want them or the venue going up in flames so she tossed the flag to her audience and recommended that someone rip it apart.

After the drama, the deluge: A photo of Gen's protest made national news and incited apoplexy. Death threats found their way to her cell phone. If the would-be assassins had her number, did they also have her address? That's what I would've wondered in her place. But Genesis grew up "occupying" KKK rallies with her father, where they'd be the only objectors. Frankly speaking, she feared nobody now.

Genesis scoured her bulging social media feeds. In the fusillade of comments, she picked out a message from Louis, a classmate from middle school. Within days, she reached out to him directly because she wanted to learn from someone with different lenses. You see, Lil, he's the descendent of a Confederate soldier who fought to keep the Southern way of life, slavery and all. He, too, takes history personally.

Louis disagreed with Genesis when it came to the flag, but he also rejected the calls to muzzle her. As he later told me, "I'm a Christian. That word translates into 'Christlike' and that's the kind of life I choose, helping others without judgment." Oh, but he has prejudged. Immigrants. Muslims. Garden-variety "others." To look at Louis is to expect nothing less, Lil. He's a white guy in a red beard and a dusty ball cap.

Engage Louis, however, and you realize that he's no odious "redneck." He's an unpredictable plural. A person of faith but not of dogma. A member of the Sons of Confederate Veterans, but one who risked becoming radioactive by responding to Genesis after she contacted him. A self-described "blue-collar garbage man" who runs a business installing trash compactors for twelve hours a day, six days a week, but who made the time to meet up with Gen.

In Genesis, I witness another plural. That's not merely because her father's black and her mother's white. Gen's a plural because you can affix any label to her and she'd still color outside the lines. Here's a hip-hop artist who openly challenges fellow rappers to cherish people, not things. A Muslim who takes seriously her father's teaching to think freely. An antiracism activist who dignifies the Other even before the Other proves himself deserving.

Why does Genesis go in first bestowing dignity? Because, she says, "If you're unwilling to listen to someone's point of view or empathize with where they're coming from, you're not really adding anything new to the table." A genuine movement doesn't simply regurgitate its demands of society, then rinse and repeat. An authentic movement *moves* to meet with the holdouts.

Soon after they reconnected on social media, Genesis invited Louis to get together for a face-to-face conversation. Not a debate, she assured. A conversation. They'd neither seen nor spoken with each other since adolescence. Trust, if any, had to be developed in real time. And so began an uncertain afternoon for them both.

35

Listening without Agreeing

"When you see the Mississippi state flag," Genesis asked Louis, "how does it make you feel?"

"It's definitely a symbol of home," Louis said. "What about you?"

"Makes me feel unwelcome. . . . Makes me feel a little embarrassed for my state."

"I hate that you can't see something as pretty as I see it," Louis replied. "Something that is so pretty to me has been used in a negative way and has been made so ugly for so many."

Louis figured that the flag's true purpose was to distinguish Confederate troops on the battlefield because, before the Civil War, each regional flag looked much like the next. If he's in denial about history, Lil, he has no illusions about the present: "There *are* Mississippi Southerners who are racist to the core and fly that flag as a symbol of their hate, not their heritage."

Genesis nudged Louis to consider making his voice public. "What I would love to see is white Southerners who are not white supremacists, but who identify with their Confederate heritage, speak out more against those white supremacists who use the Confederacy—and I think that's a dialogue that people nationwide don't see. When they don't see that, they take it as you being complicit."

Louis agreed. "Just like we don't see your friend who's against radical Islam and who is Muslim." Ugh, Lil. He meant me. That's the cost of being a recovering media slut. If you're not everywhere, you're nowhere. Sad!

Genesis valued Louis's point that extremists of any cause get showered with airtime, which plants the assumption that voices of reason don't exist. Maybe her own extreme antics to protest Confederate Heritage Month upstaged her intent to sing the praises of inclusion? "I was angry," Genesis admitted to Louis. "I was so angry."

"You were so peaceful," he twice reminded her, at least compared to her haters on social media. Louis knew who, besides them, are responsible for the blithe brutality of our culture. We the people are responsible. The media mirror us. "People love violence," he said soberly.

Louis had been thinking about the taunting threats that Gen received. They made him feel "ashamed." He noted that Christians came to America "to escape persecution and set up a country for freedom. As a Christian and an American, with those values as a whole, how can we force our opinions and beliefs on others? That's not right. It goes against everything American."

Everything? I silently asked myself. If that's so, why don't more Americans confront their hypocrisy? In the end, it seems, "American" is a label like any other. It's unexceptional when the people who drape themselves in it then mutilate their spirits with moral mediocrity. Being American doesn't inoculate you from being human, and Louis reckoned that "pride is humans' greatest downfall"—Confederate pride, meaning *pridefulness,* as only one example.

Louis caught Genesis by surprise. "Yeah, pride," she mulled over. "Any kind of pride." She'd curbed her pride enough to be moved by Louis throughout their conversation. In turn, his own pride receded, clearing the way for a thought process that took him from being aggravated by her protest to being enamored of her integrity. "At first, I was kind of upset," Louis leveled with Genesis.

And then . . . then I start thinking about it from your point of view. And I start seeing that this [flag] has been used as a symbol of hate for many years. I can see why it offends her, why she wants it down, why she doesn't want it to represent her home state.

And then the respect came. This is something she truly believes in. This is somebody who's actually doing something about it, not just sitting on the sidelines. You know, people voice their opinion all the time but do they take the action to do something about it? No, they don't. It doesn't happen often.

To know that I might have been offended by your protest? Here I am honored to know somebody who is actually daring to make a change, doing something, putting her name, her face, out there; taking the time to talk to me, to hear my side of it, not just blindly say this needs to be changed and not want to hear people who support it, their side of it. You're doing everything respectfully.

As a result, Louis "went from upset to understanding to respect."

Voilà, Ms. Lil, the power of "taking the time to talk to me, to hear my side of it." That's what plurals do. They initiate respect more out of sincerity than strategy. If listening changes the Other's mind, so be it. Ain't nothing wrong with being judged right. For plurals, though, the spur to listening is their integrity. Since dynamic plurals are the opposite of inert things, they stay true by not staying stuck. To not stay stuck, they go out of their way to encounter different points of view—giving their Other an incentive to grow with them.

Hit me up, Ms. Lil.

Good, let's cut to the chase. You want to know whether Louis reversed his position on Mississippi's slavery-sympathizing flag.

No, he didn't.

Lay off the victory lap, though. Louis did something else. He acknowledged the fact that this isn't about him. Louis told Genesis, "As much as I would like to have [the flag] remain, who's to say my wishes should outweigh the wishes of another? That's part of equality. Will I lose my heritage if that flag is changed? No, I won't. My heritage is in my heart."

See what's staggering about this, Lil? Louis demonstrates that identity doesn't have to be zero-sum, as in "for me to win, you must lose." Cutthroat competition permeates American culture, which may be why we analyze so much in zero-sum, or win-lose, terms. Not just who wins college seats, but also at whose expense. Not just who won on the Senate floor, but also who failed to obstruct them. Not just who's winning the sprint to break news, but also who's losing eyeballs. Zero-sum is heroin for emotional euphoria, and it's ruinous for sane results.

Jay Rosen, a prominent scholar of media, thinks journalists should admit their part in amping up our egobrains. Reporters, he says, are hooked on chronicling "the game aspect of politics." So they "explain who's winning and how they're winning" by bringing us "inside both the strategies and tactics of political players." The effect of zero-sum journalism? "It teaches citizens to look at their fellow citizens as objects to be manipulated."

Wow, Lil. Just wow.

Of course, the winner-take-all mentality makes sense for games that are meant to be games. Sports, that is, in which you earn the championship only by besting the rest, round by round, match by match, playoff by playoff. But happiness? Liberty? Justice? Applying the win-lose lens to these ideals garbles our pursuit of them. I wince when politicians tiptoe through the question, "Do black lives matter or do all lives matter?" It's a false choice. It's false when the police make it and it's false when activists make it. Black lives matter precisely because all lives matter. Zero-sum presumes that only one or the other can have dignity in our depraved system of justice. Is the corrective really that black and white? Is life?

Genesis and Louis are now inviting people from each side of the divide to a physical table. There, they'll discuss the design for a new flag, drawn by an artist whose grandfather was an arch-segregationist. How will Louis talk about it with his Confederate band of brothers? "Better to be part of the decision-making than shutting ourselves out of it and then taking offense as if we'd never been consulted. If that's what happens, it's on us and nobody else."

Once again, Louis speaks a truth that grown-ups will grasp: If all you care to do is play the blame game, then, as they said in the 1960s, let your freak flag fly—on your own lawn. You have that right. Just know that your wailing about being oppressed won't get sympathy in the public square. Nor should it, since you opted to enclose yourself in the child's sandbox.

Weeks after his conversation with Genesis, Louis confessed that he still prefers the Mississippi flag as is but, he added, so what? He's realized that he cares more about Gen than about a piece of cloth, as redolent with memory and identity as it may be. "Genesis looks at the flag and sees torment and terror," Louis told me. "I want that flag to represent my friends. She's my friend. We all have to make sacrifices and she's done her share."

Louis said as much to his father. "Why should African Americans let it roll off their back?" the son asked the elder about historical trauma. "Why don't we let it roll off *our* back?" It's wise that he's giving the elder time to think. Necessary, too. As Louis is learning, "People have to discover the hard things for themselves. But I can raise the questions so that some of us will think."

This, Lily, is how plurals tribe out differently. Like Genesis did with Louis, they respect the Other by asking what makes the Other more than a patchwork of labels. Then they pass the respect on by assuming that more people, when encouraged and not humiliated, will take the permission to branch out. If that assumption flops, no new harm done. If it flies, then pluralism has won.

Every day that we've been together, cream puff, you've shown me that you're a plural. The time you spend listening, tilting, and teasing out what I'm trying to express—it inclines my heart to view you as more than my dog. You're Lilybean, my daughter. Liliko'i, my sweet. Ms. Lil, my mentor. Lilyboss, my tormentor. Lilpill, my all-natural upper.

There's no hack, no shortcut, for creating that kind of relationship. It's a patient journey. And, in our case, an investment in your service to a disenchanted nation. This nation, tired and torn, could stand to follow in the paw prints of a plural. Will you inspire us, Madame President?

36

Lily for President?

No bones about it, Lil, you'd be a sensational candidate for President of the United States—one nation, under Dog, irresistible, with jerky and justice for all.

In your ceaseless search for all meats grilled, you'd be the belle of the Texas ball.

Your exquisite intelligence would get the East Coast intellectuals buzzing.

With your propensity for leaning into the wind, the Midwest wouldn't get enough of you.

Yet your free spirit would have New Hampshire swooning.

The Pacific Northwest would hike to the polls when the folks there watch your fearless expedition into every inhalable terrain.

And once you're seen for the party animal that the beach brings out, Florida will be drinking out of your cup. (Hawai'i, too, but that's an end-of-election-night bonus. Get your hula on, girl.)

Yes, ma'am, you'll make diversity great again! True, you don't have proof of being microchipped in America, but you'll insist that you've never wandered far from Compton, California. After all, you'll jest, that's where a "wretch" like you was found. (Voters will get the musical allusion. And they'll adore the self-deprecation. Trust me.)

The best part is, as a plural you'll have accumulated some vital political experience: listening to voters who'll initially regard you as a flimsy candidate. "Fabulous fur," they'll concede, "but can she govern?" They'll have learned from previous Oval Office occupants that big hair only achieves so much.

Those voters, burned as they are by politicians, will skewer your policies, mangled as they'll be by the media. But you, Lily, will already wield the skills to communicate your vision to the doubters. Over many years of exposing yourself to disagreement, you'll have expressed your values clearly to an apprehensive electorate.

You'll know what's negotiable and nonnegotiable in order to maintain your integrity. You'll have gobs of self-awareness and a cornucopia of world-awareness—the implicit understanding that viewpoints other than yours exist and that those who hold them are more likely to hear you out if you hear them first. Let's jot that down for your upbeat ads.

You won't appear defensive because, well, you're not. Your openness will lower emotional defenses both in the reporters and in the voters. Above all, you'll distinguish yourself from the pack of howling rivals, trained at elite colleges to exercise freedom of screech.

Voters will have had their fill of the shouting. Your campaign credo, "Listening—for a change," will catch on and stimulate neighborhood potlucks nationwide. Down with shrill! Up with Lil!

After you win, Madame President, your well-groomed capacity to absorb and engage will alleviate the perennial gridlock in Congress. Mark Lilla, a political scientist, explains the advantage you'll be trotting in with:

> To pass legislation you need to persuade very different sorts of people that it makes sense, which might require compromise but also helps ensure that the law will not provoke a mass reaction that leaves you in a worse position than when you began.

By cooperating with all sides, what you're really doing, Lilla reveals, is breaking the habit of turning to judges for legislative progress. Taking it to the courts "was an essential tactic in the early years of the civil rights movement," he notes, "but it has been a disaster for liberalism's reputation with the public ever since."

> *It got liberals into the habit of treating every issue as one of inviolable right, leaving no room for negotiation, and inevitably cast opponents as immoral monsters, rather than simply as fellow citizens with different views.*

Lilla (running-mate material, Lil?) rightly points out that we've become rusty at building consensus, "the most secure foundation for any social policy." Obsessed with chastising the racist, sexist, and homophobic clods on Capitol Hill and beyond, we've taken solace in the existence of beings who are like us. So have conservatives in beings who are like them. The more they hive, the more we cloister. We're forgetting how to talk to people *unlike* us. It's a peculiar way to advocate diversity.

Speaking as your Steve Bannon—er, David Axelrod—may I suggest that what America needs now is less liberalism, less conservatism, less radicalism, much less populism, and mounds more pluralism.

Too sophisticated a message for distracted voters, you say?

With respect, I'm not persuaded. Kindly indulge me once more, Lilyboss. Please RT this tweet: *Enuff polarization! Have ur opinion & express it. Then invite ppl 2 disagree & engage. It's called pluralism. #Lily4POTUS #DogHouse2WhiteHouse.*

That's 143 characters. You can determine what the other 137 will be. You're the future president.

37

Social—No, Sociopathic—Media

Mama, if nominated I will not run and if elected, I will not serve.

Where's this coming from, Lil?

You're projecting your personal political ambitions onto me, Mama. You should've learned by now that I'm **not** your bitch!

You don't understand your privilege, Lil. As a native-born American, you're constitutionally eligible to become president. As an immigrant to the land of immigrants, I'm not. Empathy much?

I'm next to you, Mama. Look up from your phone, please.

Aaack. You're right, Lily. Let's power down our devices. By DM'ing these words to each other, we've escalated our differences needlessly. How fast we stop being plurals when we have to stuff our thoughts and emotions, expectations and disappointments, desires and distastes, into tiny boxes from our small screens.

On my Facebook, a "friend" named Jeff went batty after I posted a video. It featured an iconic photo of Earth from space, overlaid with the voice of Carl Sagan, the renowned socially conscious scientist. When we contemplate our planet as a pale blue dot, Sagan says with reverence, humanity is humbled.

Stirred by his perspective, I updated my status to read, "3 minutes of Carl Sagan worth listening to—no matter what one's faith or lack of it. He cuts right through the noise, no?"

Apparently not. Jeff's a self-confessed atheist and he commented, "Lack of faith?

> *Seriously? How insulting and demeaning just because rational*
> *people refuse to believe in an invisible magic person. I'm sorry, I've*
> *followed you for years but this is where we part ways. It's insulting,*
> *Irshad, and arrogant to say the least!*

Alrighty then.

I have faith—pardon me, confidence—that in-person, Jeff and I could've hashed it out over a beer and mango juice. We would've probably clinked glasses at the end. But online, rationality goes bye-bye. Everybody's got an opinion about why social media releases the maniacs in us. What I want to point out is, those maniacs reside *in* us, not outside of us. And in *us,* not in our devices.

Tech giants take skillful advantage of the egobrain. They employ armies of designers and engineers to dissuade us from thinking through our emotions. They tweak algorithms so that we're first fed only the content that matches our biases. Then they revise more algorithms to automatically "connect" us with people who will go ninja on our content, which is how the techies measure "engagement" and sell "advertisers" on their "key performance indicators." Where does that leave us, the plurals? Navigating manipulation from the moment we log on.

Plurals calm the egobrain in order to dignify ourselves and whomever's disagreeing with us, since they're the threat that our well-meaning egobrain has detected. In the real world of eye contact and body language, we can compose ourselves quite handily. On sociopathic media, it's a lot harder to stay composed—and not just because we can hide behind handles. There's that, but there's more.

Sociopathic media thrives on my egobrain networking with yours and your egobrain networking with someone else's. The network grows so mammoth that its culture of carelessness, funneled by algorithms but produced and propagated by snap decisions of the brain, becomes too ubiquitous for us to resist. People give up on individual relationships, which require nuisances like paying attention. We give in to "the network," that gluttonous grid of egobrains reacting, pinball-like, here, there, and everywhere.

In the end, what humans are giving into is our own dehumanization. Jaron Lanier, a Silicon Valley pioneer, has witnessed the engineering of this effort firsthand. He says that we "start to care about the abstraction of the network more than the real people who are networked, even though the network by itself is meaningless. Only the people were ever meaningful."

Yeah, yeah, I know, Lil. There's nothing we can do about it because soon, bots will overtake human users anyway. So what are you saying? We should help our "friends," the tech companies, accelerate their conquest? After all, they need us glued to our screens right now—this very second—so that we're "interacting." Our interactions then inform them of how to debug their bots for a more lifelike "experience." But I've got a better idea for a lifelike experience: Get a life.

God, Lil, I just realized how old I sound.

Gah! I don't give a whizz. Yes, Lilpill, let's get a charmingly analog life to complement our digital existence. Let's meet fetching plurals. Let's dance with brassy mutts. In person. Where we can't be spied on as readily as we can by the tech snoops who enlist us as unpaid interns and count on us to use others for "likes" and "follows," all to bloat our personal networks and their corporate profits.

Stand back, Lilybean, I'm on a roll! Mama doesn't "like" exploitation. Neither does Jaron Lanier. In *You Are Not a Gadget: A Manifesto*, Lanier argues that your individuality and mine have a lot more value than do lines of code. By definition, our gadgets won't rehumanize our culture, whether in the virtual or in the actual spheres. Only people (and our furry gurus) have that power. If we want to keep it, we have to quit idolizing technology as though it should do our thinking for us.

"People degrade themselves to make machines seem smart all the time," Lanier explains. For example, before the financial crash of 2008, "bankers believed in supposedly intelligent algorithms that could calculate credit risks before making bad loans." How'd that turn out? In education, too, data-deifying policymakers thrust standardized tests onto teachers. Why? So that students "will look good to an algorithm."

In venerating technology, humans are humiliating themselves. As Lanier asks, "Did that search engine really know what you want, or are you playing along, lowering your standards to make it seem clever?"

Drop mic. Exit Lanier.

Stop, Mama!

'Sup, Lil?

Mama, every last aspect of social media can't be labeled "sociopathic."

Why the hell not?

Because without YouTube, Mama, I wouldn't have learned about Bruce Lee and consequently I couldn't have taught you about him.

Touché, my little cream puff.

Come to think of it, Mama, we might never have met in the absence of Facebook. The shelter lady came across my photo there. Mama Laura follows the shelter lady, so she received the post about me and showed it to you. The rest is our love story.

Oh, Lil.

Keep your accounts active, Mama. Deleting them would be extreme. And as you say, extremism on one side can't be moderated by extremism on the other side. So sally forth! Tally ho! Delight in your digital platforms! Just don't sedate your mind when you use them.

Right on, Lilyboss! I won't split up with technology; I'll just shake off my servility. Because I'm not Twitter's bitch. Or my egobrain's.

Ms. Lil, will you help me get clear on my values so that I'm practicing them in my feeds? From time to time, will you also warn me that the conveniences tech providers come out with are mostly meant to rope me into their software so they can scrape and sell more of my personal data? And do you want me to remind you that your attention shouldn't come cheap?

You talking to me, Mama?

Yes, love. Your attention shouldn't come cheap. Would you like me to remind you of that?

Did you say something, Mama?

Your attention, Lil, your attention. It shouldn't—never mind, smart-ass.

38

Sassy but Classy

Yours is an apt question, Lil. Since most of us will use sociopathic media for a while yet, let's get practical. Those haters—what do we do with them?

First, remember that disagreement on its own doesn't equal hate. Let me illustrate. Shortly after your mamas got married, I tweeted some photos from the wedding and asked my tweeps, "Which pic is your fav?"

A woman from Pakistan tweeted out the wedding album and remarked, "Like desi men, desi women also have admiration for white women." (*Desi* refers to someone with South Asian roots who lives abroad.) Now, I didn't mind being labeled a Desi, but the woman's tweet sounded judgmental to me. Like I'd betrayed my brown peeps by marrying a white chick. Was I reading too much into it? If so, why would the Pakistani woman bring up your Mama Laura's skin color?

A lifetime of being told that I'm insufficiently South Asian, or Muslim, or feminist, or queer, or Canadian heightened my defenses as I thought about whether to reply. I sat with it as I went about my day. If I could come from a place of grace, I reasoned, why not ask the woman what she meant by her tweet? So I did. Here's how our dialogue went down.

ME: *With respect, why reduce people to skin color?*
SHE: *Same gender marriages are still very new & unusual for me! I will take time to adjust to this new reality!*

ME: *I understand. But again, what does anybody's skin color have to do with same-sex relationships?*

SHE: *It was just used to point attention that woman is marrying a woman, nothing to do with skin colors!*

ME: *Then why did you use the word, "white"? I ask sincerely, not sarcastically.*

SHE: *I feel extremely embarrassed & guilty for tweeting this gibe and hurting U. Sorry! Everybody has right to live their lives.*

ME: *Thank you for engaging. Wishing you well.*

Good on her—not for feeling guilty but for admitting to the jab, apologizing, and clarifying that she harbors no hate toward same-sex couples. I, in turn, expressed my curiosity, set a tone of civility, and heard her out. Neither of us gave free rein to our egobrains. We humanized our disembodied but plural selves to each other.

Not every thread will go so swimmingly, of course, Lil. But when heavy-duty bile appears in our sociopathic media streams, we don't have to react. And definitely not right away. Better to breathe and ask ourselves, *If I reply, am I being more defensive than dignified?* If more defensive, we can take charge by depriving the haters of any fun. We can move on.

If it's important to us that we respond, as I did with that woman from Pakistan, then we can experiment. Spark conversations that would otherwise be sermons. Instead of making statements, ask questions of the commenter. And always—always—sign off with a thank-you. Being classy is a potent way of being sassy. We can be both, and more. We're plurals.

I'd like to address a final item, Lil. Can your next question wait? Not really? Go on, then.

The trolls. What can we do about those flame-hurling, emotion-igniting reprobates whom we charitably call "trolls"? That's where I was going, Lil. I've saved the trolls for last because they pose a particularly nuanced challenge for us plurals.

What's that, boss?

Keep it simple, you say, and ban them? Let's contemplate this.

39

About Those Trolls . . .

The nature of trolls isn't nuanced at all, Lil. On my media pages, they've swooped in simply to prevent my community from having healthy conversations. I don't know about yours, but my trolls tend to be fundamentalist Muslim guys who puke homophobia. Whenever they emerge from their gutter, I notice a steep drop in the number of friends and followers who engage with me. Normally, I call on my community members to ignore the pests. But in merely asking this, Lil, I've given the trolls just what they covet: attention.

Yes, I hear you, Lil: Ban 'em.

Not so fast, my endearing ego-brainiac. I swear to you, I'm not trying to overthink this; I just don't want to be a hypocrite. Plurals uphold free speech. If I put up with only the speech that I already agree with, then I'm not exercising freedom of speech, am I? I'm practicing discrimination—exclusion based on my preexisting biases.

That said, there's something else to weigh. Even if language should be free, what about tactics? Trolls don't intend to participate in dialogue; they show up just to blow up the space. From a moral standpoint, does my commitment to free expression oblige me to accept their methods?

Until I hear a better argument, I'd have to answer no. Methods sometimes give away motives. If I can ascertain that a troll is actively disrespecting *other* people's freedom of speech, then I'm not bound to make free speech my operating principle in response to the troll.

Let's take a real-world example. When white supremacists arrive at their protests with assault rifles in tow, their method hints—actually, it hails—that they're not here to fight with words alone. If they were, they wouldn't make a show of packing heat. Their weapons terrorize some, and maybe many, into running away and staying away. Which tramples on the free speech rights of counterprotestors.

The gun-toters know it, too. It's not as if threatening death is an oopsie outcome of carrying an assault-ready rifle. Enticing carnage is exactly their intention. So free speech was never their issue. I won't defend their "right" to deny others the freedom that they crookedly arrogate to themselves.

Madame President, I'd counsel you, don't ban the protestors or their speech. Ban their access to those arms.

All of this takes us back to the online trolls, Lil. They do more than usurp conversations. They drive community members away, undermining not only those members' right to speak but also my right to *listen*. And that's when trolls are at their least dangerous. At their worst, they injure their targets directly and indirectly, sometimes with lasting fallout. They're gladiators not for freedom, but for its failure. I love freedom enough to ban the trolls from my accounts. Happy, Lil?

Happier than I know? Then tell me more.

You like my point about protecting the right to listen and not just to speak because it implies that I should always exercise my right to listen—to you. Probably true. Bruce Lee, by the way, would be beaming at your subtle move just now. But keep in mind that "listening to" doesn't have to mean "agreeing with."

Got any more nimble strokes? Until you do, let's take up one outstanding item.

How do we decide who's a troll? My own test is simple: Give everybody a chance to demonstrate respect, the only ground rule for participating in my community. Those who flout this rule get a friendly warning because my respect for them assumes that they're capable of maturity. Those who again flout my rule get informed they're about to be purged from my forum. I then invite them to have the final word. Would you believe, Lil, that they're rarely grateful?

There's a reason Genesis invited Louis to a conversation *offline*. The internet doesn't do trust. At least not yet. More accurately, human beings don't do trust on the internet. We ghost. We stalk. We block. "When there's absolutely no trust," Genesis says, "it's very hard to have conversations that don't get heated or violent or abusive or abrasive."

If they'd limited themselves to interacting on Facebook Messenger, I can't imagine that Louis would've shared the details of why, and how, he's come to respect Genesis. That he confided at all meant the world to her. As Genesis explains, "To hear Louis say that he believes in me even though he disagrees with some of the things I say? That's beautiful."

Over my many years of speaking with Muslims and non-Muslims, I've learned why reviving trust is worth the effort. When people don't feel permitted to ask candid questions of one another, walls of suspicion inevitably rise. Warned that certain questions will offend Muslims, non-Muslims often lift an eyebrow. *Why shouldn't we ask questions? How can understanding come out of censorship? What's really going on here? Are they covering something up? Can we trust them?*

Where, Ms. Lil, is our vaunted diversity then?

40

Lily in the Field: Run!

Lilybean, Dr. Daffner called again. She's had a sudden cancellation in her surgery schedule tomorrow morning, so guess what? You're up. Let's head home, have an early supper, and get to bed. We need to be at the clinic by seven a.m.

Oh, the rapture, Mama! Oh, the ecstasy of an early supper!

I'm so feeling you, Lil. Which gives me an idea that I'm sure will excite you to reconsider running for president. Suppose you travel the country to have dinner with Americans who aren't yet feeling your platform? They table their disagreements, I take notes, and you eat. Of course, as you chow down your kibble and whichever delectable meat your hosts mix with it, you're listening to their concerns. Tilting. Exploring. Sifting. They're nourishing you and you're nourishing trust.

That night, we post a dishy photo of you and that family along with your biggest takeaway from the dinner conversation. Then we announce the folks you'll be lucky enough to dine with the next night. Every day, we're in a different village, town, county, parish, or city, allowing you to digest the burdens and blessings in the infinite tapestry of communities that is the United States.

And, given the frenetic pace of your tour, you're demonstrating how well you've recovered from surgery. Nobody, Lil, will doubt your physical fitness to lead us. Thoughts?

Hey, wait up, you punk! Supper doesn't serve itself, you know!

Why (and How) to Not
Be Offended

41

Lily in the Field: Trust Issues

Lilybean, so good to have you back in Mama's arms. Easy does it, now. You're going to be a little loopy as the anesthesia wears off. Don't fret about those stitches. In two weeks, they'll be out and you'll return to full feistiness. Today, just relax. Your bed's in the car and I want you to settle right in. Is there anything more cushy than your Lilypad on wheels?

When I handed you over to the medical team, I thought about the trust that you and I have. In our early days, you'd tremble uncontrollably the moment we entered Dr. Daffner's clinic. But this morning, you exuded cool. You knew I wouldn't desert you. How did that happen? Time. I don't mean letting time take its course and having faith that you and I would get used to each other. No relationship worth having aspires to be ho-hum. Rather, you made me reimagine time.

On our very first strolls, I assumed we were bonding simply by being together. I'd keep my eyes trained on my phone, using the time to catch up on my digital duties. You sensed an inattentive Mama and turned away from me. Literally, the distance between us grew.

On our subsequent walks, I pocketed my phone and got down in the grass with you. For the first time since childhood, I played. You played back. We ran and rolled and rerouted our strolls. When you craned your neck in a specific direction, we swiveled the stroller toward that new smell.

Until you arrived, Lil, I never imagined that between bursts of real work, I'd do anything besides check my sociopathic media accounts and dash off status updates. Something's always going on in my feeds and there's no time to wait before spending the time to comment. Let's take a moment to reflect on how senseless that logic is. Oh, dang. We can't take a moment. There's no time. Because now, something *else* is going on and if we don't use the time to comment, we'll be out of time. Get where I'm going?

You've taught me that, in fact, a crisis of time doesn't exist. But a crisis of trust does. And that's a serious impediment to diversity of viewpoint. Had I not trusted you, Lil, I wouldn't have cared to kick around the lessons that you've passed onto me. Especially the hard ones, like the value of going first: If I want your attention, I first have to give you mine. If I hope to be heard by you, I first have to hear you.

My progressive friend, Van Jones, took in this messy truth as he started to speak with conservatives. Now he says, "Nobody cares how much you know until they know how much you care." If diversity enthusiasts want to influence the people who don't trust us, we first have to care about them. And care sincerely, since diversity without humanity becomes its own form of bigotry.

Caring needs time. But too many of us squander it by foraging for excuses to mistrust the very people we wish would change. We careen down the quickest, easiest route to mistrust. We take offense.

42

Reforming a White Nationalist

You haven't met him, Lil, but Daniel's a friend who recently graduated from Brooklyn College. He's watched how speedily some students get offended by the questions of other students.

"I had this class," Daniel said, "in which a student presented her film about her transgender friend."

> *One of our classmates asked a question to clarify the concept of gender. He was completely earnest. He did everything possible to avoid sounding offensive. Well, the presenter berated him. The other students looked down at their shoes.*
>
> *So I spoke up to ask, "Don't you think this kind of reaction defeats your purpose to help people understand transgenderism?" She told me that she wouldn't dignify my question and that if anyone else was offended by me, there's a safe room down the hall."*

Daniel felt like he'd "overdosed on cray-cray pills." No offense to the cray-cray.

I'll bet you'd agree, Lil, that the presenter in Daniel's class overreacted. The kid with a question seemed innocent. His clarification would've been technical, not judgmental. If he leaked his neo-Nazi views, that would be a different story. Then we'd feel justified in taking offense and stigmatizing him right away.

But *should* we take offense? Right away, I mean?

Let's look at Derek Black, a former white nationalist. When he enrolled in college, Black defended the prejudices he learned from his parents—that white people need to separate from America and establish a state of their own. Many students became alarmist, took instant offense, and expected others to follow suit. But a few overrode their egobrains.

Matthew Stevenson, a Jewish student, invited Black to his dorm room for discussions over Shabbat dinner every Friday. This was no interfaith dialogue. For one thing, Black's parents, both atheists, raised him to believe in the rationality of white nationalism. Black had "facts" on his side.

Shabbat participants would read his literature and give him feedback—but never sermons. After quietly undoing his arguments, they taught Black about the repercussions of his beliefs: that people whom he'll never meet, whose humanity he'll never know, will suffer.

Over two years, Black opened his heart and changed his mind. Why? Because he came to trust this circle of critics. They "weren't just going to straight-up condemn me and tell me to get out of their face," he says. "It was that personal relationship, that somebody was willing to listen to me." From the get-go, Shabbat guests took an unambiguous stand against Black's supremacist views, but they also offered a shame-free hearing.

Crucially, too, Stevenson never exploited Black's presence to notch a win for diversity. "I was legitimately friends with Derek," he emphasizes. Even before Black was outed as the resident racist on campus, he and Stevenson talked, strummed, and crooned. "He lived downstairs from me," Stevenson remembers, "and I would sing along when he played country-and-western songs on his guitar." As a result of his soft spot for Black, respect—just enough to discuss the difficult stuff—felt like less of a leap.

A few of Stevenson's Shabbat regulars dropped out when Black dropped in. New people broke bread with him and, inevitably, some of them also vamoosed. Regarding the mainstays, though, Black will never forget the big-hearted choice that they made. By engaging him, they trusted that there's more to his back story than they knew.

Good call. It turns out that Black espoused white supremacy not out of a targeted animosity for people of color, but out of an instinctive affection for his family. "[T]he conversations that led me to change my views started because I couldn't understand why anyone would fear me," he explains. "I thought I was only doing what was right and defending those I loved."

I can anticipate, Lil, what you'd be wondering if you had your wits about you right now. You'd be asking, should we trust the intentions of *militant* white nationalists, too? Like those who descended on Charlottesville, Virginia, in August 2017, one of whom drove into the counterprotest and murdered Heather Heyer?

I said it yesterday to you and I'll say it again: When they're armed, they're communicating that they've got no interest in dialogue. Although the hooligan who killed Heyer did so with a car, not a gun, the glaring visibility of guns screamed that the nationalists' stated intentions can't be trusted. As your Mama, I'd have asked you to leave the counterprotest stat and meet me for a bite at the nearest burger joint. However, if the paraders carried tiki torches only, I'd have asked them why they're plugging a cultural staple from the brown people's republic of Hawai'i. But that's just me.

Would Derek Black talk to the tiki-torchers? "I don't want people to take my story as, 'Oh, we should just listen to white nationalists; we shouldn't shout them down," he says. "There's a time for talking and the Charlottesville rally is not the time to say, 'Oh, we just need to listen.' We should counterprotest, too, so it's complicated."

Complicated only in the sense that honest diversity needs diverse forms of advocacy. Voting. Street demonstrations. Voting. Consumer boycotts. Voting. Petitions. Walkouts. Sit-ins. Strikes. Satire. Formal deliberations. Voting. And the piece that makes any spurt of social change endure beyond the moment: grassroots diplomacy, like that of Matthew Stevenson, since diplomacy brings down defenses and dignifies people, entrusting them with the capacity to evolve.

As another instance, Lil, think about the Florida high school students who've galvanized America's gun control movement. They took an exceptionally mature step in their first televised town hall forum. Several thanked their Republican senator, Marco Rubio, for appearing despite knowing he'd be submerged in boos. Can I tell you what their diplomacy accomplished because they practiced it from the outset?

It's made the students impossible to vilify. The usual conspiracy theorists ginned up rumors that they're actors-for-hire and gun lobbyists pooh-poohed them as children. But by publicly reaching out before digging in, these students elevated the moral authority of their protests—and mobilized hundreds of thousands of teenagers on the brink of becoming voters. Let's hope they have the grace to hear out some of their responsible, gun-owning peers. Bringing more of their peers on board won't require students to compromise with fellow students; just to care about them.

I grant, Lil, that protest is much sexier without diplomacy. Mass rallies display the strength of our numbers. They catalyze solidarity. They encourage the discouraged. True, all of it. By the same token, protesting caters strictly to our egobrains. Through the defense mechanisms that our egobrains work up, we glory in our blind spots—such as a culture of shrieking rather than speaking, a protocol of sanctimony, and an arsenal of exclusionary tactics. On its own, protesting doesn't transform a soul.

What does? From Derek Black's perspective, "that kind of persuasion happens in person-to-person interactions and it requires a lot of honest listening on both sides." Most of the research I've reviewed backs him up. According to Katherine Cramer at the University of Wisconsin–Madison, "People are only going to absorb facts when they're communicated from a source that they respect, from a source who they perceive has respect for them."

She'd know, Lily. Despite being based at an urban university, Cramer has earned the trust of rural voters in her state by continuing to swing by and asking yet more about their lives. That's handy when an election's on the horizon and it's caring—simply, powerfully caring—in between elections.

Then there's the online space. danah boyd (she writes her name lowercase) studies interaction on the internet. She stresses how much social change relies on the quality of personal relationships. Citing facts that dispute other people's biases "doesn't actually make them more empathetic" to a new point of view, warns boyd. "To the contrary, it polarizes them. What makes people willing to hear difference is knowing and trusting people whose worldview differs from their own."

boyd illuminates why shaming, blaming, and gaming may be the worst moves we can make. "If we want to develop a healthy democracy," she concludes, "we need contexts in which the American public voluntarily struggles with the challenges of diversity to build bonds that will last a lifetime." I'll go further, Lil. As long as we're disgracing folks who mistakenly offend, any change on their part will be neither voluntary nor a struggle. It'll be imposed and superficial, which is to say ripe for unraveling.

The kind of relationships I imagine might be explained this way. Consider the distinction between religious dogma and personal faith. Unlike dogma, faith breathes. It squirms. It holds tension. My faith can do that because it's a relationship of trust between me and the Creator. I question God all the time, trusting that God knows me and therefore knows the motive behind my challenges: to understand. Our relationship makes my pursuit of truth an entirely voluntary struggle, free from stigma. If more of us had such a relationship with each other, we'd care enough about each other to struggle—voluntarily—to be together and not just to stay together.

Do you hear that groan, Lil? Somewhere in our wondrous universe, an assembly of atheists is suppressing its collective gag reflex.

Yet it may be that atheists themselves inadvertently affirm the existence of a great God. Lao Tzu, the philosopher of ancient Chinese legend, is said to have mused that the best leader inspires people to believe they've led themselves. From that perspective, an atheist who attributes all progress to the human mind could be attesting to what an effective leader God actually is.

Lunacy? If so, I'm open to changing my view. But it won't happen by humiliating me. To convert me, missionary atheists would be wise to ask themselves: What are we missing about people of faith?

In the meantime, I say to the godless: Gag on. The more unarmed expression we have, the more honest our diversity will be. Let a thousand heretics heave.

43

Tolerating the Intolerant?

You're scarcely five hours out of surgery, Lil, and still woozy from the anesthetic. Could you hurry up and heal? I don't mean to rush you, but I miss you. Call me a sap. Now's the time to do it because you've got an unimpeachable alibi. Besides being criminally cute, you're legally high.

Whether or not you can hear me, Lilybean, I'm just using my voice to let you know how much I appreciate yours. A question keeps playing in my head, and I think it's coming from you. The question is, am I tolerating the intolerant?

I've long argued that when Islam-supremacists train their hate on Jews, queers, or women, free people like me shouldn't shrug it off. Freedom flounders when we give authoritarians carte blanche. So, asks the voice of Lily, why tolerate white supremacists?

I don't. And I won't. They ought to be challenged at all times. The operative question is *how*. Derek Black wouldn't have reformed himself if Matthew Stevenson had sneered, "Go ahead, Nazi asshole, make my day." By his own admission, Black needed the personal relationship in order to ingest, then digest, the conversations coming his way.

In the wake of 9/11, my impatience flared whenever self-styled progressives said that we have to understand why some Muslims gravitate to jihadism. Only by understanding, they stressed, can effective solutions be found. Early on, my emotions equated understanding with excusing and appeasing.

I was wrong and progressives were right. Over many years, I spoke with *former* jihadists who confirmed the importance of being understood. I can't claim this for every man on a homicidal mission, but the guys I met left militant extremism after they felt heard—not coddled or swaddled; just listened to by individuals who excoriated their ideology but embraced them as people with back stories.

What I'm saying is said better by the political scientist Javier Corrales. He suggests that if we do more confronting than conversing, we could be impelling more people to vote for Donald Trump. "When the opposition adopts extreme positions," Corrales cautions, "it can expand the president's electoral base because it provokes a merger of die-hard supporters and ambivalent moderates. The hardliners respond by saying: As bad as our president's flaws might be, they are nothing compared with the excesses of the other side. Moderates, witnessing the opposition overreach, begin to agree with them."

Corrales has seen it happen time and again in Latin America. That continent's cultures differ from ours, but the egobrain works its mischief behind and beyond every border. How inept if we furnish something—anything—that Trump needs to depict us as the unhinged ones. Resisting his policies with extreme methods, we end up conveying seemingly extreme positions.

Don't be so mindless, Corrales advises us. By all means take a firm stand, but "avoid emulating the president's escalation tactic, so as not to validate the image that the president wants to portray . . ."

Let's conduct a related thought experiment, Lil. Richard Spencer, the slick frontman of the alt-right, comes to town for an event. We picket. We chant the tried and true, "Racist, sexist, antigay! Richard Spencer, go away!"

In rhyming this off, we're sure to amass small wins. First, we're registering a decent society's disapproval of Spencer's white-is-right bunk. Second, we're bagging publicity for our own cause. What reporter doesn't salivate at a naked good-versus-evil narrative? Third, we're showing that offended citizens can do something together, and can do it nonviolently. All told, we're "raising awareness" about positive action in the face of a repellant ideology.

But it's at least as likely that we've raised awareness about our own shriveled imaginations. When we shout, "Richard Spencer, go away!" we're shoring up a myth—that you can have liberty or you can have diversity, but you can't have both. Another false choice.

Suppose we tweak our mantra. It now goes, "Racist, sexist, anti-gay! Richard Spencer, *have your say!*" Picture it, Lil. The reporter asks us why we'd allow a thorough bigot to have his say. We reply it's be-cause *diversity means diversity from bottom to top. It's not just your skin color or gender identity or religion or sexuality or age or ability to live with a disability. Diversity includes the different ways in which people view a life worth having.*

The reporter asks, but what about the vulnerable? Don't you side with them? *Damn straight,* we reply. *We're not on the fence about Richard Spencer. He's racist, sexist, and antigay, as we've been yelling to anyone who passes by. But to take away his right to speak would be a huge disser-vice to diversity itself.*

The reporter tries one more time. You oppose Richard Spencer then? *Absolutely, we oppose his ideology of white supremacy.* We look right at the camera. *And we invite anybody who agrees with Spencer to tell us why. What's enthralling about his agenda to break up America for a separate, white-only safe space? For his comfort, you're willing to dismantle what all of us, including you, have built over 200-plus years? Let's hear from you. Come on down. We're open to learning.*

With that, we've practiced what we preach about diversity. We con-stantly say it's about inclusion. This time, we've behaved like we be-lieve it. We've embodied integrity at another level, too, Lil. We've stood our ground even as we've summoned people to higher ground.

Finally, we've challenged ourselves to see the Other—*our* Other—as bearers of gifts. Spencer's sympathizers will help us become better communicators. If nothing else, they'll teach us how to reframe our arguments for more ears and hearts. And when we listen with our own hearts, we'll further learn what we've been overlooking about his sympathizers. Everyone has a back story, Lil. Everyone.

Finally—and I mean it this time—we've rewritten the script of political correctness, denying ammo to those who'd otherwise have a reason to accuse us of it. Sure, they'll continue to label us that way, but the more we model how liberty and diversity can be reconciled in reality, the better our chance of attracting voters who hanker for sanity. Voters whom some researchers describe as "the exhausted majority." Voters who, refreshed by a good reason to go to the polls, can tip elections.

44

The Other "N-Word"

You're in your own dream world right now, Lil, and maybe I am, too. Be assured, though, that I'm hip to the larger fear here: that when dealing with neo-Nazis and their ilk, to launch anything less than a full-scale whooping is to normalize them.

"Normalize" has become an N-word among people with our values. We're aghast at the deteriorating public square under Trump, Spencer, and gang. We refuse to let their stunted worldview penetrate American culture that much more. We recoil at the thought of conversing with their comrades. To do so is to recognize, and therefore normalize, them.

Is it, though, Lil? I'd say that to invite conversation is to undermine their normal by broadening "us."

I experimented with this approach years ago as the host of *QueerTelevision*. As far as I know, it was the world's first digitally streamed show about lesbian, gay, bisexual, and transgender people. My team had two investors: an American tech company and a Canadian TV station. To survive, our idealism had to deliver an expanding audience.

Giving queer people our own weekly show didn't invigorate us. Too ghettoizing. We aimed to ignite honest conversations among queer people, straight people, the in-between, and the offbeat. Which meant speaking to our common, human, condition.

Even before we went to air, the team received offensive mail. Cultural conservatives tarred us as antifamily fanatics. Predictable.

But what would transpire, we wondered, if *QueerTelevision* broadcast their vitriol word-for-word? Better, what if I responded to it with a genuine smile on camera?

We tried it—and viewers couldn't get enough. Soon, they, too, wrote and voiced their responses. We then aired those. Some viewers countered the hate with lacerating logic. Others outshone it with saucy humor. "People can say what they want about queers and homos and whatnot," one guy phoned in, "but I've never, ever, ever been woken up on a Saturday morning with a group of homos knocking on my door, asking me to join their church."

People stopped me on the street, grateful to have learned what they can say when friends or family put queers down. I got invitations to viewing parties in which fans, irrespective of their sexualities, gathered 'round the show like a hearth and discussed it afterward. In its third season, *QueerTelevision* won one of Canada's top broadcasting awards in the "general information" genre—a normalizing step up from the "lifestyle" niche. A plague on all labels, Lil, but if a program about the pluralism within any group has to fit some category, then let it be "general information."

The LGBTQ movement has flowered worldwide for this underlying reason: Activists have normalized the bridging of *presumed* opposites. Queers not only in bars but also in business, in church, in politics, in marriage, in the military, in the maternity ward, many of us proud without having to be prideful. And more of us trusting our friends to be there when our haters go on the offensive.

I still think about a concerned viewer's question for me. "Why does your program allow such bigoted remarks?" he asked. "You're making it that much harder for all the honest and beautiful people who are gay or lesbian to come out of the closet." I replied that if we didn't air the hate, we might never realize how much love is also out there. Sometimes, it takes ugliness to rouse beauty from its slumber.

45

Safe Spaces for All!

Lil, I know that the lions will never sleep with the lambs. Today, the loudest voices in every tribe claim to be victimized, so agreeing on who's a lion and who's a lamb would be enough of an achievement. I'm not holding my breath, not even for the effort. That's because humans are maestros of self-deception. When we're convinced that we've done our best to create trust with our adversaries, the odds are that we've done very little.

I once held a leadership seminar for young people of color at a progressive church. Almost everybody raised a hue and cry about being discriminated against. But some of the participants also realized how eagerly they awaited the next racist incident, just so they could preserve their pain and make a show of it.

Clutch pearls, Lil. However stupefying, this is what human beings do. Lions who identify as innocent lambs roam *everywhere*.

I've met scads of conservatives who grind their axes about political correctness but go out of their way to court censorship. Such people are in the fight not to resolve it but to prolong it. The fight's their thing. It gives them purpose. Meaning. Belonging. They'd feel stranded if the fight ended. The least demanding way to keep the fight alive? Scout out more reasons to be offended.

Take the debates about higher education. Americans tend to agree on the core task of a first-rate undergraduate college: to teach students that thinking through the various facets of any issue will prepare them for an examined and adult life. No wonder most of the conservative individuals I've talked to, and quite a number of liberal people, are offended by "safe spaces" in schools. They perceive safe spaces as romper rooms where a student never has to hear opinions other than her own. Like right-wing talk radio.

But even when students dream of being that dull, adept teachers don't. For the top-notch educators I've watched in action, safe spaces are places where all perspectives at the table, offensive or bland, get an airing as long as students back them up. So, yeah, the kids in these spaces are safe—not from intellectual challenges but from immediate judgments.

It's called "psychological safety." Google tested it with their own employees because you never know who's got the next breakthrough idea. The company's tests led to a decisive conclusion: When project members trust that nobody's going to jump down throats for a harebrained thought, self-censorship fades. Even the socially awkward feel permitted to talk. They include engineers, not exactly a syrupy bunch.

Psychologically safe spaces have now infiltrated our military service academies. I heard a three-star general tell cadets at West Point, "We want to build teams where everybody feels like a valued member." As their supervisor, he underlined that "We want teams where you add value and feel respected, both physically and emotionally. That's what leaders do."

There goes victory in World War III, Lil.

Same deal with "trigger warnings." In the classroom, a trigger warning is a heads-up that the teacher gives to students about the material being assigned. A memoir, for example, might contain graphic scenes of rape. Out of concern for any student who's been sexually assaulted, the educator would warn that the text in question could dredge up disturbing memories. Should that educator excuse fearful students from studying the memoir? It depends on the situation but overall, and in my view, no.

I'm hardly the only naysayer. In my many years on different campuses, I can name only two professors who've issued trigger warnings. Here's the kicker: Each of them did it for veterans of war who'd been diagnosed with PTSD. The trigger warnings helped prepare them emotionally to read detailed accounts of combat.

Well, my conservative-thinking friends? Do all trigger warnings reek of pampering? Lily wants to know.

Now to something that you and I have briefly tackled, Lil: "microaggressions." You got me to understand how words can be invisible forms of harassment to people with distressing pasts. My question is, do we end the patrolling of language somewhere? And who's the "we" drawing that line?

During the presidency of Barack Obama, some Christians interpreted his reference to "freedom of worship" as disrespect of their faith. They said Christians *worship* within church walls, and by using the words "freedom of worship" instead of "religious freedom," Obama implied that Christians must stop praising God once they leave church grounds. Christians have a history of being persecuted. Given this fact, Lil, why can't the offended legitimately claim that the phrase "freedom of worship" is a microaggression? Why should they let it go?

I've learned that the sentence, "You speak English very well," qualifies as a microaggression when it's expressed to Latinos or Asian Americans. It connotes that they're foreigners. But isn't it possible that a recent arrival could consider that sentence inoffensive, even friendly, in that someone cares enough to offer encouragement? Who, then, decides what verbiage rates as halal? Kosher? Whatever?

If the answer's as simple as, "The individual to whom it's said decides," then woo-frigging-hoo! Sanity prevails. But what if another member of that individual's group, overhearing said comment, disagrees? It's an honest question. In 2017, the research firm YouGov and the Cato Institute, a think tank, surveyed Americans about free speech and tolerance. Among other findings was this jewel: 77 percent of the Latinos polled believed it's "not offensive" to be told they speak English well.

Admittedly, these Latinos don't speak for anybody but themselves. And that's as it should be. Microaggression monitors also speak for no one but themselves. So why are diversity advocates looking to them for guidance about who may say what to whom? Chyna, a feminist friend and recent college graduate, tells me why. Inside the pro-diversity posse, "It's cool to be offended."

This, Lily.

Increasingly, the labels of the "marginal" make someone cool. If you have those labels, then your proclamations about what offends are prone to be trusted without question by diversity's umpires. In effect, you're vested with the power of cool purely on the basis of your innate traits or group affiliations. Privilege, anyone? Honest diversity requires paying attention to how easily human beings fall in line with power—no matter who exercises it.

A suggestion to the next generation: Unfollow the fad of taking offense as an avenue to power. On any issue that incites outrage in your peers, ask yourself: *Should I be offended? What if I'm not? Does disagreeing with my friends make me a horrible person?*

Of course, just because something's not a barrier for you, it doesn't cease to be a barrier for others. Your friends may be incensed for valid reasons. Before joining them, ask about those reasons. If you find yourself too fearful to ask them, then ask yourself: *Am I censoring my questions because I'm afraid of being thought stupid? Is it possible that my friends also don't know why they're outraged? By asking for their reasons, aren't I inspiring them to become better communicators so they can inspire more students?*

Suppose you go along with your friends regardless of their reasons. In that case, ask yourself: *Am I taking offense sincerely or am I trying to stand out? Am I chasing the attention of a clique that wouldn't care about me unless I became an ally in their cause? By agreeing that something's offensive without contemplating it first, am I conforming to fashion in a way that I wouldn't with clothes?*

Let's say you've reflected deeply on the issue at hand—and, in all good conscience, you're not offended like your peers are. If they label you evil, ask them the capstone question: *I'm offended by the fact that you're offended. Where do we go with that?*

People are a strange breed, Lil. Humanity needs your help to cut through its self-spun nonsense. Recuperate smoothly, girlfriend. We have a presidential run to explore.

46

Lily in the Field: Blunt Talk

You want me to do what, Lil?

You want me to repeat after you.

Silently.

Zipping it now, honey.

Mama, you see me sitting?

Good. Read my hips: I'm sitting out any presidential run that you organize for me. You enjoy learning, so I'm alerting you to a concept from social science: "egocentric bias." That's when you believe others will acquiesce to your oh-so-savvy ideas.

I think you suffer from egocentric bias, Mama. Your political fable is not the future that I choose for myself. Although I want the best for all the critters of America, I need to spend my days doing what matters in the end. You hear me?

Loud and clear, Lil. I'm profusely sorry for the pressure that I've put on you. Is this why you haven't been eating for the past thirty-six hours? Or is it the stress from having your tumor removed?

You were doing so well after the operation, Lily, and a week later, without warning, you start limping. As suddenly as you stop, you walk again. But you walk away from the kitchen, your all-time favorite hangout. I come to you with your bowl but you turn your back on breakfast, then breakfast and dinner, then water, too, and now I can't even tempt you with a hunk of peanut butter.

When I carry you to the car, you shudder. While it's obvious that you don't want to leave the house, and while doing so might worsen your condition, and while I respect your right to be consulted, and while you're my elder, the fact is that you're also my daughter. At what point do I take charge and bring you back to Dr. Daffner?

I'm scared, Lily. We both know that in this relationship, I have the power. But I'm feeling powerless at the moment.

Mama, breathe. Fill those lungs. In through the nose, out through the mouth. Nice and slow. Atta girl.

Thank you, Lil. That helps.

Listen to me, Mama. You say that in our relationship, you have the power. When you communicate my thoughts to your fellow humans, you rely on man-made language. It would be inconceivable for humans to learn my native tongue. Yes, you have power.

In my stroller, I'm at your mercy. You push me around—literally! Yes, ma'am, you've got power.

If you willed it, you could tie me to a tree as punishment for rejecting your leash. My former owner did much, much worse. She pinned me down for the carnal pleasure of feral studs. She sold my babies for profit. She had power, despite telling herself otherwise.

Historically, your philosophers and scientists classified creatures such as me with rigged categories. Dogs, mules, termites, pigs, pigeons— you name 'em—have all been designated lesser forms of life because you humans judge other animals by standards stacked in your favor.

"The Great Chain of Being," your species once termed it. At the summit of that chain: God and His angels. At the bottom: nonhuman animals, plants, and minerals. In the middle: humans, the center around whom everyone and everything revolves. Now your society's doing away with the God-and-angels part of the chain. But the chain itself remains, with the human being as top dog.

How often has your species gloated that the capacity to feel or do or remember or imagine is what separates man from beast? People, please. Why do you insist on separating yourselves from us and pronouncing yourselves supreme?

You've answered this, Mama, yet it's worth paraphrasing one of America's literary titans. James Baldwin asked white folks why they need to invent the "nigger." (See? I do like books. Just not the books that you slobber over.)

In the spirit of Mr. Baldwin, I ask humanity why, almost universally, you view furry or feathered or spotted or striped beings as property. For all of your awesome power, you humans are more desperate for vision than I'll ever be.

Preach, sister.

You, too, have to shed your blinkers, Mama. You say that between the two of us, you have the power. *The* power? Does power come in just one configuration? I mean, when we're out for our walks, who picks up whose droppings?

I never thought about power that way, Lil.

You once feared my kind, Mama. But you learned I'm no threat. Does this mean my power has vanished? Or is it even greater since you're willing to learn much else from me?

In our conversations, Mama Dearest, I've peppered and sometimes pelted you with questions. On occasion, I've been blunt, and intentionally so. Because you must prepare for a rockier path ahead. Let's retrace our path so far:

We've called for a shift from dishonest diversity—labels—to honest diversity—relationships that recognize the plural sides of each being, including the different points of view within any group.

We've explained how honest diversity can dissolve rock-solid divides between humans.

As well as outfox some treacherous political forces, Lil!

Spectacular, Mama. If I could, I'd reward you with all manner of treats. Take the hint. But I digress. On the path we've walked, we've also illustrated what democracy could look and feel like when honesty defines the future of your species. Speech, for example, would be exercised by haters, but overwhelmed by lovers, who didn't realize how much their love mattered until the hate surfaced.

And we've offered tips—questions to pose, tactics to try, online and off, collectively and individually—for pets and their people who share the dream of honest diversity. What am I missing?

Gorgeous touch, Ms. Lil, smuggling that question in. An exquisite summation of our trek together. Hint taken, too.

I'll believe it when I savor it. Now, Mama, it's time to fix your sights on the next twenty years. As best you can, prepare America for its post-Trump life, when the conditions that empowered this president will have to be addressed remorselessly. "Not everything that is faced can be changed," said James Baldwin, "but nothing can be changed until it is faced." Sensible, isn't it?

Sensible but scary, Lil.

Then show your fellow human beings that they're capable.

Show them? How?

By going first, of course. You, Mama, are ready to challenge three near-sacred ideas that our diversity tribe must rethink. Be mindful. You're entering the most emotional territory yet. Bring my vote of confidence with you. And pack a dose of humility because, with respect, you're as much of an err-head as anybody else.

Which is why you're coming with me, Lil. Aren't you?

Mama, I'm entering a new chapter of my own and will need the space to sort myself out. Physically, I have to step back from our journey. But you got this. You really do. Don't be afraid for me or for you. Power on.

Rethinking Power and Privilege

47

The Elephants in the Room

Lily, my guide, may I keep talking to you? You're preoccupied with other matters, I know, and I'm proud of you for focusing on your needs. We can't be of lasting service if we disregard our own well-being. You, sweet bean, are the author of your story. I trust you'll make it clear when, or whether, we should visit Dr. Daffner's clinic again. Meanwhile, feeling your presence will help me to steel my spine for what's to come.

There's an elephant in the room, Lil. Two elephants, in fact, and they demand to be addressed. One is named "Power"; the other, "Privilege." Wherever people are teaching, discussing, or doing diversity, ideas about power and privilege loom large.

After studying various definitions of power, I've arrived at one that encompasses how power can be used by an individual or a group, whether for personal objectives or for social purposes. *Power is the capacity to set expectations about what should be and to translate those expectations into what will be.*

Here's the contentious bit: A lot of people who think of themselves as marginalized actually wield power. And a lot of the time, they're unconscious that they're wielding it. As a result, power's exercised poorly, even destructively.

Some mad hopping may be in order. Am I blissfully unaware that, on the whole, women of color in the United States have it so much harder than white men, what with minorities still underrepresented at college, pay equity yet to be achieved, childcare an unthinkable luxury, and health insurance out of reach? Haven't I discovered that white men tend to enjoy more *material* power than the rest of us?

They do indeed. But this fact doesn't erase another: White men, like women of color, are individuals before they're data points. As individuals, they're capable of making honorable choices that statistics paper over. Remember Louis in Mississippi? "I've never felt terror or torment from our state flag," he confessed to Genesis, "and you know why? White privilege." Louis didn't have to be so transparent. He chose to be.

Off-camera, he told me more:

> *The other day I was paying for something. There was a black guy in front of me—sharp, shaved, good-looking guy. He puts down $20 and the cashier marks it to see if it's counterfeit or real. I was going to pay with my credit card but I decided to pay with cash, just to see if she'd do the same with my money. She didn't. Here I am, looking like a bum, and she still took my money without any suspicion. It's not fair. It's just not fair.*

The store clerk saw the black man as a stereotype, not as an individual. That's why, although Louis would prefer to leave the Mississippi state flag alone, he understands the odds stacked daily against those whom the flag excludes. He also supports their movement for change.

Unearned advantage exists. Very few American employers would read the résumé of a Kevin and make the split-second decision that customers will feel uncomfortable dealing with him. Does the same truly go for a Khaleel?

Police stop and search black men startlingly more often than they do white men. Black parents know to have "the talk" with their sons: "Do what the officer tells you, even if it's for no apparent reason." That talk is optional for white parents. Why?

Plus this: An epidemic of cocaine has plagued America since the 1980s. In their "war on drugs," the feds targeted inner cities—not for treatment but for arrests. Thus began the mass incarceration of black and brown men. But no such crackdown on users and pushers in the suburbs. Why not?

Today's coke is opioids. White men have been the chief victims. So when Donald Trump declared opioid addiction to be a "national health emergency," I had to ask myself: *If the primary victims were people of color, would the government have yawned as usual?* As it is, Trump's declaration of this emergency has amounted to diddly; an extravagantly empty gesture to his base. Yet it's a thicker slab of nothing than men of color would've been thrown.

Without a doubt, Lil, power and privilege are unjustly distributed. The most exasperating part is, when an underdog fully cooperates with a skewed system, there's no guarantee that she'll be treated as an individual.

This reality hit home as I tried to cross the U.S. border one Saturday night.

48

Welcome to America—Not

I'd reached a milestone on the road to American citizenship. The State Department approved my application to become a permanent resident of the United States. Required to pick up my documents in Montréal, I had only to submit them to U.S. Customs and Border Patrol at the airport, collect a stamp for my permanent status, and catch my flight home to New York. "It's a formality," shrugged the young man who interviewed me at State.

The U.S. side of Montréal's airport was practically deserted. No lines, no unruly throng, no huddled masses whom federal agents could bawl out. I gave my passport and papers to an intake officer. He welcomed me to the country. "Thank you, sir," I chirped. He then handed my documents to Officer Garcia, who instructed me to take a seat. Thirty minutes later, Garcia motioned me into his office.

"You have a big problem," he said, engrossed in his computer screen. "I don't see any adjustment to your status in the system." I pointed to the pile of State Department paperwork sitting on his desk. One particular document would allay his concern and I requested that he inspect it.

He postured. "How do I know it's not Photoshopped?"

I must have worn a dazed gaze as I stared at Garcia. My impulse was to remind him that the State Department sealed the papers so they couldn't be tampered with. But when Garcia started trash-talking State itself, I held back. Fortunately, his own agency had emailed me a copy of the document for my records. "It's on my laptop," I told Garcia. "I'll show it to you."

"We don't do computers."

"I'm not sure what else to say," I replied. "May I call my immigration lawyer?"

"We don't do lawyers."

After more psychological ping-pong, Garcia dispatched me to the waiting room. I forced myself to stay buoyant. *It's a slow night,* I thought. *Garcia must be bored. He's killing time.*

An hour elapsed and he waved me into his office again. "Your existing work permit expires in one month," Garcia verified. "My supervisor, who is a nice guy, will allow you passage into the United States until expiry." He then began enunciating each word:

> But if it were up to me, I'd not only detain you indefinitely; I'd have you charged with fraud. And the burden of proof would be on you, not me. I'm inputting these notes into the system as we speak. You are declined for permanent residency.

Shocked and shamed, I shuffled to the flight gate. Just before midnight, as I unfurled the cover of my bed in New York, my numbness gave way to grief. In that moment, I sure could've done with a tight hug from you, Lil. "Please, Allah," I wept. "Please help me to see this obstacle as an opening. Do I need to understand something that I still don't? Teach me. I'm willing."

Over the next week, I kept in close touch with my immigration lawyer, my family, and my God. Six days later, on the Fourth of July, I received a call from U.S. Customs and Border Patrol. While hesitant to admit any wrongdoing, the agency arranged another opportunity for my government-generated documents to be accepted.

At Liberty International Airport in New Jersey, I met with Officer Jansen. She presided over a painless process, green-lit my status as a permanent resident, and accompanied me to the airport exit a few floors down. We stood alone in the elevator, lamenting the "glitch" that brought me there. Aiming for a more positive send-off, Officer Jansen chimed, "So, you teach Islam?"

"Leadership," I clarified. "I've written books about reforming Islam, but I teach leadership."

She frowned. "It's all over your file that you teach Islam."

We paused. "Officer Jansen," I queried, "do you think that's why . . . ?"

She, of course, couldn't react. But in hanging her head to avoid more eye contact, she let the cat out of the bag.

That "glitch," Lily, is an example of "systemic discrimination." It's when people act on the biases that are baked into their institution's culture, regardless of who's running things at head office. Officer Garcia's rejection of me had nothing to do with Donald Trump's reprehensible immigration policies. My slapdown took place during the presidency of Barack Obama, whose administration deported more migrants at the southern border of the United States than previous ones and deliberately separated children from their detained parents.

Speaking of presidents, George Washington emancipated his slaves when he retired. But Washington's admirable decision put no dent in the institution of slavery. That's because the culture of enslavement was systemic. Its legacy, in some ways, still is.

During my harrowing encounter with Garcia, I tried to follow the advice I've been dispensing. Calm yourself. Ask questions with an open heart. Listen with the intent to understand, not to win. Between individuals, these good faith attempts at relating can channel destructive conflict into breakthroughs.

But in this conversation, neither Garcia nor I would be individuals with unique histories and complicated emotions that might overlap. Rather, the system ensured that we played roles. I was marked as the incarnation of foreign antagonism. He was cast as the incarnation of domestic tranquility. Garcia could act out this delusional script because he had state-backed power over my Muslim ass. To my relief, he also had a supervisor who would overrule him. Temporarily.

Within days, my immigration attorney turned the situation around.

What, though, does this say for any number of migrants who can't yet pay for a dedicated lawyer?

I'd taken three weeks off from work to wait for my documents in Montréal. Where does the process leave those who can't afford to stop working, assuming they've got gainful employment at all?

During my wait, I stayed with family who fed and comforted me. How can most migrants do it if they have to cover all those nights at a hotel?

I grew up in Canada, which shares a language with the United States. What hope do less lucky folks have for defending themselves against cold-blooded agents of the "deep state"?

When I beseeched Allah to teach me the lesson, Lil, I might have gotten more than I prayed for. First, I learned to expand my empathy for people in upheaval, a wake-up call that couldn't have been timelier. Now for a second, more layered, lesson: that I can be monumentally privileged at the same time as I'm momentarily powerless. My privilege as an English speaker with a pistol of an attorney decided the outcome of my immigration fiasco. Garcia's privilege within the system didn't.

You clinched it, Lil: Power shows up in fluctuating shapes and flows in unforeseen directions. This truth matters for the sake of honest diversity. Social justice obsesses with the system in our external, material universe. That obsession often diverts us from asking game-changing questions: *As I fight the system in which I live, am I ignoring the system that lives in me? In situations where I have power, am I using it all that differently than Officer Garcia did?*

49

Power "Out There" and Power "In Here"

"I have no power," Vanessa stated at a leadership workshop for NYU students of color.

I'd just explained that, from my perspective, she's putting white students in an impossible bind. On the one hand, she wants them to be educated about racism as she defines "educated." On the other hand, she's sick of sharing her story with white students; going forward, they'll have to educate themselves. And no, she won't recommend books or articles that reflect her views because that would amount to doing white students' work for them.

"Suppose they don't read the correct sources—'correct' from your point of view?" I asked her.

"I feel that it's their problem," Vanessa replied. "They need to be uncomfortable. I've been uncomfortable all my life because of racism."

I understand how taxing it is to educate, I affirmed. I've been sharing my story as a reform-minded Muslim for twenty energy-siphoning years—as I did at the start of this very workshop. But if I don't, I'm not helping people relate to the issues that I want them to think on afterward, in their own time. Why would they care about what I want them to do if I haven't cared enough about them to be reassuring?

Then I told the story of my brush with Garcia. It left me feeling miniscule. Scrutinized but unseen. Vanessa nodded sympathetically. I said that his abuses evoke what many of us do when we've got the power to "approve" certain people. I locked eyes with Vanessa. When you "disapprove" of white students for lacking the proper education, are you using your power well? When you put on their shoulders the entire "burden of proof" for being educated in the way you want them to be, are you exercising your power justly?

She kept looking at me, expressionless, but for a trace of jaundice that might've only reflected the jadedness I felt.

I stopped my questions, deepened my breathing, and lightened up. Organically, the participants and I returned to the takeaway lesson: If you treat white students as individuals, not as avatars of racism, you'll set expectations that they're far more motivated to meet. That's a form of power.

Two students from Nigeria gestured their mini-epiphanies. But Vanessa swatted the notion of having *any* type of power. In her classes, she'd been taught "critical race theory," which denies that individual actions can lead to palpable change.

According to critical race theorists, white supremacy infests the basic structure of American society. We need only examine the Constitution's original premise that black people have just three-fifths the value of property-owning white men, a "compromise" agreed to by representatives from the U.S. North so that the slave-holding South would sign on to a "free" republic—that is, free from Britain's whims.

Mercifully, the Constitution's been amended. On paper. But the past isn't over, critical race theorists argue. America's founding sin persists in the culture of its systems, from public education to criminal justice. This, some of them add, explains why affirmative action policies and desegregation laws haven't delivered more than paltry progress. A few well-intended laws don't hold a candle to a debauched structure. Since the system's pre-inscribed with antiblack racism, no individual who's black can be said to have power.

What, however, is power to these theorists? As individuals, they differ on the details, but they agree on a foundational aspect. Having power is having the ability to "otherize"—to taint people not like you as the malevolent stranger, the unidentified foreign object, the It, the Other. And they take as a given that the "othered" are people whom the system has historically repressed, especially people of color.

Having received this information from Vanessa, I decided to re-frame my point in a way that I hoped she could hear. I empathized that in the system "out there," she wields little power. In most cases, she'd be straight-up subordinate to authorities. But in the system "in here," between herself and those white students who'd like to be seen for more than their pigment, she's the power who "represents."

Vanessa has the cultural capital to direct what inclusion looks like on the ground. She can decide to include white students as fellow travelers in the antiracism effort, or she can otherize them by signaling that we're not in the struggle together. You're on your own. Don't speak until you've learned what I won't tell you that you need to learn. On this front, if on no other, Vanessa carries the power of a Garcia.

There is, I must emphasize, a cardinal difference between Vanessa and Garcia. When Garcia misuses his power, he's not forfeiting it. He's in the business of being feared. But as an antiracism advocate, Vanessa's in the business of breaking down fear. When she props up fear, even unconsciously, she throws away the better part of her power.

All the more reason for Vanessa to be mindful; to acknowledge that "in here," she's got enough power to otherize. By waking up to her privileged status, Vanessa can marshal her power in ways that enthuse her peers to subvert injustices "out there." After all, how else do we reform the cultures of institutions unless it's through people? Cultures don't make decisions. People do.

To face the hideous underbelly of any culture, humans need to muster our guts by first becoming the captains of our egobrains. Which is easier to do when we feel that our leaders have our backs. And such a feeling can be cultivated only when the Vanessas of this generation exercise "relational leadership." That's when you concentrate on relationships so that you're humane, tactful, and tactical all at once. You focus not only on what's owed in the name of justice, but what *you* owe the wider public in order to improve the likelihood of receiving what's owed.

Vanessa has learned to criticize without the responsibility—dare I say, the power—of being constructive. Critical theorists arm students with tools to unmask the system. To "interrogate," or question, long-held truths. To "problematize," or find problems with, conventional wisdom. To "deconstruct," or pick apart, the assumptions behind society's latent beliefs. So far so good, if you ask me. Education ought to release us from thoughtless conformity.

Yet much of critical theory has itself become a drill in thoughtless conformity. Students learn that facts are "constructed"—orchestrated by the elites to strengthen rigged structures and systems. When authorities assert what's true, they're exerting the raw power to frame reality and to fake truth. Therefore, the enlightened must foil the "facts."

Where have we heard that before, Lil? I'm not faulting our universities for Donald Trump's conspiracy-peddling. I do, however, believe it's time to mature out of the bad habits that critical theory shares with delirious Trumpitude. By treating criticism as the endgame, they're both infatuated with demolishing. They each make a personal virtue of feeling oppressed. And they outright ignore the question, *What do you improve by acting ruthlessly powerless?*

I have a story that helps answer this question.

50

Did Women Co-Create the Alt-Right?

This, Lil, is the story of how horrendously things can go "out there" when we deny our power "in here."

Vanessa's generation spawned the digital culture in which we're swimming today. Young women, in particular, carved out a space for their voices. A triumph of empowerment? I wish I could make that claim.

Angela Nagle is a scholar of the alt-right. She leans progressive, maybe even radical, and she flinches at how her side gave ammo to opportunists like Richard Spencer. Nagle says that years before the alt-right's sewage spread to the masses, its culture sprouted on the web "in opposition to its enemy online culture"—that of identity politics and its BFF: cyberbullying. Together, they became mean girls.

This virtual partnership of group and gripe germinated from the keyboards of young women more than anybody else. As fans of superstar critical theorists, they "transgressed," or liberated themselves from, cramped gender frames such as male/female and gay/straight. In place of those binary, overly binding labels, the transgressors came up with "gender-fluid" categories. And, boy, did they have power: Within a decade, Facebook would ask subscribers to self-identify by choosing from fifty gender-fluid labels, a smarmy way to monetize more of our data.

Looking up to the gender-busters, other young women, and some young men, began adopting gender-fluid labels for themselves. Then,

Angela Nagle discovered, more and more of them added mental illnesses to their online identities. "[V]ery often," they "lashed out at anyone for not reacting appropriately to their under-recognized, undiagnosed, or undiagnosable" conditions. (She's referring to anyone in the progressive community. The alt-right hadn't coalesced on the internet yet.)

Likewise, many of these women banished community members whom they judged as "lacking sensitivity" to their labels. Which is how "check your privilege" became a cornerstone phrase in identity politics. It's also how this subculture, intended to be avant-garde, adapted the age-old game of abusing one's power while pleading powerlessness. Only later would such manipulation be challenged for what it is: "cry-bullying," to quote Nagle.

By 2013, one longtime advocate of justice had seen enough. In a notorious blog post, the British writer and labor activist Mark Fisher revolted against "Left-wing Twitter," a frequently "miserable, dispiriting zone" populated by "sour-faced identitarians." He recalled how progressives of late had been persecuting people who sympathized with their causes but who slipped up in their word choices:

> *What these figures had said was sometimes objectionable; but nevertheless, the way in which they were personally vilified and hounded left a horrible residue: the stench of bad conscience and witch-hunting moralism. The reason I didn't speak out on any of these incidents, I'm ashamed to say, was fear. The bullies were in another part of the playground. I didn't want to attract their attention.*

Fisher's blog post turned heads and the public shaming of him followed like clockwork. Eight months later, he killed himself for unknown reasons. In the obituaries I've read, nobody implies that he'd committed suicide over the foul reactions to his essay. Still, some cyberbullies took their pound of flesh even after his death.

Angela Nagle highlights an influential Twitter feminist who hate-tweeted about Fisher's suicide. "This response," Nagle notes, "is a fairly typical example of precisely the sour-faced identitarians" whom Fisher anguished over. "The left's best critic of this disease of the left had just died and dancing on his grave was a woman who once blogged about baking bread using her own vaginal yeast as a feminist act."

Nagle emphasizes the cruelty of progressives for one reason: It "undoubtedly drove so many young people to the right." In retrospect, the nascent alt-right offered a safer online space to kids, boys especially, who wanted to find their voice, whether by commenting intelligently or clowning around. I'm not arguing that boys will be boys; just that insecure boys can't become secure men if they're constantly being monitored and reprimanded.

Today, some of these kids talk about themselves in terms best reserved for refugees. They've "fled" the online "firing squads" of identity politics, only to fall in, flirt, or keep distant company with another battery of identity politics: hatred of women and nonwhites.

Will we make the same mistake yet again? Will we categorize all of these kids as toadies of white supremacists? Or will we engage when it won't physically endanger us to do so?

My conversation with a seventeen-year-old named Pascal opened up an opportunity for both of us. Pascal split with progressives online because they're "the worst kind of power-trippers, the ones who think they're victims."

"But isn't that what your alt-right buddies do, too?" I asked him. "Don't they moan about being victimized by political correctness?"

"They're not exactly my buddies," Pascal said. "I talk to them, but I'm not brainwashed by them. Not yet. Mmmwwwwahahaha!" We joshed for a bit, then I reminded Pascal that he didn't answer my question. I asked it again. "Don't people on the alt-right also promote themselves as victims?"

"Oh yeah," he nodded.

"You said you don't comply with false victims who throw their power around. Did I hear that right?"

"Yeah."

"So why not challenge a bully from their side?" I explained to Pascal that he could use his "in" with the alt-right, his privilege, to do what others wouldn't have the credentials to pull off. This isn't a setup for some ugly showdown, I swore. He could choose to challenge bullies compassionately. Pascal asked for a few pointers and agreed to try them.

Weeks on, I checked in with him. Pascal reported a couple of surprises. "I didn't realize how isolated some of these dudes are," he said. "I mean, they need friends. Real ones. Offline." Why offline? "Whenever someone has something serious to tell me, like I'm being a douche bag, they can grab my arm or kick my butt and I get it. It's hard to have that kind of impact anonymously. Unless we talk in person, I don't know that these guys will get what douche bags they are."

Okay, so Pascal didn't make progress "out there." But he did experience a breakthrough "in here." The more we spoke, the more he understood the power of relationships in the actual world. If that realization gets his head out of the cloud for one extra hour each day, just as my relationship with you did for me, Lil, I'll take it.

Pascal's other discovery? Until this experiment, nobody he knew had framed his white male privilege as a positive, as a blessing to do some good with. His privilege has only ever been dumped on as "the reason I should shut up." That's a loss for decency as well as for diversity.

51

Privilege as a Blessing

You still with me, Lilybean?

I've been thinking about what Pascal said. That he'd never been told how his privilege could be a blessing, let alone a blessing to be pressed into action rather than be ashamed of. Privilege left to rot emits the fumes of egomania.

Imagine, Lil, that Martin Luther King Jr. sits in a college classroom today. Nobody knows him to be the future "Dr. King." He's Martin, a junior majoring in, say, sociology. During a heated class discussion about race and poverty, Martin volunteers information about his own upbringing:

> *I was born in a very congenial home situation. My parents have always lived together very intimately, and I can hardly remember a time that they ever argued (my father happens to be the kind who just won't argue) or had any great falling out. The community in which I was born was quite ordinary in terms of social status. No one in our community had attained any great wealth. Crime was at a minimum, and most of our neighbors were deeply religious. . . .*
>
> *It is quite easy for me to think of a God of love mainly because I grew up in a family where love was central and where lovely relationships were present. It is quite easy for me to think of the universe as basically friendly, mainly because of my uplifting hereditary and*

environmental circumstances. It is quite easy for me to lean more
toward optimism than pessimism about human nature, mainly
because of my childhood experience.

King wrote these words in 1950. If "Martin" said them on a contemporary campus, or posted them online, would he be pilloried for
having class privilege? Would his ideas for social change be disquali-
fied because he could never understand those without privilege? Would
Martin feel discounted enough to nix the possibility of leading a justice movement, and leading it as a Christian witness?

In truth, Martin didn't realize by himself how his Christianity
might serve a greater, earthly, good. He enjoyed the mentorship of his
college president. Would Martin be bad-mouthed for his respectability
within the system?

After Dr. King's assassination, radicals took up civil rights as their
cause. The iconic poet and essayist, Audre Lorde, was among them.
Lorde, she loved her labels: Black. Feminist. Lesbian. But she didn't
fetishize those labels so that she could feel powerless. In fact, Lorde
believed in professing her privilege as "the first step in making it available for wider use.

> *Each of us is blessed in some particular way, whether we recognize*
> *our blessings or not. And each of us, somewhere in our lives, must*
> *clear a space within that blessing where she can call upon whatever*
> *resources are available to her in the name of something that must be*
> *done.*

Even as she came to grips with her terminal cancer, Lorde counted
her advantages. She entered in her journal:

> *I have been very blessed in my life. I have been blessed to believe*
> *passionately, to love deeply, and to be able to work out of those loves*
> *and beliefs. Accidents of privilege allowed me to gain information*
> *about holistic/biological medicine and their approach to cancers, and*

that information has helped keep me alive, along with my original gut feeling that said, "Stay out of my body." For me, living and the use of that living are inseparable, and I have a responsibility to put that privilege and that life to use.

Rethinking Multiculturalism

52

Lily in the Field: Live and Forgive

Forgive me, Lily. The emergency room's the last place that either of us wants to be. You had a bloody accident early this morning and you still hadn't eaten or gone near your water bowl in seventy-two hours. You didn't even quiver when I brought you to the car. You just lay in my arms, listless. Now I know why.

The vets say you've got acute pancreatitis. I looked it up.

Oh God, Lil. It may be that you're at the ER because of Mama. Abruptly, in the past ten days or so, your system took in too much fat. I can't think of any other culprit than the wads of peanut butter in which I wrapped your post-op pills. But without that incentive, you wouldn't keep your meds down. When I shoved them into your mouth, you spat them out. Even when I tucked the meds in your food, you managed to eat around them. I didn't know what else to do.

Now I want nothing more than to rip out your IV drips and hit your power button. But we're not devices. We can't just reset ourselves or each other. We can only commit to learning from our mistakes and hope hard that they're not fatal.

Please, Lily. Please rebound. Your brothers and sisters miss you. Their home is *our* home because of you.

I wish I felt comforted by your doctor's assurance that you're safe in your hospital bed, somewhere at the back of this building, among all the other cages and their occupants. Nobody will take advantage of you,

I'm told. Each dog has a crate to him or herself. And yet, knowing this doesn't assuage me. Instead, it calls to mind another mistake I recently made with you.

We drove to an animal shelter, you and I, so I could help a friend adopt her Lily. After parking and rolling the windows down, I left you in the car because I didn't want you feeling anxious, what with all the barking mad mayhem around the kennels. But I completely forgot that you could smell the dogs. You shook all the way home, triggered by the memory of having almost been euthanized.

Lily, I had no intention of abandoning you then and I have no such intention now. You're not mine to treat like another disposable doo-hickey. You're a living, breathing organism with an inner life who has slyly made Mama's life richer. If it's the last thing we do, we'll go home again.

53

Diversity Day at *The Office*

Lily, my mentor, your doctors have advised me to keep talking to you. Hearing is the last sense to go, they've said. I can't believe we're discussing the "last" anything. It's just not possible.

Your eyes, they're looking up! You're following my voice! Go, Lily, go! There's hope, honey. Stay with me. We'll pull through together.

I've been reflecting on how we began bonding. The day after Mama Laura and I brought you home, I placed your bed next to mine and we binge-watched *The Office* on Netflix. Well, I watched and you listened. In *The Office*, a video camera follows the sales team at a branch of the paper manufacturing company Dunder Mifflin. You immediately perked up at the voice of Michael Scott, the boss. How could you not? The man has no filter.

In season one, *The Office* holds Diversity Day. Michael, a white guy, is facing staff complaints about his insufferable impersonation of Chris Rock, the African American comic. Corporate headquarters sends in a consultant who trains the office to "celebrate diversity." All you have to do, he says, is be a HERO: honest, empathic, respectful, and open-minded.

Human Resources doesn't want to single Michael out. So it mandates everyone at the branch to participate in Diversity Day. Privately, though, HR requires only Michael to sign the HERO pledge. And he complies. Sort of. Michael's signature reads, "Daffy Duck."

When the consultant leaves, Michael leads a diversity training session of his own. First, he hands out note cards with a label written on each. Black. Jewish. Italian. Asian. But not Arab—"too explosive," Michael figures.

Then he pesters his staff members to wear a card, any card, on their foreheads. But they're not allowed to read what it says. Their conversation partners will know the label on the card because they can see it. Unless, of course, they're blind, in which case they'll simply have to bump along.

That's a joke, Lil. The kind that would come out of Michael Scott's mouth. Just making sure you're still responding to his voice—and mine.

With identity cards plastered to their foreheads, Michael's coworkers approach each other and enter into dialogue. Sort of. They're supposed to say the first thing that pops to mind when they see the label of their dialogue buddy. Pam, the office receptionist, encounters Dwight, the office ogre. She stands frozen in front of him, with Michael pressing her to "stir the pot—the melting pot."

"If I have to do this," Pam stammers to Dwight, "based on stereotypes that are totally untrue and I do not agree with, you would maybe not be a very good driver."

"Oh man, am I a woman?" Dwight squeals. The card he's wearing reads, "Asian."

In the office-wide debrief, Dwight points out that some minority groups don't tolerate gays. "Paradox," he smugly suggests. But who cares that he's right? Nobody wants to agree with a prick. Whatever Dwight's occasional wisdom, it goes nowhere thanks to his snottiness.

Diversity Day ends on a stinging note. Kelly, the all-American girl born to immigrants from India, is fed up with Michael's loud, butchered imitation of an Indian accent. She slaps his face. Silence descends on the office. Sort of.

Recovering his swagger before the stunned staff, Michael declares,

"Alright! Yes! That was great! She 'gets' it. Now she knows what it's like to be a minority."

Lil, don't take his clumsiness for cluelessness. Michael has deciphered something with profound implications for our society: Multiculturalism, which many of us equate to diversity, undermines honest diversity.

54

Humans Are Groupies

A society that revels in multiculturalism resembles a room full of folks buzzing around with identity cards stuck to their foreheads. The first thing you see is their labels. As you've personally shown, Lil, labels can deceive. That's because they represent groups, not individuals, and groups are where complexity goes to die. Our egobrains prefer it that way. Less information to process. And more security in the pack. I'd say that humans are packies, but that would sound boorishly Michael Scott-ish.

Now I sound anti-Scottish. I'm not. I love the Scots. The Irish, too. Humans, Lil, are groupies.

Michael Scott makes another understated point: Multicultural America won't adapt to him; he's adapting to it, fumbles and all. In real life, I can attest, more white guys are striving to get with the program. Cast your mind back to Sam, the young man I met at the University of Virginia. He wants to be part of the multicultural mosaic because, he says, he agrees with diversity. So why, Sam asked me, doesn't multiculturalism include people like him—whites in the U.S. South? You know my answer by now, Lil. It's fear—not Sam's, but ours.

Despite our intention to welcome different people, many diversity-lovers ignore humanity's most primal instincts: to fear anyone or anything that our brains perceive will hurt us. So, we extend multiculturalism's welcome only to people whom we believe are like us—

sometimes in color and always in victim status. If a community's routinely stereotyped (like ours), we usher them into the multicultural fold. Until we don't: Today, Sam worries about his status and that of his culture. But most of us aren't inclined to think about them.

There's a reason we're not. Cass Sunstein calls it "the law of group polarization." When people with a particular viewpoint surround themselves with like-minded folks, they tend to become that much more confident in their identity. Confidence easily devolves into over-confidence, a mark of becoming exclusionary.

We can stop that slide. We can grow secure in having a nuanced identity. Instead, most of us let our egobrains shelter us from growth. It's a lot less work to know what we're not than to know all that we are.

This, Lily, is how noble ideas curdle into intolerant ideologies. From Christianity to Islam, from free speech to social media, from democracy to diversity, our best propositions get overtaken by the human impulse to segregate into in-groups (Us) and out-groups (Them).

Multiculturalism's *especially* vulnerable to the law of group polarization. Culture's all about the habits and customs of communities, right? By its very nature, then, multiculturalism appeals to the groupish instincts in people.

Add the chemicals of a defensive egobrain and you've got the stuff of tribalism.

Spike it with extra dollops of defensiveness and you've got a recipe for violent tribalism.

That's why, in the hands of white nationalists, multiculturalism's a weapon. *As long as everyone else can have "their" group, they protest, we can have ours. America's becoming a majority of minorities, they remind us, and y'all are good with it. You know how that shakes down, don't you? The white nation is the new minority. By your multicultural logic, white lives matter. Enjoy your ghettoes as much as we'll defend our homeland.*

We can't afford to be blasé about groupiness gone wild. As we discussed way back when, black and brown folks won't be the ones in need of integration twenty years from now. Everybody will be minorities. Competitive victimhood could mushroom into a national sport with no referee.

Going forward, let's ask young people a few questions. What do you want more—to be seen for your individuality or shown off for your labels? Would you rather own yourself or be owned by groups that claim you as "theirs"? In short, which is better for you: honest diversity or multiculturalism?

55

Should We Celebrate Bad Traditions, Too?

As a kid, Lil, I oozed patriotism for my adopted home of Canada. Almost every morning, I thanked God for orienting my family to a free and peaceful part of the world; a place where I could phone the police when the violence in our house spun out. For a little brown girl to feel the power of voice? So unforgettably fly. I attributed my good fortune not only to Allah, but also to Canada's multiculturalism, which steered me to one overarching insight: *If I don't have a vision for my life, someone else will have an agenda for it.*

It's an invaluable lesson that I extricated from costly circumstances.

In the Canada where I came of age, multiculturalism wasn't a description of society, but a prescription for it. The national government adopted it as policy—a first for any country anywhere. Whatever else it aimed to do, the multicultural policy funded immigrant groups to maintain their traditions. But I don't think enough people asked, "Does that include the harmful traditions within cultures?"

I told you about my mother, Mumtaz. In her hellacious marriage, she struggled mightily to stay alive while her family stayed quiet and her husband's family stayed away. On both sides, our relatives accepted patriarchal customs. Canadian politicians did, too. For them, multiculturalism meant that all differences should be applauded and protected, which in practice meant that myriad women and children would be owned, like livestock, by "their" communities.

"Her" community didn't represent Mumtaz, the individual. The individual who attempted to break free from a loveless engagement. The individual who became the first in her congregation to divorce. The individual who blessed her queer daughter's marriage. Mumtaz, the renegade, thrives today in spite of multiculturalism and not because of it.

I trust you understand the spirit in which I say this, Lily. I'm not minimizing brown cultures or sanitizing white ones. Sam, you might recollect, told me that his culture of the U.S. South can teach us about kindness to the visitor and compassion for the neighbor in dire straits. Well, Arab culture also valorizes hospitality and generosity. It's one of a thousand examples demonstrating that white people don't have a lock on decency.

That said, Mumtaz needlessly suffered because of a tradition shared by various parts of the world, from the U.S. South to Latin America to Mediterranean Europe to the Middle East to the Asian subcontinent. This tradition, group honor, turns individuals into the property of their families, their tribes, and their nations.

Group honor legitimized slavery and segregation in the Southern states of America, since mixing with blacks would've sullied the blood of the white nation. In reality, mixing would've desecrated only the self-image of the white nation, a self-image utterly contrived in the first place. Group honor is what Mumtaz bowed to after her grandmother begged her not to sabotage the engagement so that the family's self-image may be spared from stain. Group honor's a blight on individuality and therefore diversity, yet multiculturalism tolerates it. The upshot: dishonest diversity.

Hence the lesson, Lil, that if I don't have a vision for my life, someone else will have an agenda for it. When you're born into a community that expects you to fit its mold mindlessly, you've got to ask yourself whether you're made for that mold. Godspeed if you are. But if you're not cool with a predetermined agenda for your future, then you'll have to develop a vision for it—one that can change as you change.

That's precisely what I did one night as my father waved a kitchen knife at me, threatening to slice off my ear. I ran into my second-floor bedroom, jumped out the window, and got comfortable on the roof. There I sat for hours, eventually making a pact with myself: I'd use my education to ensure that neither I nor any woman I know would have to settle for the nightmare unraveling below me.

Should cultures be protected more than the individuals living in them? Pierre Trudeau, the prime minister who announced Canada's multicultural policy, didn't hold much regard for group rights. When it came to identity, he championed "individual freedom of choice."

So why did Trudeau introduce multiculturalism? I'll tell you a story about the eccentric politics that led to it, the dazzling case that Trudeau made for it, and the reality that vandalizes multiculturalism everywhere. Even in Canada.

56

Even in Canada

In October 1971, a year before my refugee family arrived at the port of Montréal, Pierre Trudeau rose from the prime minister's seat in Parliament. Canada, he proclaimed, would adopt multiculturalism as a "conscious support" for the individual's freedom to choose. That is, the freedom to choose who you are, what you stand for, and how you'll conduct your life. The "more secure we feel" in whatever cultural group we belong to, the prime minister explained, "the more free we are to explore our identity beyond it."

Like I said, Lil, dazzling. Trudeau turned the tables on those who feared that multiculturalism, which protects groups, would throttle the rights of the individual within any group. He reasoned the opposite: If the government regards your minority culture as equal to that of the majority, you won't have to become defensive about your group. You'll use your personal liberty to transcend the group and flourish as an individual, eventually even as a citizen of the world. The plural in me cheers.

But the daughter in me doubts. Trudeau soft-pedaled the risks of being an individual in a situation like my mother's. Despite his impressive intellect, he didn't think hard enough about the restrictions on women in honor-based cultures, where exploring beyond the group's confines can be punishable, sometimes lethally so.

As I watched Mumtaz disentangle from the family's tentacles, the beginnings of an idea pawed at me: If my society sanctifies the tribe over the individual, then we're heading for tribalism, and at some point it's sure to become manic. Human nature will see to it. This inkling ballooned after I thought about the story I'll now share.

When he declared the policy of multiculturalism, Pierre Trudeau had an urgent reason to harp on the individual's dignity. At the time, Canada threatened to come undone over tribal emotions—not among recent immigrants but among French-speaking nationalists. Their objective: to sever the province of Québec from the rest of Canada. To survive, all of Canada needed a novel look at itself and a new conversation about its future.

Trudeau took the challenge more than seriously. He took it personally. The prime minister had grown up in Québec, an intensely Catholic and conservative province back in the day. Although educated by broad-minded Jesuits, he knew how it felt to have his identity owned by the Catholic tribe. Masses of Québec youth resented the Church's decrees about who they had to be, what they had to believe, and how they had to behave.

Starting in 1960, Trudeau's generation rebelled against the priests and their political stooges. Electing an unapologetically liberal government, young Quebeckers propelled the "Quiet Revolution," a movement to become the "masters of our own house." The devil lay in the definition of "our."

Casting off the shackles of the Church inspired in young Quebeckers ever-more confidence in their ability to leave Canada. As we now know, Lil, collective confidence can congeal into zeal. And it did. Many Québec nationalists campaigned not just against Canada, but also against the "Anglos," or English-speaking citizens, within Québec itself. Drunk on dogma, the movement's militant wing kidnapped a prominent politician while planting bombs in spaces large and small, from the Montréal Stock Exchange to mailboxes in sleepy neighborhoods. Anglos got the message and left in droves.

How could this happen in a country known for keeping the peace in war zones worldwide? A nation that gave sanctuary to my family, and untold more, who couldn't scram quickly enough from civil unrest in our native lands? And how could the French in Canada, a minority par excellence, harass their own minorities?

At root, it's straightforward: When the egobrain creeps in, the law of group polarization kicks in. When we defer to the biological urge to have our identities constantly affirmed, we listen less to voices from outside our group. When we hear voices from inside our group over and over and over again, most of us don't get bored; we get more extreme. And we influence the people in our orbit, so that members of the in-group, Us, incrementally harden our hearts toward the out-group, Them.

Bigotry then becomes a blood-rush. "If a nation aims to prevent terrorist activity," writes Cass Sunstein, "a good strategy is to prevent the rise of enclaves of like-minded people." He refers to this as the "simplest and most important lesson for law and policy."

I'd say there's a simpler lesson still: Never underestimate the furnace that is emotion. Even for Quebeckers who rejected violence, as most did, separating from Canada made engrossing emotional sense. They treasured their motto, *Je me souviens*—"I remember." They'd always remember their ancestral French heritage. They'd forever be rankled by France's defeat by Britain in 1759 and the subsequent surrender of Québec. Now that they'd overthrown one master, the Vatican, why should their French identity be compromised, contaminated, by remaining in a country that *felt* like enemy territory?

As if the tinderbox needed it, emotions ran that much higher because of France's pompous president. Charles de Gaulle visited Canada in July 1967, the country's centennial. He supposedly came to celebrate—his ego, not Canada. At Montréal City Hall, de Gaulle stepped onto a balcony, surveyed the throngs below, and delivered a speech in which he cried out, *Vive le Québec libre!* Long live a liberated Québec! The nationalists went nuts.

Eleven months later, Canada elected Pierre Trudeau as prime minister. Being a nonconformist, he didn't swap one tribe for another.

Whereas nationalist Quebeckers traded a frigid group identity imposed by the Church for a rigid group identity dictated by the separatist campaign, Trudeau prized the individual. Ever the romantic, he believed that individual rights would keep Canada together.

To this day, Lily, I melt at how Trudeau integrated individuality and social cohesion:

> *National unity, if it is to mean anything in the deeply personal sense, must be founded on confidence in one's own individual identity; out of this can grow respect for that of others and a willingness to share ideas, attitudes and assumptions.*

Of course, rhapsodizing about the individual didn't impress Québec nationalists. They branded Trudeau a traitor. And multiculturalism? To hell with it. They idolized "pure-wool," as in white, French-Canadians.

Pierre Trudeau had a needle to thread. He needed to slice through the nationalist clamor and show everyday Quebeckers that Canada accepted—*non*, cherished—the "French fact." Here's how he did it, Lil. Two years before making Canada officially multicultural, his government passed a law making Canada officially bilingual. From the Arctic to the Pacific to the Atlantic oceans, any Canadian could receive federal services in English or French. Their choice.

The winner, according to Trudeau? Not any single group, but every single individual. Nobody had to feel "locked for life within a particular cultural compartment by the accident of birth or language." Two years later, as the prime minister finished addressing Parliament about the bilingual, multicultural Canada of tomorrow, he brought home his core conviction. "We are free," he assured, "to be ourselves." This time, "our" would be defined as each Canadian wished.

A decade-plus on, in 1980, Québec separatists held their referendum to exit Canada. They lost. In 1995, they tried again to Quexit. They lost again, with no recovery in sight. This might have something to do with the unseemly underside of their fight: When the second referendum failed by a thin margin, the face of the movement blamed "money and ethnic voters."

It could've been a misstatement from a sleep-deprived leader. Or it could've been a peek into more: Recently, the nationalist government of Québec attempted to pass a "Charter of Secular Values" so that Muslims would know their place. "We mean it only for Muslims who are a menace to secularism," one of the bill's supporters said. But as another defender of the charter divulged, "we" *excluded* secular Muslims like me. Why? Because I remain a Muslim.

In the rest of Canada, multiculturalism has grown as central to national identity as hockey. And it results in fewer broken noses. Yet I can't say that Pierre Trudeau would be proud of multiculturalism today. Its purpose has been revised to "preserve and protect" the cultural traditions of minorities. "Preserve" and "protect" are words that freeze, not free, individuals. These words also speak volumes about Canadian society. It conflates diversity with labels and rewards ongoing cultural anxiety, since only the anxious need their labels preserved and protected.

That approach resonates with the white nationalism of Richard Spencer. Believe it or not, Lil, Spencer founded the alt-right while briefly living in Canada's most multicultural city, Toronto. He cunningly told a Canadian journalist that "[b]eing a minority is very difficult. We have recognized this when we look at minorities and yet we, as white people, seem to want to become minorities in our own homeland." Of course, no Canadian (or American) territory can rightly be viewed as a white person's "homeland." At best, Spencer's a squatter.

But let's get honest about something more. Multiculturalism excuses his desire to *preserve* and *protect* white people of European stock. Which raises yet another reason to be skeptical of labels. Liberals who back multiculturalism are, in a crucial sense, conservatives. They want to conserve the traditions of groups that might otherwise feel alienated. It's what Richard Spencer wants for his group, as well.

Defending multiculturalism won't spring us from this snare. Its logic led us there. It always will, in light of multiculturalism's first principle: group before individual. Far healthier, I think, to rediscover the individuality that Pierre Trudeau stood for.

Amendment: far healthier for you, Lil, to rediscover sleep. Collect your energy, my love. I'll be back first thing in the morning.

57

Ben Franklin, Founding Farter

My little cream puff, Mama's waiting for you to be brought out for our morning visit. You're at the back of the hospital right now, in a box among a dozen other kennels. The fact is, though, you're too much of a cowgirl to be boxed in. I see how seriously you take the revolutionary American creed, "Life, liberty, and the pursuit of happiness." When you're well, you're implacably independent and when you're ill, you're stubbornly stoic.

Yet being American doesn't stop you from epitomizing Canadian attributes at the same time. North of the border, people aspire to the ideals, "Peace, Order and Good Government." In mentoring me to balance impulse and introspection, you reveal the peace that comes from good government of the self. A peace that emanates from "the order of the soul"—that haunting phrase sung by Leonard Cohen.

In your quirky integration of virtues, you demonstrate the difference between individuality and individualism. Or, if you like, between Trudeau and Trump.

Individualism is the belief that I'm here to serve myself and I don't care if my society benefits. That's Donald Trump. Individuality is the principle that by being myself, I can enrich my society. That's Pierre Trudeau. Your individuality glistens and because it contributes to the common good, it doesn't rust into individualism.

Now, Lil, I respect that you're an American patriot. Could I have imagined you as President of the United States otherwise? So let me assure that I'm not laying some pretext for Canada to colonize the United States. Nothing that I'm saying telegraphs a code to the current prime minister, who happens to be Pierre Trudeau's son. Fishy, I know.

But Canada just doesn't seek power for power's sake. It could've spun a grandiose story about itself in 1967, when Martin Luther King Jr. described Canada as "the north star" for fugitive American slaves. He even disclosed that some of the Negro spirituals *did* contain code:

> *We sang of "heaven" that awaited us and the slave masters listened in innocence, not realizing that we were not speaking of the hereafter. Heaven was the word for Canada and the Negro sang of the hope that his escape on the underground railroad would carry him there.*

I was taught (barely) about the underground railroad. But the covert "heaven" bit? News to me. That's how much Canada spurns grandeur.

Which is smart in light of the facts that Dr. King *omitted*. In the seventeenth and eighteenth centuries, the Dominion of Canada auctioned black and indigenous slaves to white settlers. Mother England routinely overpromised and under-delivered to her loyal Canadian subjects—white, black, and brown. In 1784, poor whites in Nova Scotia turned their anger to the British monarch, but took it out on their black neighbors. Mobs burned down the nearby settlements of blacks who worked for wages that whites wouldn't. Canada became the site of the first reported race riot in North America. Who knew? Not me, until I researched it a few years ago.

Unlike the United States, Canada doesn't have nationally accepted myths. Nor does it have an appetite to propagate them. It's largely ashamed of the bad in its history and typically torn about the good. Maybe that's why it feels at home with a multiculturalism that commits the country to no supreme truth. In contemporary Canada, diversity's an end unto itself. Bonus that it hatches just enough unity for the nation to skate by.

In America, diversity's a means to an end. It has to serve the primary mission of unity. After all, the republic's founding narrative, never mind its name, mythologizes union: Self-made men of courage, dedicated to the law of liberty and the rule of reason, defeat corrupt overlords and, with the practicality of citizen-leaders, the most ingenious of the revolutionaries passionately debate, pragmatically compromise, and ultimately constitute these *United* States.

I reiterate, Lil, that much of it is myth; more hat than cattle. But myth makes for shared purpose. In a nation that's increasingly unsure of its identity, neither multiculturalism nor individualism caters to the sharing of purpose. What can? I vote for a squarely American alternative—pluralism.

It would start in school. Broadly speaking, both conservatives and liberals tell me that civics needs to be taught again. Conservatives want to include white guys and statues. Liberals want fellow Americans to learn about a lot more. So let's experiment with learning *more about white guys and statues*. Teach all of them as the plurals that they are.

Take Benjamin Franklin, one of America's most beloved founding fathers. The usual portrait follows a paint-by-numbers template. He was an entrepreneur, writer, inventor, civic activist, diplomat, philanthropist, scientist, and so on. But that's Franklin, the Renaissance Man. It's not Franklin, the relatable human. A pluralistic classroom would rejoice in his oddities.

Franklin was a fartful, I mean artful, jokester. This side of him seeped out in a letter that he penned to protest a trend: that scientists were publishing research without caring how their discoveries could improve the lives of people. Franklin believed that science should add value to the real world. Instead of delivering public goods, it was becoming a private playground for snobs.

To push back, Franklin considered pulling a wee prank. He drafted a letter to the leading body of scientists in Europe. (That's where the top research came from in his day.) In that letter, Franklin proposed to study how science could eliminate the stench of our farts. Better still, he wondered, how might science make our farts so perfume-like that someone may "give Vent to his Griefs" even in polite company?

Franklin listed two benefits of fragrant farting. First, it's physically better to let one rip than to store one up. Second, in doing so, we'd become more hospitable friends. Say you're hosting a dinner party. You're going to offer your guests a choice of beverages, aren't you? Similarly, as this "whirlwind" of an evening gets underway, you could ask your guests what bouquet they'd prefer to breathe: "Musk or Lilly, Rose or . . ."

The letter closed with gusto:

> [S]urely such a Liberty of Expressing one's Scent-iments, and pleasing one another, is of infinitely more Importance to human Happiness than Liberty of the Press, or of abusing one another, which the English are so ready to fight & die for.

As a fellow patriot, Lil, you can't blame Franklin for raising a stink about Britain.

But there's a twist. He didn't mail that letter to the bigwig European scientists. He wrote it while serving as America's ambassador to France and he figured that a potty mouth wouldn't reflect well on the revolutionary spirit. Still, he had legitimate concerns about making science matter.

A question for seven-year-old students: *If you were Ambassador Benjamin Franklin, would you have sent the fart letter?*

For older students, too, civics and ethics converge in almost all the founders. Thomas Jefferson is a provocative plural. Apart from the obvious reason—his contradictions on slavery—the life that he led lends itself to a major dilemma for young Americans today. Jefferson had an unbounded faith in the people. He trusted them to make the right choices at every turn, which is why a "Jeffersonian democracy" limits the powers of the federal government. Yet in his later years, Jefferson watched America's character coarsen. He died embittered and fearful of the future.

Question: *Would you rather have high expectations of your country and risk being let down or have lower expectations and risk taking part in a meritocracy of mediocrity?*

Even the Statue of Liberty can be taught as a plural, Lil. She originated in—wait for it—Egypt. Her sculptor envisioned Lady Liberty as an Arab woman holding high the torch of progress at the entrance of the Suez Canal, where she'd welcome ships en route to Asia. As it turns out, the sculptor's funding dried up and, with no fixed address to her name, the fine lady eventually wound up in New York Harbor.

Imagine the questions about American identity and global citizenship. Think about the opportunities for diversity of thought. Extrapolate individuality to every historical figure, whether woman or man; whether black, white, or green; whether flesh, stone, or copper.

I once asked an auditorium of students if they identified themselves as global citizens or American citizens. Almost half raised their hands for "global citizen." This, in the U.S. South! After scraping my jaw off the floor, I informed the students that "global" versus "American" is a phony choice. You can choose to be a global American.

You'd be loyal to the values of a traditional patriot, and to infuse citizenship with humility, you'd take one step more. You'd speak truth to the most global power of all: the ego that inheres in you; the brain that could be causing you to fear those who identify only as American citizens; the egobrain that needs to know them, not just of them.

To engage and enlarge your Us: That's about as revolutionary as it gets.

Rethinking Courage

58

Lily in the Field: Letting Go

They just gave me the news, Lily.

Your doctors said we can shift into overdrive with no guarantee that you'll survive, let alone bounce back to full health. The only assurance would be that you'll continue to suffer. I can't let it happen.

In that case, they tenderly told me, "Let Lily go." They don't realize that I've needed you incalculably more than you've needed me. To be honest, Lil, you'll have to let me go.

Yesterday, I whispered your many names. You looked right up at me. Today, your eyes peer straight ahead. Are you letting me go, Lil?

When you ruled out running for president, you explained it's because you need to focus on what matters in the end. If this is the end, Lily, please let me know.

I'm listening.

I trust you.

I thank you.

59

The Killer Cuddle

Lily, my angel, please excuse me for going AWOL these past two weeks, but I've been wrecked with grief. Yesterday, I picked up your ashes along with your paw print. We came home together, as promised.

Is heaven all it's hyped up to be, Lil? Do my prayers reach you? Are you finally free of pain? That would make one of us. Last night, I held your bed to my chest. It was all I could do to keep the pieces of my shattered heart intact. You dug a deep tunnel into it, sweet bean. I never thought that I'd fall madly in love with something—someone—whose very shadow I'd feared most of my life.

Soon after your Mama Laura and I met, she introduced me to your siblings, Lucy, Ricky, and Rocky. I froze in their presence, certain that they'd rip my hand off if I held it out. Our neighbor, Jim, was there. When we got back to his place, I made myself comfortable in his La-Z-Boy. Then, plop! Jim's fanged-toothed rescue dog, Romeo, landed in my lap.

Oh God, I thought, *get me out of here*. As if in a slow-motion dream, I saw Jim form the word, "Relax." And you know what, Lil? I did. You know why? Because I trusted Jim. I had faith that he wouldn't put me in harm's path.

As I loosened my back and exhaled, ravenous Romeo went in for the killer cuddle. Almost instantly, I felt the touch of *tawheed*—the oneness of God and all of God's creation. My fear suddenly competed with grace. I found my twitchy hand migrating to Romeo's head. With a pat from me and a lick from him and a nuzzle for the ages, I went for broke. Eyes shut, I pursed my lips and pressed them on Romeo's ear.

Yes, Lilybean, I kissed a dog and I liked it!

No longer could I remain a species supremacist. What higher a being is there than the one who challenges my lifelong prejudice and does so with love? In mid-snuggle, I chose courage over fear. Life, as I knew it, changed forever.

But when you died, life changed forever again.

The father of evolutionary theory, Charles Darwin, taught us that whether we want it or not, see it or not, trust it or not, change happens. We're perpetually evolving in ways that serve the purpose of species survival. To progress, we must reconcile ourselves to the ebbs and flows of reality. You're not returning to my arms, Lil. As marooned as I feel, I accept that you've departed and another precious being will turn up. I'll survive and so will our memories. That's the best I can do, for now, at adapting.

Of course, sometimes we're summoned to question change, not adapt to it. But in those moments, how do we prevent our perspectives from degenerating into yet more rabid dogmas—those that trample on life in all its variety? For me, the answer's hidden in plain sight. We need to rethink courage. It's not just about standing up *for* ourselves. It's first about standing up *to* ourselves.

60

"Ballsy"?

What I so loved about you, Lil, is that you asked me more questions than I would've asked myself. I'm not impervious to the influence of my egobrain. It limits the aperture through which I see everything. Most of us need others to point out that our lenses are clouded by mental cataracts. The ballsy among us then look clearly at ourselves.

A highly educated woman I know forwarded me one of those rant-filled email chains. The subject line read, "Ballsy." Normally, I delete these things but this time I opened it, curious to learn what qualified to her as balls. The link led me to a video of three men in suits denouncing Muslim extremism, their audience clapping copiously. She singled out one of the speakers for "saying it like it is."

When I finished listening to him, I wrote this woman back. To be candid, I told her, I don't think the speaker's all that ballsy. He's embedded himself with people who have the same views. It's just another safe space, isn't it? I didn't expect to hear back and in that regard, the woman didn't disappoint.

In diversity circles, too, it doesn't take much courage to speak up about social ills if we surround ourselves only with people who'll applaud. At a liberal all-girls academy, I assigned student leaders to pick a controversial issue that deserved more honest conversation within the school's walls. We'll organize a forum around it, I said. Try, I added, to choose a subject that makes your peers a little uncomfortable so that you have a reason to build up your bravery around them.

The students picked "rape culture" because "the statistics are shocking" and talking about sexual assault is a "social taboo." I tensed up. Was choosing this subject their way of reporting personal experiences? No, each insisted. They also knew they could come to me confidentially.

Now, Lil, kudos to these students for identifying the issue that would set off the earthquake known as #MeToo. They're right: Going public if you've been sexually violated can be daunting, especially outside of cosmopolitan society.

But I was asking the girls to bust a school-specific taboo. That's because their day-to-day community is made up of fellow students, not the general public. This matters since they'd be learning the skills to speak, hear, question, and negotiate with the people they encounter every week, all week.

Would theoretical conversations about sexual assault truly demand courage inside their liberal school? Wouldn't such conversations elicit beams of pride (or at least rays of responsiveness) from administrators? Wouldn't it get "Go, girl!" cheers from friends?

I pledged that I wouldn't take offense if they condemned me as a mouthpiece of the patriarchy. Just accuse me in person, I requested, so we can have that discussion.

Ultimately, the girls chose a topic far more controversial within the school—and a magnet for diverse perspectives. They'd noticed that most of the boarding students from China ate lunch in a room separate from everyone else. The girls had a question for them: *Are you self-segregating or are we excluding you? Or both?*

The whole exercise taught an ancient, real-world truth that intellectual bubbles can't convey—courage entails sacrifice. It requires giving up some of our emotional comfort, lest we end up exchanging one dogma for another.

How can the old-fashioned principle of sacrifice make sense to a new generation? I turn here to my friend, Payam Akhavan. He's an international human rights lawyer who's prosecuted war crimes. "The problem with the world is not a shortage of brilliant theories or feel-good slogans," Akhavan says. "The problem is that we confuse the proliferation of progressive terminology with empathy and engagement. We say the right things, but we fail to act on them because we want to feel virtuous without paying a price."

But paying the price of a sacrifice isn't the same as getting ripped off. What you learn in return could well become your saving grace. "In responding to injustice with genuine empathy and meaningful engagement," Akhavan adds, "we are nobody's savior except our own."

I have a suggestion for diversity's champions. Let's break the first rule of tribalism. Instead of assuming that it's "mission accomplished" when we've offended those who fear diversity, let's offend ourselves.

I'll go first.

61

Offend Yourself

To offend myself is to acknowledge, upfront and out loud, that someone who profoundly disagrees with me has at least a kernel of wisdom that I can grow from. With that in mind, Lil, I'm swallowing hard as I embark on a story.

For years, my face has gone flush with shame about a calamitous public appearance I made. On Martin Luther King Jr.'s birthday in 2010, MSNBC aired "Obama's America," a LIVE event revolving around one gimmicky question: Is the United States post-racial now that it has elected a black president? The resounding answer was Lily-esque: Yeah, right.

Chris Matthews, the host, asked me why young people voted over-whelmingly for President Obama. "Because he's black," I stated. Don't flip out, Lil; I clarified that I'd polled students at my campus. None of the NYU kids I spoke with seemed to know Obama's policy positions. They only wanted, they said, to right a historic wrong by ensuring that an African American would finally be the country's chief executive.

Matthews scowled. My co-panelists, media icons in black communities nationwide, glared. Each responded to me with disdain. On cable TV, you're tapped to be a performer, not a listener, so I followed protocol and threw shade right back. For all my confidence, I could feel the judgment of the full house. It made me paddle up the creek harder with my hands.

Afterward, in and among a torrent of viewer reactions, I received a note from an old, now deceased, friend—Howard McCurdy. We'd met in the Parliament of Canada, where he sat as only the second black man elected to the House of Commons and where I formulated ideas for how our party could sparkle in Question Period. McCurdy would razz me warmheartedly back then. This time, he scorched:

> *I was embarrassed by [your] performance of overbearing arrogance as you attempted to defend the indefensible position that you had solved the question of Obama's youth support on the basis that "he's black." As one who has far more understanding of the black experience and white attitudes towards blacks both in the U.S. and Canada than you can ever hope to have, I believe that any assertions you make in that regard should be proffered with far more modesty than you displayed.*

My defense mechanisms went into high gear. *What about the brashness of the men onstage? Shouldn't they be called out, too? If I'd been a guy, would they have torn a strip off me or would they have differed respectfully?* As I speculated, my egobrain sneered, "You've got nothing to learn from a sexist crank."

But, to give diversity of opinion its due, I must offend myself and explain why Howard McCurdy had something to teach me. To many viewers, I came off as a precocious carpetbagger—swooping into black America, flinging a verbal grenade, and acting as if it's no big deal. During my exchange with the guys onstage, my face conveyed to them, *Cope. Just cope.* Body language does more talking than words themselves do. In that respect, Howard McCurdy spoke truth. I behaved vainly. Out of self-defense, I self-destructed.

On issues that polarize, Lil, heartfelt humility goes a long, long way. I won't always remember this when I'm burning with the white heat of emotion. But I'll keep striving to check my egobrain.

Some might snort that we shouldn't give a rat's rear what our critics think. That's legit if the critics want only to eviscerate us. At all other times, though, their criticisms can be useful in honing us as communicators. We're likelier to discern those times when we step back rather than fight back. And if we realize later that we ought to have fought, it takes no emotional sacrifice to settle scores. The sacrifice comes in trying the alternative first.

Here's hoping that future Howard McCurdys take a lesson, too. Raking people over the coals doesn't motivate. When repeated, it humiliates, and the scars of humiliation can be years in the healing, if at all. Unless we transform trauma, we'll transmit it, the Jesuit brother Richard Rohr instructs.

He's supported by the emerging science of epigenetics, which looks at how we pass onto our children and grandchildren some of the damage that we, ourselves, never healed from. If it's true, this idea of transferred trauma helps explain a lot. Like why so many people have a tough time getting over what others would rather consign to the distant past. It's more than possible that the sediment of slavery shows up today as medical issues in the descendants of slaves, leaving such kids disadvantaged in the race for success through no doing of their own. Telling African Americans to "move on" from slavery makes no sense if, in certain instances, their cells and molecules haven't. It might just make matters worse, ensuring that a lack of healing in this generation gets handed over to the next.

Same with white people whose family histories are rife with addiction, famine, poverty, genocide, war, and the like. Mothers who kept a lid on their tragedies could've secreted their fears to the embryos growing in their wombs. Under those conditions, any privilege a white male enjoys might very well be counteracted by the trauma he inherits. Since we can't know every person's back story, it's all the more reason to make grace our first response to disagreement.

Don't get me wrong, Lil. I'm not trying to depict all folks with privilege as marionettes of their biology. Biology *influences* but doesn't have to *determine* everything. What each person does always has some kind of context, and there's more to the canvas of context than genes. As an individual, my context includes who I consider to be my community and what its culture is, as well as my personal upbringing and the values it instilled in me, if only by virtue of my rebellion.

Nurture cooperates with nature. This pairing helps decide whether I'll be more or less rash than someone else who's feeling as threatened as I am. The difference lies in the choices I make as my egobrain processes the threat.

Even when our trauma's etched into us, humans have agency. We're capable of developing habits that heal us—and heal our future families. The science behind generational trauma points to why lasting social change begins from the inside out. Systems, structures, and institutions, laws and policies, theories and ideologies, won't work for us unless we work on ourselves.

Friends of honest diversity, lend me your ears. In moments when you'd likely to go off on others, gently offend *yourselves*. Here's a three-step guide:

- Sacrifice a few moments of melodrama so that you can breathe.

- After the first intentional breath, resolve to communicate in a way that at least some of your detractors can relate to.

- Keep breathing—consciously.

Your emotions are evolving as you breathe. You started with fear and the hysteria it produces. Now you're recalibrating to the constructive emotion of compassion for others. Or gratitude for this opportunity to present your perspective. Or pride in having conviction without the pridefulness of having certainty. Each step of the way, you're working with your built-in biology to cultivate grace—the highest form of courage.

Take it from a sleuth for truth. In 1273, after a lifetime of reconciling pagan, Hebrew, Christian, and Muslim thought, St. Thomas Aquinas delivered the *Summa Theologica*, a guide for living with grace. In it, Aquinas conceives of courage as "a disposition of the soul to stand firm with what is in accord with reason amid sundry assaults of passion or the hardships of practice."

Ms. Lil couldn't have said it better if she tried. She didn't try because she's frolicking with Thomas and the other saints up there. What's our excuse for not trying?

62

Coward for Congress

Since you're cavorting with the angels, Lil, and I'm in the land of the imperfect living, I need your celestial supervision to address another question. It's a vexing one. What do we do when They don't have the courage to engage with Us?

My short answer is, walk away. The cowards had their chance; it's time to jet. The danger of such certainty, though, is that we'll give up on Them too soon. I imagine that sounds overly generous—groveling, even. I don't mean it to be. Let me explain my thinking with two stories.

A colleague of mine, Adam, tried to exchange views on Facebook with a brazen anti-Semite named Paul Nehlen. This Nehlen guy had posted cryptic messages like "Pass the bikes. Race far now"—code for "Gas the kikes. Race war now," as alt-right websites allude. Nehlen had also claimed that Christianity "correctly identifies the followers of the Talmud as the children of Satan."

He wasn't being a prankster, Lil. He was being a candidate for the U.S. Congress. Nehlen shared this drivel, and more, as part of his campaign to win Wisconsin's first congressional district—until recently, the seat held by the Speaker of the U.S. House of Representatives.

A number of Jew-baiters ran for Republican nominations in 2018, and Adam contacted this one for two reasons. "Nehlen has a large, young following on social media, unlike several of the others," he told me. And "I was raised to understand that asking questions is usually the only way to learn about something or someone."

The campaign deleted his queries. "Funny," Adam says, "that Nehlen found my polite and simple questions more offensive than his followers' statements about my nose." Which extended Adam's list of reasons for communicating: "I thought that some of his followers might be capable enough of critical thinking to recognize that he's less about freedom of speech and more about freedom of his own speech."

After a few arduous but civil exchanges with those followers, Adam was blocked by Nehlen himself. Had Adam wasted his time over this aspiring Nazi-like legislator? Not for a second, he believes. Because good came of it. Some of Nehlen's fans bleated that Adam's questions were scaring possible followers away from the campaign. Let me stress that Adam didn't threaten anybody physically or verbally. He just posed questions. By staying consummately courteous, Adam accrued power. But he couldn't have harvested that power had he given up on Nehlen too fast.

My second story's about the perils of prematurely walking away— in person. Think of it, Lil, as an update on Genesis and Louis. They're the friends from Mississippi who feel very differently about their state's flag. Genesis, descended from civil rights activists, abhors the flag's slavery-era symbolism. She advocates a redesign. Louis, descended from a Civil War soldier who defended the South, wishes the flag would stay as is.

The curveball is, Louis's heart has opened to Gen's point of view thanks to her respect for his point view. They had a brutally honest conversation in which she asked questions about where he's coming from and why. Each time, she listened with the intention to understand, not to win. And she expressed her own perspective with no apologies— not that Louis wanted any.

That's where we pick up their story.

Impacted by Gen's courage, Louis volunteered to promote dialogue about an all-inclusive state flag. He'd draft his own friends and help lead a conversation, on-camera, with Gen's friends. As they say in Mississippi, the good Lord willin' and the creek don't rise, honest diversity would have its day.

Well, the good Lord seemed reticent. The creek, so to speak, rose: Besides Louis, only one individual from the "old-flag" side attended the conversation. You should know, Lil, that Gen and Louis recruited participants not by how hard-core they were, but by whether they wanted progress. If you said you did, you got invited. Yet most of the old-flaggers bailed at the last minute. By contrast, on the new-flag side, all who signed up showed up.

Genesis anticipated the no-shows. Two days before the conversation, she told me that a handful of the recruits already had cold feet. "There's a difference," Gen sighed, "between saying you're ready for progress and actually acting on what you say. The work on the other side isn't being done."

We can conjecture 'til the creeks rise about why they never arrived. Maybe some feared being demonized. Others might've feared being filmed and edited unfairly. It could've been that they feared being educated and therefore having to reckon with their consciences. Whatever the factors, most of the old-flaggers prioritized feeling safe over using their freedom to teach others about their perspective. But that's no surprise. According to Clay Routledge, a professor of psychology, "fear causes people to privilege psychological safety over liberty."

Why did Genesis go through with an experiment that appeared to be fizzling before her eyes? Why didn't she cancel and relieve herself of a headache? Why not just walk? "I'm a representative of the South," she says. "I wanted to show younger Southerners that in between elections, there's still a lot more democracy to do. I wanted to role-model civic engagement at its most basic."

But, I pushed, "You're a touring rapper. You're curating an exhibit of your paintings on top of that. You're busy enough! Why tolerate this time-suck?"

It's then that Gen's willingness to sacrifice found specific words. "I

don't mind being exhausted or uncomfortable," she asserted. "I'll live."
Gen riffed some more:

> *We were shooting a video, right? We had our cameras, we had our audio, we had the room, and we had whoever was brave enough to come through that door. I didn't know the outcome and that's okay. I knew it would tell the truth about what young Mississippians are working with. Facing the truth is a precondition for success.*

With that, the conversation took place.

63

Friends on Opposite Sides, Part 2

"First of all," Genesis announced over pizza, "I just want to commend everybody for being here."

Louis explained, "We're trying to prove that people with differences can come together and reconcile for a solution peacefully. Violence isn't the answer for anything. There's always a way around it."

Gen then laid down the law: "I want everyone to feel like they can be *honest.*"

One of the sharpest points came from Tyrus, a new-flagger. Had the South won the Civil War, he said to the two old-flaggers, "We would never be at this table right here." That's because blacks and whites would've been prohibited to mix as equal citizens.

Diving headlong into the culture war, Tyrus asked, "Can you see the discontent we have when we see statues of individuals" who prohibited "people like you and I from getting together?" He won't stop anybody from displaying slavery-era flags and statues on personal property or in museums. But on publicly funded grounds? No way. "These are symbols of terrorists!"

"I think you're embarking on a slippery slope," intervened Kyle, an old-flagger. "Honestly. Take the American flag, for instance. That flag represents tyranny to the Native American people of this country. We put them off in these reservations and we forgot about them. Nobody's questioning that." He implied that if Americans exhumed everything about their past, recrimination would overwhelm reconciliation.

So you know, Lil, I disagree with Kyle. The soul of America has room for a truth-and-reconciliation effort in which white folks can be heard alongside members of historically persecuted minorities. Free speech would never know a friendlier forum. The egos of the insecure will balk at that idea, but traditionalists such as Kyle bolster my hopes. Sure, he's an old-flagger; nonetheless, he recognizes Native Americans and their mistreatment by the U.S. government. Kyle's a plural.

That afternoon, the plurals from both sides vetted a redesign of the state flag. It's prototyped by an artist named Laurin Stennis. She's the granddaughter of a U.S. senator who voted against every prominent federal law aimed at integrating blacks and whites. Genesis read out loud the artist's statement, in which Stennis testifies how her colors and shapes co-mingle to capture the honest diversity of Mississippi: its indigenous cultures before the colonists arrived, its attempt to secede from the Union, even the *ongoing* "passionate differences we sometimes harbor," signified by blood-red bars on opposing ends of the flag. A masterstroke, in my view.

Most participants found the redesign unifying. Louis quibbled with, of all things, that reference to "passionate differences." He wondered, "When do we stop classifying as African American, Irish American,"—he tapped Kyle—or "Indian American and say, hey, you know what? We're American. We're Mississippi."

His fellow Mississippians discussed how "American" they feel these days. Not much, some confessed. Not in light of the invective cascading out of the White House. Genesis gingerly countered their hesitation to identifying as Americans. Black people sweated buckets, broke their backs, and lost their lives to build the United States, she reminded African Americans at the table. "We have a stake in this country."

In effect, Genesis was asking the discouraged to choose courage; to do justice to their ancestors by sacrificing the emotional safety of distrusting the Other. A few nodded solemnly. Brenna, a white woman whose ancestors include a Confederate general, opened up about her own contribution to courage. "Personally, I have been trying to"—she drew a deep breath—"be more brave" when the culture war comes up in her family. "And these days, it comes up a lot. No one's going to say the same things in front of you as they'll say in front of me," she told Genesis. "And vice versa."

"That's moral courage," Gen interjected. "Speaking truth to power when it's going to make you uncomfortable and when it's going to be tough."

"Yeah, then you can begin to grow," Brenna added by way of a tip to the other participants. Go about change from the inside out—inside yourself, then in your family, then in the wider world.

Louis clicked with Gen's call for moral courage. He shared a question that keeps him focused when he's being lambasted for standing with Genesis: "Why should she not be represented by a flag that others are, you know? Even though I support that flag, I support *her*, you know?"

He really does, Lil. When another high-profile new-flagger started receiving credible death threats, Louis offered to teach her responsible self-defense, Mississippi-style. "I said, 'I'll show you how to shoot a gun, how to clean and maintain it, how to get certified to carry it,'" he reported to me. She took him up on the offer. Had Genesis bolted too soon, Louis would've never made such an overture. He would've felt no direct connection to Gen's cause. She would've left possibilities on the table.

64

Moral Courage

Genesis and Louis exemplify "moral courage"—doing the right thing despite your fears. Both of them risked being dishonored by their tribes for talking to each other. To maintain their credibility as change-makers, they had to think about how they'd be judged. Besides, it's human to care about your reputation. What's paralyzing is to care too much.

Louis regrets nothing. And Genesis? "Ummm," she started. Not two seconds later, she took me aback. Pleasantly. "I was transformed by it," Gen said of the honest diversity that she and Louis uncovered. "It definitely gets better results than the alternative."

But exercising moral courage seems so insufficient to the task at hand, doesn't it, Lil? Here on Earth, we're in a war for planetary survival. Biodiversity's getting bulldozed and that's a superb reason to be afraid. Why expend time and energy to quell the justified fear that our biology has us feeling? Why engage our opponents if it's more effective to pulverize them for the sake of moving forward?

That's the pipe dream. Conquering the inconvenient Other isn't effective. It makes for losses down the road. If the Other doesn't feel heard, eventually he'll feel humiliated. Or, at least, he'll preach to his people that their accumulated wounds have scabbed into humiliation—a handy pretext for future backlash. Perceived humiliation fuels identity-obsessed warriors, whether they're rampaging for the ethno-state or for the caliphate. In aiming to decimate our Other, we in the diversity camp sow an emotion that'll negate diversity.

To last over the long term, social change has to start with difficult dialogues. Genesis respects this reality. "Probably my earliest memory, since I was itty-bitty, is watching the History Channel with my dad," she reminisces. "We would spend hours talking about world events and mass psychology." As Genesis matured, she pulled together the bigger picture behind why people rise up. "In a word," she says, "degradation. When people feel degraded, the fuse is lit."

Gen's putting us on notice, Lil: It's just not smart to be degrading our neighbors while we presume to be upgrading their society. It's smarter to show moral courage. For Genesis, moral courage takes two forms.

First, she actively acknowledges that she won't be right all the time. Even when she strenuously believes she's doing the right thing, not everyone will agree. That's the way it goes. But that's no reason to flick away opposing points of view. "Let's say we have that beautiful redesigned flag fluttering from every pole in the state of Mississippi," Gen imagines. "How did it get there? If politicians forced the flag on people, then hearts haven't changed. Why would Mississippians feel any more represented, any more welcome, under the new flag?"

Second, Genesis makes it a personal project to treat people as multifaceted. Or try to. With her artist's eye, she has innovated an anytime, anywhere ritual. "I concentrate on a stationary object," Gen teaches me.

Without moving my position, I visualize the object's relation to its surroundings—the table it's on, the bookcase behind it. Then, in a different part of the room, I take in that same object from the opposite angle. This time, I visualize myself as part of the surroundings, gauging the object's relation to me as I'm viewing it. Then I try to imagine the two perspectives simultaneously. The more I practice, the more perspectives I can combine. If I'm able to do that, I can start to understand people in a similar way.

Gen describes this exercise as "conceptual resistance." In our consumer culture, she says, "We've bought the concept that a person is a thing, a label, an image. We need ways to question what we assume we understand." It's a classy call to offend ourselves—patiently.

Her admiration for questions explains the "moral" part of moral courage. For the sake of justice, we have to choose between what's right and what's wrong. But given all the situations that contain vivid shades of gray, how can we *know* we're choosing well? How can we come close to understanding a person or topic unless we're exposed to views that challenge us to rethink?

Not in every conversation, obviously. Not even in most. Our congested brains would quit on us. But deliberately putting ourselves in front of one friend, one coach, one canine who sincerely disagrees with us on an issue we care about—that alone will do wonders for exercising the moral courage muscle. And, as happens in physical training, moral courage training soon becomes a habit. A mindful no-brainer.

In one sense, moral courage is counter-evolutionary because it demands thinking for yourself. In another sense, though, moral courage jibes with how we're wired. Our cave-dwelling ancestors had to cooperate with the community that existed right under their noses. Even when nostrils flared, cooperation continued. The tribe's success depended on each member having personal humility alongside ambition for the whole. Trust emerged from being *trustworthy*.

We still have this brain. As Genesis and Louis prove, a great good can be fulfilled if we tribe out to win trust—which is enormously different than tribing out just to win. To become trustworthy, take a cue from Genesis and start here: *Ask not how to change the Other's mind. Ask what you're missing about the Other.*

65

When *Isn't* Talk Cheap?

Brandon sat quietly in the conversation that Louis and Genesis led. I've learned from you, Lil, that silence doesn't always connote passivity. Listening can be a maverick choice.

As the discussion wrapped up, Brandon stepped up. He wanted to do more reconciling between young people right across the state. "I'm going forward with it," he confirmed. "If we—if ol' backwoods, red-dirt, cotton-pickin' Mississippi can figure it out, you know, maybe the rest of the world . . ." Genesis leapt in to cheer him on.

Weeks after, she found out that Russ, another participant, launched a service to deliver food directly to the homeless. He, too, felt a burst of optimism following the roundtable and, in thinking about that feeling, he chose to build on it. When Genesis told me that exploring honest diversity gets better results than the alternative, this is what she meant. In her experience, "It changes the community exponentially."

Talk's cheap except when it breaks new ground, which is what the conversation did for some of its participants. Far from hosting an idle gabfest, Genesis and Louis role-modeled action. Being plurals, they moved Brandon, Russ, and the others beyond sloganeering. Something else about these plurals: Unlike a lot of activists for diversity, they don't issue Us-or-Them ultimatums. Rather than perpetuate compliance, plurals urge curiosity. As Gen stated from the start, this is an opportunity to be honest. Do everyone a favor, she asked, and wring the most out of it.

I'll ask for a favor of my own, Lil. Never lowball the adventure that curiosity can be. It's one mother of an antidote to boredom. So says the writer Ta-Nehisi Coates, whom many consider today's James Baldwin. Coates bemoans our shallow media culture, which pours cold water on wonder and, instead, "expects you to be an oracle."

> I've become, in the most vulgar sense, a pundit. I'm not open to having my mind changed. I'm not trying to figure it out. I'm not curious. I'm not exploring. I'm standing on a rock. I'm sitting on a throne. I'm making pronouncements about what the world is and that is so boring. It bores me to tears.

Curiosity, on the other hand, makes us cry for the right reasons. Such as amazement. Curiosity allows us the courage of our confusions, which spells opportunity for any budding innovator of social change. Do-gooders aren't necessarily risk-takers, but innovators have to be. The most daring ones develop the courage of their confusions so they can put curiosity to *informed* use. Their questions don't end with, *Who's suffering and how do I help them?* They ask further, *Who benefits from the suffering and how do I reach them?*

Think about the dilapidated public schools across America, from urban blocks to rural tracts. Why do so many schools teeter on a knife's edge, Lil? My egobrain would rather that I not ask. It far prefers the known to the not-yet-answered. It wants me to settle for the status quo by, for example, tutoring a student in her shabby classroom and spartan library. Doing so will help her muddle through the system while polishing my CV, burnishing my street cred, and boosting my endorphins.

Notice that I get the better end of this bargain. Yet my effort is supposed to be about the student. If I want to serve a good greater than my self-interest, I'll tutor her *and* dig deeper. I'll ask, *Who gains from run-down schools?*

Is it teachers' unions? Upon reflection, that's doubtful since squalid classrooms attract more complaints about teachers and less funding from governments.

Is it small businesses? Probably not, given that they need employ-ees who can out-imagine the competition.

Is it mega-companies? Many are investing in artificial intelligence to shed human workers and hike profits. Why, then, refurbish public schools? Why should kids learn to listen, speak, and cooperate when robots will fill those functions?

Is it me who's benefiting? At the supermarket, I already use self-checkout. Before I know it, human cashiers will be outmoded. Sen-sors will charge my virtual credit card the moment I stick an item in my bag. Convenient for me, but where will locals work in the future? Should I take it on faith that we'll balance technology with humanity? Who, by the way, are "we"?

Would urban developers like to keep school buildings in a sham-bles so they can raze and replace them with parking lots (automated, of course)? Cha-ching, baby.

Have affluent taxpayers let politicians know that not a single extra penny will be squeezed out of them and thrown into those sinkholes called public schools? It's worth doing the research.

For some answers, I'll interview journalists who've covered local education. I'll be upfront about my biases—for example, that the play-ers I least suspect are teachers' unions and small businesses. Am I giv-ing them too much credit? If the journalists disagree with any of my assumptions, so much the better. "Tell me what I'm missing," I'll ask.

Because I'll now have a relationship with reporters, I'll propose that they publish a story about my quest: one tutor's search for a fair school system. If they like my idea, they'll connect me with the people they believe are prospering from our ramshackle schools so we can get their perspectives. The reporters will also come with me to the meetings that I schedule. My courage has its boundaries, you know. I'll need backup.

I won't forget the individuals directly affected. I'll ask the kid I tutor, "Why do you think your school lacks the books and heating it needs?" I'll have her introduce me to her parents, and I'll then ask them, "Why do you think your child's school is in such desperate shape?"

After I've exhausted my questions (and her parents), I'll ask them to help my quest in one final way: Please introduce me to the school principal and assure her that I'm not a stalker. I'll bounce what I've discovered off of the principal. I'll then ask her what's being done by way of solutions and whether she'd be open to a new plan of action from outsiders such as me.

If she's closed to my input, bummer. But she's not the only school official out there. A newspaper's now writing about my odyssey through the obstacle course of public education and some of the powers-that-be are bound to read that story. In our mondo-networked culture, it'll make the rounds.

As I reflect more about the lessons I've gleaned, I might have more recommendations. Can I access other platforms to reach decision-makers? Here's one idea: Given my relationships at the paper, I'll write a follow-up column. Plus, I'll share it on *Medium*. Someone, somewhere, will post feedback that prompts a new question and my next move.

Lil, the innovator's journey—ask, listen, ask, listen, synthesize, understand, contemplate, act—might sound elementary to your wizened ears. Still, I can't tell you how many times teachers have approached me about explaining to them why students do this and think that. I always reply, "Have you asked *them*?" Hmmm.

Just a second. My phone's buzzing.

Lily, your name's displayed! Are you actually calling from—?

Sure, operator, I'll accept the charges.

Lilybean!

Awww, Mama loves you as well. Big league.

No, honey, Mama loves *you* more.

Heck yeah, you can ask me a question.

It's about Genesis and Louis? About the conversation they hosted over pizza? Go to town.

What's that, my little cream puff?

Yes, they finished the pizza.

Crust, too.

The Lessons of Lily

66

POOP Time

Lily, my heartbeat, it's been six months since you crossed the Rainbow Bridge. I thought that time had licked my grief. Not yet, boo. Excuse my whimpering but I now have to decide what to do with your stroller. Mama Laura and I are packing for the family's move to Hawaiʻi.

You loved the Aloha State, Lil. Never before had I seen you skip through grass. During our long walks, you jumped up on your hind legs, clutched the edge of your stroller, and thrust your nose in the air. Such a jamboree for the senses! In California, you sniffed the world go by but in Hawaiʻi, you inhaled. I'll remember to thank the plumeria trees for making you so happy. Rest assured, Lil, I'll take the time to respect them as you did.

Truth is, I'm in no rush to get over you because even in death, you teach. More than ever, I understand why we can't hold it against people who need to mourn the passing of their particular America. Their America defined their routine, and routine comforts us in ways we barely register.

Every day, you stirred at seven a.m. I carried you downstairs at 7:30. Breakfast at 7:45. Our first stroll at eight. Our second at one o'clock. Dinner at four and our final outing at six. In between, I taught, wrote, researched, and organized—always with my heart fluttering as my mind buzzed in anticipation of our next break together. For all my resistance to conformity, Lil, I'd grown attached to our habits. For all of my professed openness, my attraction to adventure, my premium on fluidity, I've realized how much I value familiarity.

The morning after you died, eight o'clock felt excruciating. One o'clock came around and I had no place to go. The routes you traipsed, I made extra efforts to avoid. Otherwise I'd find myself gravitating to them, only to be stabbed with sadness that nobody needed me there.

And it sunk in, way, way in, why our neighbor Jim can't curtly be told to suck up the loss of his America. When Jim wonders whether he belongs, he's actually wondering whether he's needed. To do what, you wonder? Anything that affirms he has something to teach a republic of plurals. Because he's one of them. One of us.

Brené Brown, the noted researcher of vulnerability, says that to develop trust in a relationship, don't just stand ready to help; proactively ask for help. Establish the other party's worth before making claims about your own. Suppose we took her guidance when working toward honest diversity. Imagine if more of us asked our Other, *Will you help me understand what I'm missing about your point of view?* Jim would consider this question corny. But he never laughs when I ask it. Rather, he wants the chance to be seen—by being relevant.

Jim will have to integrate into a new generation's America. But it doesn't have to be on my time. It can be on POOP time. POOP stands for "Perspective On Other People." Roi Ben-Yehuda, a leadership scholar and educator, came up with this silly phrase to explain a serious idea: Many Americans can set aside one hour a week to help peers, neighbors, whomever, with a task that would mean a lot to them. Jim reserves POOP time for me regularly.

Ben-Yehuda schedules POOP time with his coworkers. A couple of days before his free hour, he blasts out a message to ask colleagues how he can lend them a hand. "The reaction to POOP time has been great," he wrote me. "I've gotten to experience different facets of people's work and worries. Most important for me is that they've felt cared for." It doesn't hurt that the guy's got a sense of humor: He signed off with, "Warmly ('cause, you know, POOP)."

Lil, in the days following your death, my mama, Mumtaz, took the time to become my core support. I'd call her every afternoon for consolation and she readily gave it, knowing that's what I needed. The daily POOP time she spent drying my tears convinced her of how deeply it's possible to feel for a dog.

Her newfound understanding surprised both of us because Mumtaz had always conceived of nonhumans as things. When she first met Mama Laura, she warned, "Don't let your dogs touch me. My prayers won't be valid to God!"

Mama Laura glumly instructed Lucy, Ricky, and Rocky to avoid their grandmother. "Your souls," she informed them, "will be damned if you touch a Muslim." Mumtaz got the joke but hung onto her belief that dogs have nothing pure to offer people. Until she realized firsthand the influence you've had on me.

Several months into your arrival, my uncle observed that I'm "so much more patient and kind" toward Mumtaz. I told him it's because of you. Lilybean, our daily POOP times helped me to meet my biggest challenge ever: putting on the brakes, looking around, and pursuing happiness in what's immediately present.

Mumtaz called these the lessons of Lily. She connected them to my overall lightness and, like a wall of rocks immersed in water, her fear of dogs is now crumbling. Last night, your brother Ricky sidled up to her in bed. Today, Rocky shimmied onto her lap. Of all your siblings, he's the one who wags Mumtaz's tail because he's as spastic as she is. "Mum," I exclaimed, "you're so good with the dogs!"

"I love those people," she effused. *Those people*. She may be a species-supremacist, Lil, but may Allah love Mumtaz for evolving. If this is how change happens, through grace building on grace, I've got a thought about your stroller. How about we donate it to a shelter and keep the wheels of grace moving.

Sound like a plan? I'll clear our stuff from the stroller's pockets. Let's see what's in them.

Poop bags.
More poop bags.
An abandoned collar.
Ah, that lonesome leash.
An envelope. Postmarked, "Eternity."
Eternity? Oh, Lil.

67

Amazing Grace

Mama, my everlasting companion,

Good news: Up here, the rivers abound with peanut butter and I alone can fix my portions. Be at peace. I have a new leash on life.

More good news: I'm engaging my neighbors and I can confirm that you don't have to be a saint to move into the hood. You merely have to accept that you're neither God nor God's ambassador, and act accordingly. If you don't believe in God, it's perfectly alright as long as you bring a scientific skepticism to your disbelief, which is to accept that you might be wrong.

The other week, I ran into Charles Darwin and I thanked him for his courage. He denied having any. "You must remember," he said, "that my most famous work, *On the Origin of Species,* stopped short of discussing *human* origins.

> *My discussion would have directly contradicted Christianity's teach-*
> *ing that God designed human beings to be the most special of all*
> *creatures. I would have relished puncturing human arrogance but I*
> *was frightened of the backlash that would ensue from Christian*
> *men and women.*

I howled, "That's courage, Mr. Darwin! Rather than choosing si-lence, you introduced your findings. But you did so in ways that allowed your culture the time to assimilate a countercultural paradigm. You tamed your ego."

Mama, he went beet red. Or I think it was red. I can see again, but I'm still a novice with the color palette. The nose is so much more clever.

"Mr. Darwin," I continued, "I lived my final years well because your courage subverted the hubris that once classified me as a soulless creature. To you, sir, I remain grateful."

He said, "Thank you, young lady.

Please, however, may we dispense with this 'sir' rubbish? I was born a Victorian Englishman but these are only labels, and an ill fit besides. Ask my children, whom my wife and I raised with an affection that belies the Victorian stereotype. Now then, call me Chuck. And your name?

Such amazing grace, Mama. Charles Darwin is a plural who epitomizes the "how" of fighting for truth: To rumble effectively, be humble immediately.

We got to chatting, Chuck and I, and he left me with more to think about. He emphasized that correlation is not causation. Therefore, my passing might have had nothing to do with peanut butter. Thank the Lord, since I'm always dying for some.

Furthermore, because correlation is not causation, Chuck's humility might have played no role in the success of his ideas. It's possible that at a different time or in another society, Chuck's modesty would have undermined his impact. The converse is also possible. *Origin* could have opened even more minds had it explicitly panned the belief that God created humans to be all that. The fact is, we can't know how history would have changed if Chuck had been less humble.

So, Mama, let *us* be humble. In taking our message to the next generation, let's proceed as if we're right, then let's listen as if we're wrong. In that spirit, I've written two more letters. Would you retrieve them from the other pouch of my stroller so I can read them?

Thank you, Mama. You go back to packing. I'll keep the wheels moving.

Mushily ('cause, you know, all those poop bags),

Lily

PS: When you feel settled in Hawai'i, please ask the Pacific Ocean if you may sprinkle my ashes in its surf. I'll bob along as you paddle. We'll be like water as never before.

68

CCRAP Time

Dear students,

Lily here. I want to speak with you myself because Mama has a lot on her plate. Me? I have nothing but time.

When I lived among you, I learned something about being human. It's no walk in the park! Now that I'm roughly thirty jillion feet above the ground, I enjoy a much wider perspective and let me tell you: labels are good for jars but not for much else.

Back in the day, Mama taught me this truth. Mind you, I resisted a lot of her wisdom because I was a rebellious twelve-year-old (which made me a youthful eighty-four-year-old in human terms). Lucky me, Mama respected my individuality and encouraged my questions. That's why I've taken the time to think about what she said. Strictly between you and me, I see the validity of her message more than ever. It's become *our* message, and I wish to relate it directly to your life.

The older ones among you have been labeled the "millennials." Doggie dung. You're individuals. Of course, by now the industries that make bank from clumping and targeting all of you have begun eyeing the post-millennial generation, dubbing them the "plurals." I hope you understand that when Mama and I invoke the word "plural," we mean something altogether different. For us, "plural" isn't a category reserved for young consumers. "Plural" is the reality of pretty much every being.

Bruce Lee. Audre Lorde. Charles Darwin. Ben Franklin. Sarah Silverman. Frances Lee. Genesis. Louis. Jim. Mumtaz. Mama. Me. You.

Most beings aren't aware that they're plurals, so they let others define them. But when you're a self-aware plural, you commit to three actions:

- You embrace the fact you're more than your labels and you treat others as if they are, too. Because it's a safe bet that they are.

- You lift the lid on different points of view without pretending that all views carry equal moral weight. They don't. But before judging your own perspective to be superior, you find out why your Other holds the beliefs that you don't agree with.

- You take disagreement as an invitation to engagement. You can't do this with everything that interests you, but to be true to yourself, you must do it with the one issue that moves you like nothing else does.

Your teachers can help. I encourage you to eavesdrop on my letter to them later. Meanwhile, just as I'm learning portion control at my pantry (which, by the way, is out of this world), you have to take a certain amount of responsibility for yourself. As Mama and I view it, the biggest barrier to being a successful plural is "CCRAP time."

CCRAP is our acronym for "Consumer-Centric Reactions Accelerated Pronto." CCRAP sums up your one-click culture: Buy and sell instantly so you can get on with the next click. And the next. By "consumer-centric reactions," we mean people's hair-trigger judgments about each other, as if they're scanning a shelf of grab-and-go items. Pick this, skip that, and fly out the door. "Accelerated" and "pronto" point to the expectation that accelerated checkout isn't enough. Accelerate your acceleration or lose my business, consumers signal to entrepreneurs. You can see how this CCRAP-y mental model of time leads anybody to privilege transactions over relationships.

CCRAP time debases relationships. For example, are you a friend or an "ally"? As Mama and I developed our relationship, she confided to me that in high schools and universities, socially conscious students are forever scouting allies for their causes. Nothing wrong with that, I woofed. Strength in numbers. Except, Mama said, those allies tend to get valued only for their usefulness to the cause, not for their intrinsic humanity. And certainly not for their ideas or questions.

She tipped me off to an unspoken rule of allyship: that listening means unquestionably agreeing with how victims perceive their situation. Mama's been told that seeking simple clarity from victims amounts to challenging them, which revictimizes them. So, the rule of allyship states, sit down, shut up, and follow the script about how to support victims.

In all of these ways, allies serve as showpieces. They're tasked to be like consumer products—performance-ready, suitable in the moment, and expendable once they become inconvenient. Their involvement with causes is more transaction than interaction, verging on exploitation. Mama wondered: *Do we honestly advance diversity by making products out of people?*

Mama also wondered if she was being a drama queen. She took that concern to her friend Brie Loskota, who won the "Fearless Ally" award from an American Muslim foundation in Washington, D.C. "All too often," Auntie Brie confirmed, "people treat their relationships with allies as a transaction of political goods.

But as an ally, I'm not in a relationship with an abstract cause, I'm in a relationship with people. And if you see me as a person, too, then any tension between us can be constructive because we've got a commitment to each other.

Just one hitch: Commitments demand lots of time. Transactions typically don't. Most can be settled with a yes or a no. But commitments are honored by becoming curious about the space *between* yes and no. Many activists, Auntie Brie says, "foreclose on curiosity with snap judgments about whether someone's in or out. How do they look? How do they speak? We tell everyone else to interrogate their biases. We fail to ask why they should if we don't question our own prejudices."

Students, you didn't invent CCRAP time. You inherited it from generations past. I speak mainly of those individuals in the 1930s and '40s who have been heralded as the "Greatest Generation." They braved sixteen years of austerity, withstanding the Depression and winning World War II. Afterward, the survivors let loose as consumers. Mothers and fathers splurged on labor-lite, time-saving devices. Mama and I laud them for earning their conveniences.

But a lot of their children took convenience as a birthright. For the most part, their children and their children's children did, too. As do the assimilated children and grandchildren of immigrants. Here y'all are.

Mama and I will never slag you as "entitled." Labels stink anyway, but that one stinks to high heaven. We don't blame or shame any of you for acting as the founder of Me, Myself & I, LLC. That's what more and more employers force you to be. Not for nothing do so many of them crow that "people are our best *assets*."

Companies that lust after growth, quarter over quarter, will be mercenary about subjecting you to CCRAP time. In *Kids These Days: Human Capital and the Making of Millennials*, Malcolm Harris writes that "we"—he means *you*—"didn't happen by accident. . . . :

> *Over the past forty years we have witnessed an accelerated and historically unprecedented pace of change as capitalism emerged as the single dominant mode of organizing society. It's a system based on speed, and speed is always increasing. . . .*
>
> *The growth of growth requires a different kind of person, one whose abilities, skills, emotions and even sleep schedule are in sync with their role in the economy. . . .*
>
> *In order to fully recognize the scope of these changes, we need to think of young people the way industry and government already do: as investments, productive machinery, "human capital."*

As an asset, you're most valued when you're low maintenance: performance-ready, suitable in the moment, and expendable once you become inconvenient. Ring a bell? Isn't this the way "allies" often get treated in social movements?

The gig economy productizes people, and people productize their encounters with other people, even within movements that aim to "change the world." You might oppose capitalism, yet in the way you oppose it, ask yourself whether you and your network have adopted the market's logic of equating beings to things.

How viral has the logic of CCRAP become? Mama and I think that it festers not just widely, but also deeply. So deeply that in the name of resisting imperialism, many of you have been colonized by CCRAP. Pull up your big-people undergarments, friends. I'll explain.

69

Colonized by CCRAP?

Students, let's have a word about "cultural appropriation." Certain cultures belong to certain groups, many of you say, just as things belong to this or that individual. Consequently, lifting from "other people's" cultures without paying due props is tantamount to thieving someone else's things. By this logic, such an act ought to be labeled cultural appropriation and judged as an offense worthy of shaming.

If Mama and I may also judge, that's CCRAP. Only a transactional mind-set would suggest that cultures can be owned and therefore embezzled from their owners. Finished products can be owned because they are, indeed, things. But cultures? They're endlessly kinetic, combining influences from near and far.

Cornel West, the celebrated philosopher-activist, makes this point about one of his loves: jazz music. It's an emblem of American culture, he confirms, and yet "there's no jazz without European instruments or African polyrhythms." Brother West urges us to "give up all quest for pure traditions and pristine heritages" so that we place more value on being factually correct than politically correct.

Do you know about *haiku*, a form of traditional Japanese poetry? The three-line poem originates in Ancient Japan, but modern haiku takes a leaf from nineteenth-century European art. In the Japan of the late 1800s, haiku (*hokku* at the time) was dying. Its revival happened at the hands of Masaoka Shiki, a poet and essayist who borrowed from French realism.

Realist art portrayed ordinary objects and events as they literally were, unadorned by flights of emotion or metaphor. That's how Shiki conceived of *shasei* haiku—sketches from life. Japanese poets wrote what they directly experienced by seeing, hearing, touching, smelling, and tasting. According to his biographer, Shiki claimed that this approach "promised an unlimited source of new materials and themes, as varied as reality itself. If one observed from multiple points of view, near and far, high and low, then subjects for numerous haiku poems could be found everywhere. . . ." By fusing innovations from Japan and France, Shiki gave haiku poetry both a makeover and the life support it needed to stage a comeback.

Who, then, "owns" haiku?

As Mama mentioned, the Statue of Liberty, constructed in France, has an Arab pedigree. What's more, the U.S. Constitution takes inspiration from recorded history's first advocate of religious freedom. We're referring to Cyrus the Great, an emperor of Persia—today's Iran. Thomas Jefferson profoundly admired Cyrus. Does the First Amendment, with its protection of religious liberty, belong to Iranians? Does Lady Liberty belong to Arabs?

If they do, then we must also ask about suitably crediting Iranians and Arabs. When Lady Liberty's image appears on a kitschy shot glass, what does proper attribution to Arab culture look like? If Mama gifts that souvenir to a friend, should she require him to toast Arabs before he guzzles his shot? What if that tribute offends Arabs who don't drink alcohol, but charms Arabs who do?

Mama and I pose these questions sincerely because groups consist of individuals and individuals will disagree. In April 2018, a Utah student attended her high school prom in a traditional Chinese dress. She got taken down on Twitter for appropriating Chinese culture. Conducted primarily by Americans—Chinese and not—the shaming impressed few people in China itself. There, many felt honored that a

Midwestern girl would introduce a thread of Chinese culture to her peers on such an auspicious night in her young life.

Could she have satisfied everybody by pinning a "Thank-you, China" note to her prom dress? Or, between dances, distributing pamphlets to educate her peers about the history behind the dress design?

Sounds cumbersome, doesn't it? Alternatively, she could've gone the consumer-centric route preferred by some social justice campaigners at Reed College in Oregon. Not long ago, "Reedies Against Racism" (RAR) proposed that white students fork over $5 apiece before heading into the school ball. To be collected at the door by RAR activists, that money would serve as reparations for enjoying the music of black and brown artists. Maybe the Utah student should have donated five bucks to a Chinese historical association and, at her prom, worn a sign saying, "Cut me slack. I paid for this dress twice."

In which case, should people in China pony up $5 to the Levi-Strauss Foundation every time they wear jeans—an American creation first manufactured during the California gold rush?

To repeat, friends, the transactional mind-set isn't your doing. But buying into it is. Don't feel too crappy. You keep expert company. I still face-pawm when I think about the night that Mama commodified herself. Let me confide that story to you.

70

You're Not Alone

During a friend's lecture at New York University, Mama stepped out for some air. Suddenly she started to hyperventilate. A colleague heard Mama gasp and sent for an ambulance. Within minutes, it hustled her to the hospital.

Soon, Mama's immediate boss swung by. They both felt sheepish, this being the third emergency room visit in a few weeks. "We must stop meeting like this," Mama joked. The boss smiled and waited with her for a nurse.

Then a higher-up from the university arrived. *How kind*, Mama thought. As the nurse moved her to a gurney and prepared to push it behind a curtain, Mama thanked both of her colleagues for spending friendly POOP time with her. That's when the higher-up leaned in. "Listen," she whispered to Mama, "our commencement speaker has dropped out and we need to identify a substitute right away. Can you do it?"

In almost any other circumstance, Mama would have been thrilled to consider the request. But in Emerg? On a stretcher? Already afflicted by anxiety and about to undergo an examination? Was she a machine, as Malcolm Harris puts it?

"Yes," Mama replied. Yes, she would replace the commencement speaker and yes, she consented to be manipulated like a machine. Feeling vulnerable, awkward, pressured, and indebted to her employers for stopping in, Mama succumbed to that extractor of value, that bludgeon of dignity: CCRAP time. It would be the last time.

I'm not shocked that a university colleague would try to exploit Mama's condition. In America, elite education is all business. Students, whenever you rate faculty on public platforms, you're effectively posting a Yelp review about yet another consumer service. When professors are prohibited from assigning graduate students a grade lower than B−, as Mama was, it's because the university wants your repeat business—if not as a student, then as an eventual donor. Seems to be a sweetheart deal for you, right?

But overindulge this deal and you'll sell yourselves short as social reformers. Mama has lectured at campuses whose diversity and inclusion officers call themselves "customer service agents." Aggrieved students outsource conflict resolution to them. Petitioners for or against a speaker never have to work it out; the diversity office comes up with a remedy that rankles everyone equally.

Students, how do you expect to heal your divided country unless you roll up those sleeves and learn the art of negotiating with your Other?

How will you cultivate the moral courage to replace transactions with relationships?

How radical is it to imitate—ahem, appropriate—market culture?

A decent future depends on freeing yourselves from the CCRAP trap. Otherwise the market and its norms will do the thinking for you. Has that worked for protecting the environment? For improving access to health care? For humanizing both inmates and guards inside private prisons? Why would the results be any different in a posthuman landscape, where algorithms will reproduce the prejudices of people?

If most of you decide to linger in the CCRAP trap, have fun restraining the worst excesses of artificial intelligence. But if you believe, as Mama and I do, that some unintended consequences of A.I. can already be anticipated, debated, and prevented, then here's the scoop: Be ready to POOP. To get A.I. on the political radar, you'll need to persuade local authorities to take your generation's quality of life seriously. You'll have to arm legislators with your proposals. You'll want to take the innovator's journey.

When you do, you'll develop the skills to listen as much as to lobby—and listen not only to office-holders, but also to the varied points of view within your network of peers. Beauty is, this repertoire of skills will enhance your gutsiness in any context, from civic activism to family politics to team leadership to global citizenship.

Throughout our dialogue, Mama and I have thrown you bones. Tips, that is, for creating conversations where none would have existed before. In the hope that you'll POOP yourselves out, we'll now give you a step-by-step guide to doing diversity honestly.

71

Honest Diversity, Step by Step

You feel strongly, very strongly, about an issue. A friend or relative holds the opposite point of view. If you talked it through, you could teach each other something. But it would be so much easier to do what everyone else does: nothing. That way, you can't lose.

Oh, yes, you can.

Mama's pal, Scott Mercier, has experience with winning and losing. A person of moral courage, he was, for a time, the only cyclist on the U.S. men's Tour de France team who refused to dope. "Everybody cheated to turbo their performance, to gain that edge," Uncle Scott says. "Staying clean almost guaranteed that you'd lose." Instead of falling into line, Uncle Scott chose to maintain his integrity and resign his jersey. Lance Armstrong took his place. We know how that ride ended.

Uncle Scott's guidance for students? To rattle the status quo, draw on your moral courage and break out of the group. He followed this principle as a racer. "You can be sitting in the peloton—the large pack of cyclists—and you will literally get nowhere," he explains. "Or you can pour on the adrenaline, leave your comfort zone, and find out what you are made of." Besides benefitting you, the choice to stretch yourself will set a new bar for the people around you.

In that sense, moral courage isn't just a virtue or attribute; it's a skill. Moral courage equips you to become socially constructive, mentally focused, and emotionally aware. Consider this your moral courage training regimen.

1) Self-Evaluate. Habitually.

In chapter 29, Frances Lee offered tips for staying true to your values. First, though, how do you figure out what those values are and what they say about who you are? Social media might contain the answers. For Dog's sake, don't tell Mama that you heard it from me.

Every three months, review your news feeds and record your responses to these questions:

- When I'm on social media, what stories do I pause for?

- What stories move me enough to share with my friends?

- What gives me joy when I watch, listen, or read about it?

- What makes me mad when it's in the news? (Concentrate on issues, not individuals.)

- What should be in the news much more than it is?

- What does all this suggest about the ideals that I stand for?

- Why do I stand for these values and principles? Are they choices I've made for myself? Or the way my family has raised me? Or an "aha!" moment inspired by others? (Details, please!)

Students, you can keep your responses completely private. The point is for *you* to begin knowing you.

You'll revisit these questions three more times over a year. Each time, store your answers and compare them to your previous answers. Soon, you'll start to see if and how you're changing. That's vital information for two reasons. First, to confirm that you're living your values. If you don't have integrity, how can you ask it of your society?

Second, to identify the issue you're so passionate about that you're going to advocate for it.

Advocacy necessitates that you engage your Other, someone who just as passionately disagrees with your opinion. Which in turn requires a plan for outwitting your impetuous egobrain. Mama and I address that in steps 2–11. Here we go.

2) Defy the man for one hour a week.

Of the 10,080 minutes that make up a week, set aside sixty to be face-to-face and in alert discussion with your Other.

More, dare yourself to be device-defiant rather than compliant. Power down your phones. In so doing, you and your Other will be sticking it to the machine man. Your energies won't be choreographed by algorithms. Your gestures will elude surveillance by the profiteers of your personal stats. You'll assert your independence from the merchants of CCRAP.

In *You Are Not a Gadget,* Jaron Lanier writes, "Giving yourself time and space to think and feel is crucial to your existence . . . You have to find a way to be yourself before you can share yourself."

Try the next set of steps with an opinionated parent or relative. Why family members? Because they can't just jilt you. Peers can, and we'll come to them shortly.

3) Launch the conversation by asking, "Could you help me understand what I'm missing about your perspective?"

With a question like this, you're achieving three things at once. Immediately, you're showing that you care about your Other. After all, you're curious about where they're coming from. Genuine caring fosters trust, which lowers emotional defenses, opens hearts, and motivates the Other to share information with you.

Next, you're demonstrating humility. By asking a question rather than making a statement, you're indicating that this is a conversation in good faith, not a debate in disguise. Consequently, your Other doesn't have to feel threatened.

To top it off, you're displaying *confident* humility. By being the first to step up, you're setting the tone of the conversation. As a result, you're expanding the power that you already bring to the encounter. With power comes the responsibility to use it fairly, leading Mama and me to the fourth tip.

4) Listen to understand, not to win.

While your Other speaks, clear your mind of opposing points and what-aboutisms. Since this is a dialogue, not a debate, you don't *need* to win. And because you've claimed power up front, *you* don't need to win. So relax and listen carefully to what your Other says. Remember: To listen doesn't oblige you to agree.

5) Ask more questions based on what you've heard.

According to psychologists, it's wise to reiterate your Other's position so that they know you're listening. Brie Loskota, Mama's researcher-friend at USC, adds a related tip: "Try to articulate your opponent's view without sarcasm or hyperbole."

That's what Mama did when I brought up the theory of white fragility in chapter 13. She outlined her understanding of this theory and then asked me if I accepted how she outlined it. When I did, we both knew we could springboard into the next bit of our conversation.

Here's a second way to assure your Other that you're listening: Ask questions that stem from what they've just said, not from any agenda that you might secretly harbor. Whatever your stereotypes of Them, you're talking to one person. One. Don't assume this individual believes everything that you associate with "their" label. Ask. The more you ask, the more clues you'll pick up about their values.

And with these clues you can reframe your beliefs in ways that resonate with your Other. Go back to chapter 17 and read how Mama reframed Barack Obama's accomplishments so that Uncle Jim, a Trump voter, could hear her.

You'll need time to figure out how to reframe your opinion so that your Other can hear it. This won't happen in the moment. But something else *is* happening: Your Other is generously giving you insights. Stay grateful by staying attentive. Ask spontaneous, unscripted, follow-up questions.

6) Express your gratitude with tone and body language, too.

Somebody should have drummed this into Mama before her pitiful TV appearance in chapter 61. Nonverbal cues express a lot more than words do. And a lot more memorably. Research shows that people will forget most of what you said, but they'll never forget how you made them feel.

When your Other stumbles through an explanation, will you sympathize or capitalize? What about your voice—aggressive or appreciative? If you stand up mid-conversation to get a glass of water, will you offer to bring them one? At the close of the conversation, will you thank them for taking the time to teach you something?

At this point, Mama and I would like to remind you of a few general steps to follow throughout your conversations.

7) When dealing with your Other, don't berate. Relate.

Your egobrain wants to lunge for the jugular. There are three reasons to face up to that instinct and then breathe your way through it:

- Moral: As right as you believe you are, you don't own the full truth. None of us does.

- Psychological: In relationships, slam-dunk arguments rarely resolve issues. More often, they drip with condescension— tempting your Other to turn the disagreement into something of a war (assuming you haven't already done that yourself).

- Strategic: When you're unwilling to hear, you won't be heard. Where does that doom-loop get you? Where does it get any of us?

8) Take a breath or three.

Mama and I mentioned it in step seven, but we can't stress it enough. By breathing, you're slow-jamming your brain and outwitting your ego. The brain takes shortcuts to save energy. Human beings can't process the incalculable shards and bytes of information flung their way every day. Sucks to be you, people.

To prevent "cognitive overload," your brain reaches for prefabricated categories—labels. But if you truly support diversity, then labels can't be the final word because labels can lie. They flatten each of us to one dimension, vaporizing all the rest that makes us plurals.

9) Be open to changing your mind.

When you enter a conversation with your Other, it's counterproductive to ask yourself, *How can I change their mind?* That's an excuse for treating your Other as an object, a prop, an instrument. Nobody likes being played. Keep doing it and you'll be busted. Wave bye-bye to your power.

But changing your own mind? Audacious. Mama and I don't mean flipping 180 degrees to the other side. We don't even mean compromising your basic stance if, on balance, you remain persuaded that you're right. We *do* mean acknowledging a solid point when your Other makes one. After all, you're role-modeling the culture that you want for the conversation. There's power in being the first to say, "I never thought about it that way."

Leading by example reveals your integrity. Witnessing your integrity inspires people to care about you. That's when they'll care about co-creating a vibe and ultimately a society that respects you alongside them. Think Mama and her mother, Mumtaz.

Also think Genesis and Louis, whose friendship has survived the emotional triggers emblazoned into the Mississippi state flag. Mama and I know that friends can be far more nerve-racking to disagree with than parents are. It's as if you have to abide by a hidden rule: "Friends don't let friends think."

Take comfort. According to a recent study, the people you regard as friends don't necessarily feel the same about you. What a relief! This is why you should never be afraid to lose "friends" by dissenting with them if your integrity demands it. Just dissent in a healthy way by taking the steps that you've read so far.

Now let's turn to handling the potential outcomes.

10) Be cool with non-closure.

We fully anticipate that a few weeks from today, some of you will complain to us, "I've tried getting through to a friend who has whacka-doo beliefs. Your steps didn't work." If you measure what works by how often it converts people to your point of view, then kindly reassess your intention. You're not in this to change minds. You're in this to humanize your Other. En route, you're exchanging information that can induce both of you to think. May it be so, because thinking can curb the emotionalism that incubates and exacerbates dogmas.

Again and again, some of you will doubt your decision to have disagreed with a friend. *Did I offend?* you'll wonder. *Has the trust between us tanked? Will she/he/they ever speak with me again?* You might not get the answer for a while because your friend needs time to reflect on what you've said. Use that time to think about what your friend has taught you. Send them a handwritten card about it.

But don't force a response. What you can be sure of is that both of you are breaking ground, a tiny but illustrative patch of it, for a pluralistic society that belongs to each of you, and to many more.

11) **Walk away if you must, but not prematurely.**

The human species crawls with conspiracy theorists, psychopaths, and bullies. If you're threatened with physical violence, bolt and tell someone immediately.

In most other cases, give grace a chance. The world has a whole lot of introverts, for example. By nature, introverts don't engage as speedily as extroverts. It's not personal; it's dispositional. But you won't know who's who unless you breathe and let others do the same.

If a friend hurts you with language, be honest with them about how you feel. Assure them that you're happy to continue the conversation once they apologize. If they won't, then offer a handshake before you exit. And if they do apologize, no matter how grudging it may sound, accept it. Then keep your promise to move forward. It's in your power to be gracious.

Shady "friends" won't reciprocate your good faith with theirs. But trustworthy friends will respect your individuality and accept disagreement as natural. Allow them to see your many dimensions so that they'll feel permitted to revel in theirs.

Congratulations on your moral courage, you precocious plural, you. Yes, I just labeled you. Take it up with Mama.

Peace out,

Lil

72

Educating for Honest Diversity

Dear educators,

Thank you for rescuing Mama. When she was growing up, "school" stood in for "safety." Not every teacher understood her, but many tried. In the second grade, Mrs. Lightheart watched Mama unload the same four encyclopedias from her knapsack each morning. "Why do you haul them all home and bring them all back every day?" she asked. "Do you read all four at one sitting?"

Mama admitted, "I don't read them. I just carry them." Mrs. Lightheart appeared perturbed. Mama clarified, "I'm in training." For what, she didn't know, but the teacher suddenly did. She cracked a grin and nodded. Rare for prickly Mrs. Lightheart.

Only much later did Mama realize that physical stamina helps you persevere through life's pain. This includes violence at home, which two high school teachers mentored Mama to bounce back from. For her, Mr. Martens and Mr. Goldman defined manhood. There's no telling what would've become of Mama had they not been her teachers.

Fellow educators, look up. I'm waving at you, and you, and you. Out of gratitude, I'm putting in a good word for all of you—even for the atheists. Especially for the atheists.

This brings me to our subject of honest diversity. Let me confess that Mama and I have misgivings about how diversity is being practiced in schools. For example, most educators teach that human DNA is 99.9 percent the same, regardless of people's skin tones. Logically, then, "race" can't be real.

Yet too many educators sponsor "affinity clubs" that divide and subdivide young people into races. Why are we imitating racists, the inventors and connivers of the race ruse? Could you help us understand what we're missing?

(It may seem farcical to be tutored about dangerous fictions from me, a talking dog. Take it up with Mama.)

Further, since race is a construct, and most educators teach it as a fact, aren't we akin to distributors of fake news? Wouldn't it be more truthful to teach young people that they, like nearly all people (and talking dogs), are plurals?

Mama and I recognize the academy's attempt at pluralism: "intersectionality." This theory, developed by the illustrious legal scholar Kimberlé Crenshaw, evokes the image of two roads that converge to form an intersection. According to intersectionality, identities crisscross similarly, in that many of us inhabit multiple categories at once.

Women of color, for instance, are affected not only by our race but also by our gender. Within the gender-race intersection, some of us are wage-earners or out-and-out poor, highlighting a third category of difference: class. In yet another subset dwell lesbians of color—whose struggles shouldn't be confused with those of bisexual women of color or transgender women of color, still less of cisgender heterosexual women of color. Mama and I appreciate the plethora of additional intersections. To us, no one is roadkill.

But combinations and permutations of labels still leave labels calling the shots. If the concept of race is conjured up, and it is, then intersectionality only embellishes the ruse. Moreover, intersectionality needlessly confines our minds. Sentient beings don't stay stationary at an intersection. We move through it. We live beyond it. Speaking metaphorically, many of us thrive amid the sweeping expanse of mountains and meadows, prairies and forests, jungles and waters.

Often, these are the very places to which we retreat in order to discover who we *really* are. Why there? Because such places don't fence us in as intersections do. They let us figure out, in time, where we're at. They give us room to breathe and be. And become.

Mama and I have discussed why you humans will never pry yourselves from labels. They promise the illusion of control, and humans covet control. Intersections, where labels hook up, reinforce your controlling natures. A grid locates you in such a structured and dependable manner that you itch for further direction. On guard for threats, your egobrain admonishes, "You've come this far by following what's been charted for you. Why start thinking for yourself and risk getting lost?"

Relieved, you take it at face value that the signs erected at intersections tell you all you need to know about your journey. It may be all you need to know for a jaunt around the corner. But there's so much more to the journey of living honestly, never mind living honestly with others. On that map-less, app-less, mostly negotiated quest, constructed signs, like contrived labels, mislead. At critical junctures, intersectionality is both limited and limiting.

How, then, might educators equip young people to question labels? To think independently while collaborating for commonality, not for difference as an end in itself? It would be rich for me and Mama to ply you with instructions. Nor would we want to saddle a polarized world with yet more dogma (more dog mamas, yes; more dogma, no). Instead, we'll share three conclusions that shape our teaching.

First, kids deserve to learn about the neuroscience behind their egos. This way, they'll know that everyone has the egobrain as a frenemy. It's a friend because it'll save them from mortal danger. It's an enemy because it can't distinguish between mortal danger and mere discomfort. That's where students' higher selves enter: When asked to check their egobrains, students never have to feel shamed, blamed, or gamed. Since the egobrain is a universal reality, managing it is a universal responsibility.

Second, given half the chance, shame will squash courage—not least the courage to be curious. Students have to hear, repeatedly, that they can be honest about being human. To that end, when Mama teaches about brave icons, she tries to humanize them as plurals. She brings up not just their accomplishments but also their quirks, their failings, or—thank you, Ben Franklin—their fartings.

Third, a *culture* of courage will only be nurtured on POOP time, not CCRAP time. Start before the college years. At university, earth-shattering ideas can be introduced. Theories can be propounded and debated. Specialties can be learned, practiced, and refined. But moral courage is a missed opportunity if it's taught only as an idea, a theory, or a specialty. Its value is in the doing. The more people "do" moral courage in their relationships, the less random it'll be that people respond in kind.

And exactly because doing is the hard part, to teach moral courage is in fact to coach it. Mama has never doubted why most kids need years of coaching to shine in a sport. She's realized that this is equally true for kids to excel in the ultimate team activity of repairing a fractured humanity. Mama looks forward to joining you, the moral courage mentors, and your students on this odyssey.

As for me, I've received a message from Chuck Darwin that my latest pun miffed Ben Franklin. Best, I think, to track Mr. Franklin down and clear the air. Maybe I can buy him a drink at our neighborhood watering hole, "Bruce Lee's Bliss-Out."

Maybe Mr. Franklin will tell me to go fly a kite.

Maybe he'll let me call him Benny.

There's one way to find out.

Good luck to us all,

Lil

Epilogue

Lilybean, can you hear me? I know you've earned your rest, cream puff, but this will take only a minute.

I couldn't stop thinking about you last evening. Mama Laura and I went to a dinner party where we said the first of our goodbyes to Californian friends. Jim and Liz attended, too. You would've had a ball, Lil, because the sparks flew.

Our host brought up President Obama and the racial divisions that he somehow instigated. I respectfully took issue with her, explaining that Obama regularly and publicly asked African Americans to empathize with white Americans and vice versa. The host told me that she'd never heard such sentiments from him. I'm not surprised, I replied. The media's most lucrative business model—play to what threatens this or that group—insulates Americans from the truths that heal. On this, she and I agreed.

Another guest then excused the lies that pour forth from a certain commentator on Fox News. Lil, do you recall the name Sean Hannity? If not, no loss. I've got a feeling you won't be running into him up there, although that's Somebody Else's decision. Anyway, according to this dinner guest, Hannity's liberal abuse of truth can be justified. "The guy has to make a living," she argued.

"A living?" I frothed. "Why should I care about *his* living? What I care about is the country living on!" I was dumbstruck, Lil, that I'd have to say this to someone who considers herself a staunch patriot. She undeniably is one, so I know she didn't mean to place Hannity above country. She just obeyed her reflex to defend rather than to think.

A third friend rehashed Obama's "apology tour"—the president's early visits to Middle Eastern countries, where he acknowledged that the United States needed to be a better international partner. My friend bellyached that "Obama bowed to the Saudi leader and kissed his ring."

Mama Laura interjected. "But Trump kissing Putin's ass is okay?"

"Talk about an apology tour!" I cackled as I slurped mindlessly from the well of what-aboutism.

Jim took a swipe at Democrats, we went back and forth, and I tried—oh, Lily, I tried—to be constructive. "I'm not aiming to score points for my team," I assured the Republican majority at the table. "I'm just pointing out that each of us, me included, needs to take responsibility for spoon-feeding the Us-against-Them troll."

Look at what we'd done in a matter of minutes, Lil. Look at how blithely we'd all blamed the other side and discounted our own inconsistencies. "But," I added, "we're among friends. At this table, we can say, 'I'm human. I'm inconsistent.'"

"You're inconsistent," Jim deadpanned.

"Watch this," I told him, turning to everybody else. "I recognize the hypocrisy of my fellow liberals and progressives." Scanning the rest of the faces, I asked, "Will you say the same about your tribe?"

There wasn't one taker. What a waste of a dramatic pause.

"Well," I sighed, "then you'll have no credibility, none, in holding liberals and progressives to account. And you'll be complicit in the very problem of hypocrisy that you claim to oppose. And you're sowing the intensity of a backlash that, one day, will wipe out a bunch of the gains you think you've won." What goes around comes around, somebody once said.

The table remained quiet. Hesitantly, Hannity's fan nodded her head. That's all I needed. "The democracy that the framers had in mind—it's so doable," I pleaded to her. "Accept your piece of it and I'll accept mine. Simple, right?"

Later, I apologized to the host for any rudeness on my part. "Shush," she finger-wagged. "It was a spirited conversation. How else do we get to hear different perspectives? We had a perfect night." This from the woman who accused President Obama of inflaming racial tensions. I couldn't have disagreed more with her opinion, yet I admired how sincerely she welcomed my dissent. On her turf, no less. That's grace.

While I've got you on the line, Lil, some news: Louis has decided to stop flying his Confederate flag. "I'm keeping a patch of it in a box with other things of the past, a reminder of where I used to be," he told me. Then he said, "I just try every day to be better."

The founding genius of America still flickers. Now if only more of us would tune out the carnival barkers and click-baiters to do an evening's worth of research—pro, con, and in between—on whatever's riling us up. If I'm asking too much, it's because asking too little is worse.

Rest in peace, sweet bean, but not in complacency. Mama sends you undying love.

Acknowledgments

God is great, we Muslims say. Let me add that dog is great.

I'm referring not only to my beloved Lily, but also to an eighteen-year-old Chihuahua named Jasmine. Laura and I adopted her after she'd been hit by a car, her right side split wide open, her back and hips permanently jacked up. Jazzy's need for human care pulled me through Lily's death.

Lil, please take Jazz under your wing. Without her, I'm not sure I could've finished writing about us.

I'm blessed to have worked with my editor, George Witte, at St. Martin's Press. He patiently heard my feedback on all aspects of this book. A special shout-out to George's assistant, Sara Thwaite, who saved me grief even as I added to hers.

Dr. Geoffrey Cowan welcomed me to the University of Southern California. Through the Annenberg Center on Communication Leadership and Policy, which he directs, I had the support to study and float controversial ideas. That's equally due to Team Cowan, led by Susan Goelz and further energized by Ev Boyle, Anna Blue, Skye Featherstone, Danielle Balderas, and Justin Chapman.

Ra'idah Noohu served as a sounding board no less than as a research assistant. Thanks as well to the critics of my early drafts: Dr. Patrick Finnessy, Antonia Marrero, Joseph Bennett, Roi Ben-Yehuda, Romy Ashby, Diederik van Hoogstraten, Adam Grannick, Teresa Hall,

Rev. Bill Green, and Paul Michaels. I benefited from the vast spectrum of their views and the honesty with which they challenged mine. Even more, I thank them for trusting me to receive their criticisms well.

Gratitude galore to the students and teachers with whom I've had the honor to work and learn over the past decade. From middle schools to universities, you've each contributed to my belief about the purpose of educators: that we're not here to help our students feel safe; we're here to help them feel safe *in their discomfort*.

Above all, the family. I'm in awe of my mother's courage. Thank you for sharing it with every reader, Mum. My sisters, Ishrat and Fatima, fortify my faith in the power of honest relationships. Special kudos to Fatima for starring in the audiobook. She's the voice of Lily—sassy yet sweet. Two plurals in a pod.

A final acknowledgment. My ex-wife, Laura, was my portal to canine companionship—a world I never could've conceived on my own. One day, I took Lily and Jazzy out for a walk together. Bear in mind that Lily had no sight. Jazzy had no hearing. And apparently I had no brain: As Laura saw us off, she remarked, "There go Deaf, Dumb, and Blind!" It's the only time I let her label me. To laugh at ourselves is to subvert ego with the power of humility. Bruce Lee, I think, would've approved.

Index

Rene Clement

Recipient of Oprah Winfrey's first Chutzpah Award for boldness, IRSHAD MANJI is the founder of Moral Courage College, which teaches people how to do the right thing in the face of fear. She is also the director for courage, curiosity, and character at Let Grow, a nonprofit promoting independence and resilience in kids. A prize-winning professor, Manji currently lectures with Oxford University's Initiative for Global Ethics and Human Rights.